Praise for *Designing Effective Database Systems*

"Designing a database is not a trivial subject. Riordan brings experience and clear explanations to a fundamental part of software development."
—Patrick Birch, database and technical writing consultant

"A book that will expertly guide you in how to develop a database for a client— and how to do it right the first time!"
—Kenneth D. Snell, Ph.D., ACCESS developer
and Microsoft Access MVP

"Riordan has produced a unique book that brings together a formal, yet commonsense, approach to relational database design. And then goes further! Many database designers will find immense value in the steps to developing practical data warehouse designs. If you are seeking a framework for designing transactional databases, or want to step out into the world of analytical databases, Riordan's book excels at bridging both worlds."
—Paul Irvine, vice president, engineering, Via Training

"If you buy only one book on database design, make it this one. Riordan has a talent for explaining technical issues in simple language, without over simplifying."
—Brendan Reynolds, developer, Dataset IT Systems,
and Microsoft Access MVP

"Riordan takes a complex subject and makes it easy. If you're over your head on a database design project, this book will help bail you out!"
—Mike Gunderloy, contributing editor,
Application Development Trends

"This book covers a wide range of database design and data modeling topics in a well-organized, easy to understand format."
—Amy Sticksel, Sticksel Data Systems, Inc.

"In *Designing Effective Database Systems*, Riordan's style, wit, and attention to detail are outstanding."
—Sandra Daigle, Microsoft Access MVP

"More than just a book on database theory, Riordan gives us a practical guide to developing a database application from negotiation to completion."

—Dirk Goldgar, president, DataGnostics,
and Microsoft Access MVP

"Riordan covers core skills for any developer—database design and development—in a perfect amount of detail, including fundamentals such as normalization but also teaches you how to architect your system to allow for reporting and future expansion. This book should be on every professional developer's reading list."

—Duncan Mackenzie, developer, Microsoft (MSDN)

Designing Effective
Database Systems

Designing Effective Database Systems

Rebecca M. Riordan

✦Addison-Wesley

Upper Saddle River, NJ • **Boston** • **Indianapolis** • **San Francisco**
New York • **Toronto** • **Montreal** • **London** • **Munich** • **Paris** • **Madrid**
Capetown • **Sydney** • **Tokyo** • **Singapore** • **Mexico City**

The publisher offers excellent discounts on this book when ordered in quantity for bulk purchases or special sales, which may include electronic versions and/or custom covers and content particular to your business, training goals, marketing focus, and branding interests. For more information, please contact:

U. S. Corporate and Government Sales
(800) 382-3419
corpsales@pearsontechgroup.com

For sales outside the U. S., please contact:

International Sales
international@pearsoned.com

Visit us on the Web: www.awprofessional.com

This Book Is Safari Enabled

The Safari® Enabled icon on the cover of your favorite technology book means the book is available through Safari Bookshelf. When you buy this book, you get free access to the online edition for 45 days.

Safari Bookshelf is an electronic reference library that lets you easily search thousands of technical books, find code samples, download chapters, and access technical information whenever and wherever you need it.

To gain 45-day Safari Enabled access to this book:

- Go to http://www.awprofessional.com/safarienabled
- Complete the brief registration form
- Enter the coupon code CPNM-GG3O-AF5F-FUOL-1O62

If you have difficulty registering on Safari Bookshelf or accessing the online edition, please e-mail customer-service@safaribooksonline.com.

Library of Congress Cataloging-in-Publication Data

Riordan, Rebecca.
    Designing effective database systems / Rebecca M. Riordan.
        p. cm.
    Includes bibliographical references.
    ISBN 0-321-29093-3 (pbk.: alk. paper)
    1. Database design. I. Title.

    QA76.9.D26R54 2005
    005.7'4—dc22

                                            2004023319

ISBN 0-321-29093-3

Text printed in the United States on recycled paper at Courier in Stoughton, Massachusetts.
First printing, January 2005

To my parents.

Contents

ix

Preface

Relational databases are tricky beasts. Other kinds of commercial software are infinitely easier to understand. Word processors are really just high-tech typewriters, and it's pretty clear that the backspace key beats that little jar of white stuff cold. Spreadsheets present a familiar enough paradigm, even to non-accountants, and email is close enough to the postal system for the model to be comprehensible.

Databases are different. Other kinds of software have a real-world analogy. Sometimes, as in the Windows desktop, the analogy is a little tenuous, but the analogies are close enough; you can get there from here. But relational databases are completely artificial. They're like geometry: They can be used to build models of the real world, but they don't exist in the real world. When was the last time you poured some wine for you and your sweetie and went out on the front porch to watch the geometry frolic on the lake?

Now, I'm talking about databases here, not tables. Tables exist aplenty, from the telephone book to the dictionary. But relational databases? Nope. Unh-unh. You're not going to find them frolicking on the lake, either. The card files at the library, which contain author, title, and subject files, come close to being a database but they're still separate sets of data that are only correlated by the good graces of the local librarian.

This book is about designing database systems. My intention is to give you the knowledge you need to take a messy, complex, real-world situation and turn it into an effective database design. I assume that you have some development experience and generally know your way around a computer, but I don't assume that you have any background in databases.

After reading the book you still won't be able to watch the databases frolic on the lake, but if I've done my job well you'll be able to design and implement a relational model of the fish, the seagulls, and the effects of the plankton on them both.

The book is divided into four parts. Part I, "Relational Database Theory," covers the fundamental principles of the relational model. This is where the really ugly, theoretical stuff is. But don't worry; it will get easier. Part II, "Dimensional Database Theory," covers the same information for dimensional databases, a special type of relational database used for analysis. Part III, "Designing Database Systems," examines the analysis and design process—what you should do to get from the real world to a reliable database system design. Finally, Part IV, "Designing the User Interface," discusses the most important aspect of a database system from a user's point of view: the user interface.

Although we'll talk about implementation issues in the next few hundred pages, this isn't a "how to program" book. There are a few coding examples, but I've kept them to a minimum, and you should be able to follow them even if you've never seen a programming language before. The database examples are based on the Northwind sample database that comes with Microsoft Access. (The version of Northwind that comes with SQL Server is very similar.) By the time you're finished reading this book, you'll have picked up most of what you need to get started building database systems, and you'll be ready to turn to one of the sources listed in the Bibliography for the finer points of programming style. And you'll be confident that your data architecture is sound and unlikely to get you into trouble later in your project.

A note on English usage: As you'll discover as you read this book, I'm a stickler for terminology. But that said, I don't think syntax ought to draw attention to itself. If an author writes "he or she" or (heavens forefend) "s/he," I'm busy thinking about gender politics and no longer paying attention to the text. If I read "the data are," I'm just as likely to be thinking about the nature of the English language as whatever the author is trying to say.

Now, the pronoun issue is fairly simple to work around. You'll find a great many repetitions of "the user" in this text. But the adoption of Latin terms into English is a more complex issue, particularly in a book about data.

For the record, I had a classical education, and I'm perfectly aware that *in Latin*, "data" is a plural noun, and ought to take a plural verb. I'm also aware that in the field of statistics, one still refers to a "datum," a single data point. But this isn't statistics, and I'm not writing in Latin. In English, we have a long history of adopting plural Latin nouns as corporate nouns, and in American English, those nouns take a singular verb. It's what we do when we speak, and it's what I've done in the text.

We say "the data is reliable" not "the data are reliable." (I have actually heard "the datums are reliable," but that's just sad.) This usage has been adopted by several influential publications, and I have adopted it here. Not because I don't know how Latin works, but because I've carefully considered the issue and decided to write American English as I, as a well-educated native American English speaker, speak it. Now ain't that just about enough on the subject?

Acknowledgments

The number of people involved in getting this book into your hands would populate a small village in one of the prettier parts of England. To refer to it as "my" book is nothing more than an attractive fantasy. My undying gratitude to, in order of appearance…

Karen Gettman and Elizabeth Zdunich, my editors at Addison-Wesley, who once again smoothed an often-fraught process. Karen was on my side when lawyers said frightening things about publishing releases. Elizabeth, well, Elizabeth just fixes things. What a joy to work with someone who solves problems and shrugs.

I am humbled by the number of Microsoft MVPs who volunteered their time and talents to review the book in manuscript. Alphabetically, they are: Peter Doering, Joe Fallon, Dirk Goldgar, Henry Habermacher, Graham Mandero, Arvin Meyer, Brendan Reynolds, Sco Scofield, Ken Snell, John Spencer, and Lynn Trapp. I owe you all.

On behalf of Addison-Wesley, Patrick Birch, Paul Irvine, and Amy Sticksel added their unique technical perspectives. Their efforts, too, are greatly appreciated.

Finally, Dmitri Korzh is responsible for turning dozens of graphic files and annotated manuscripts into something that can be rightly called a book. Dmitri, you're a wonder.

To all of you, my thanks.

Rebecca M. Riordan
Santa Fe, 2004

PART I

Relational Database Theory

CHAPTER 1

Basic Concepts

So, what is this mythical creature called a relational database? Briefly, a database is a tool for storing and manipulating information efficiently and effectively. "Efficiently and effectively" means that the data is protected from accidental loss or corruption, that it doesn't use more resources (human or computer) than necessary, and that it can be retrieved in sensible ways within acceptable performance constraints. To qualify as relational, the database must implement the relational model, which is a way of describing some aspect of the real world according to a set of rules first proposed by Dr. E. F. Codd in the late 1960s.

In theory, a relational database could be coded from scratch, but in reality you'll normally use the services of a database management system (DBMS). A DBMS is sometimes called a relational database management system (RDBMS), but technically a DBMS must meet some 300 rules to qualify as relational, and, to the best of my knowledge, no commercially available system fully qualifies. The two database management systems we'll be examining in this book are Microsoft Jet and Microsoft SQL Server.

I've said that a relational database is the physical implementation of the relational model (the data model), and it's important to keep these two concepts distinct. As we'll see in Part II, the dimensional model can also be implemented on a relational DBMS, and if you muddy the conceptual and physical, you'll get yourself hopelessly confused. (And yes, that *is* the voice of experience!)

What Is a Database?

Database terminology is almost as slippery as the term "object-oriented programming." The word "database" is used to describe everything from a single set of data, such as a telephone list, to a complex set of tools, such as SQL Server, and a whole lot in between. This lack of precision isn't a bad thing, necessarily—it's just the nature of language—but it's not particularly useful for our purposes, so I'll try to be a bit more precise here. Figure 1–1 shows the relationships between the terms discussed here. We'll define these terms in this chapter, and examine them in detail in the rest of the book.

Although relational databases don't have real-world analogies, most are intended to model some aspect of the real world. I'll call that bit of the real world the **problem space**. The problem space, by its nature, is messy and

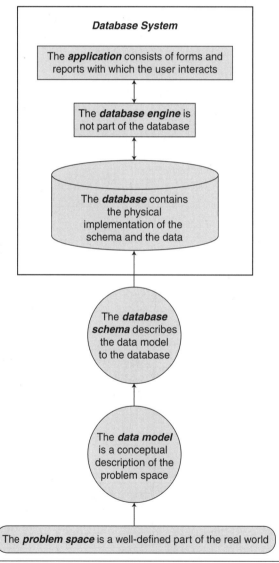

Figure 1–1 Relational Database Terminology

complex—if it weren't, we wouldn't need to build a model of it. But it is critical to the success of your project that you limit the database system you're designing to a specific, well-defined set of objects and interactions; only by doing so can you make sensible decisions about the scope of your system.

I'll use the term **data model** to mean the conceptual description of the problem space. When you're working with the relational model, this includes the definition of entities, their attributes (a Customer, for example, is an entity, and it might have the attributes Name and Address), and the entity constraints (such as, for example, that the CustomerName field cannot be empty). When you're working with the dimensional model, this definition consists of facts and dimensions, but we'll discuss those in Part II.

The data model also includes a description of the relationships between entities and any constraints on those relationships. For example, managers are not allowed to have more than five individuals reporting to them. It does not include any reference to the physical layout of the system.

The definition of the physical layout—the tables and views that will be implemented—is called the **database schema** or just the **schema**. It's the translation of the conceptual model into a physical representation that can be implemented using a DBMS. Note that the schema is still conceptual, not physical. The schema is nothing more than the data model expressed in the terms that you will use to describe it to the database engine—tables and triggers and such creatures. One of the benefits of using a database engine is that you don't ever have to deal with the physical implementation; you can largely ignore B-trees and leaf nodes and other low-level physical concepts.

Once you've explained to the database engine what you want the data to look like, using either code or an interactive environment such as Microsoft Access or the SQL Server Enterprise Manager, the engine will create some physical objects (usually, but not always, on a hard disk someplace) and you'll store data in them. The combination of structure and data is what I'll refer to as a **database**. This database includes the physical tables that store the data; the defined views, queries, and stored procedures used to retrieve the data in various ways; and the rules the engine will enforce to protect the data.

The term "database" does *not* include the **application**, which consists of the forms and reports with which your users will interact, nor does it include any of the bits and pieces—things such as middleware or Internet Information Server—used to stick the front and back ends together. The term "database" also excludes the database engine. Thus, an Access .mdb file is a database, while Microsoft Jet is a database engine. Actually, an .mdb file can contain application objects as well—forms and reports, for example—but that's a topic we'll discuss later.

To describe all these components—the application, the database, the database engine, and the middleware—I'll use the term **database system**. All of the software and data that goes into making a production system is part of the database system.

Database Tools

Although this book focuses on design rather than implementation, abstract theory isn't of much value unless you know how to apply it; so in this book, we'll be talking a lot about building relational databases using the tools provided by Microsoft. There are a lot of these tools, and Microsoft seems to introduce a new one every time you turn around, so let's take a minute now to look at what all these bits and pieces are and how they fit together. Figure 1–2 shows the tools we'll be discussing. It's easiest to think about these tools in terms of what

Figure 1–2 The Database Tools Discussed in This Book

we, as developers, need to translate a system from an abstract model to a live production system, and this is how they're grouped in the figure.

Database Engines

At the lowest level are the **database engines**. These are sometimes called "back ends," but that's a bit sloppy since the term "back end" really refers to a specific physical architecture, as we'll see in Chapter 13. These tools will handle the physical manipulation of data—storing it to disk and feeding it back on demand. We'll be looking at two: the Jet database engine and SQL Server. You may be surprised not to see Microsoft Access here. Access is technically a front-end development environment that uses either Jet or SQL Server natively and can, in fact, use any ODBC-compliant database engine as its data store. It uses the Jet database engine to manipulate data stored in .mdb files and SQL Server (or another ODBC data store) for data stored in .adp files. Access has always used the Jet database engine, although Microsoft didn't expose it as a separate entity until the release of Microsoft Visual Basic 3.

The Jet database engine and SQL Server, although very different, are both wonderful tools for storing and manipulating data. The difference between them lies in their architectures and the problems they are intended to address. Microsoft Jet is a "desktop" database engine, intended for small- to medium-sized systems. (Please note that this does *not* imply that the Jet database engine is appropriate only for trivial systems.) SQL Server, on the other hand, uses a client/server architecture and is intended for medium-sized to huge systems, scalable to potentially thousands of users running mission-critical applications. MSDE (an acronym for **M**icrosoft **D**esktop **E**ngine) is a scaled-down version of SQL Server intended for desktop use. From a designer's viewpoint, there is little difference between MSDE and the full version of SQL Server, and we won't be considering it further here. We'll be looking at the differences between the two database engines throughout this book and discussing the trade-offs between the two architectures in Chapter 13.

YUKON NOTE: As I write this in the spring of 2004, a new version of SQL Server, codenamed "Yukon," is in early Beta. It is already clear that Yukon will include significant new functionality, but it is not yet clear precisely what the changes will be. Given this (understandable) instability, I've limited my primary discussion to the capabilities of SQL Server 2000, the currently released version. Where these capabilities are expected to change significantly, I've indicated this in notes such as this one.

Data Access Object Models

Microsoft Access, and to a lesser extent Visual Studio .NET, provides simple mechanisms for binding form controls directly to a data source, avoiding the necessity for dealing directly with the database engine. For various reasons that we'll be looking at, however, this is not always either possible or appropriate. In these instances, you'll need to use a **data access object model** to manipulate the data in code.

A data access object model is a kind of glue between the programming environment and the database engine; it provides a set of objects with properties and methods that can be manipulated in code. Since this book deals primarily with design rather than implementation, we won't be discussing the trade-offs between these models in any great depth, but I believe it useful to review them here.

Microsoft (currently) provides three data access object models: Data Access Objects (DAO), which comes in two flavors (DAO/Jet and DAO/ODBCDirect), Microsoft ActiveX Data Objects (ADO) and ADO.NET.

DAO, the oldest of the three, is the native interface to the Jet database engine. The statements of Microsoft's marketing department notwithstanding, it is the most efficient object model to use for manipulating Jet databases within Microsoft Access. ADO uses a smaller object hierarchy than DAO, consisting of only four primary objects, and provides some significant extensions to the model—for example, its support for disconnected recordsets and data shaping. It is used within Microsoft Access and other products that support VBA for manipulating any ODBC-compliant database, including both Jet and SQL Server. ADO.NET is, of course, the version of ADO that is used when working within the .NET Framework.

Data Definition Environments

Microsoft Jet and SQL Server handle the physical aspects of manipulating data for us, but we need some way to tell them how to structure the data. Microsoft provides a plethora of methods for doing this, but we'll be looking at only three in detail: Access and the SQL Server Enterprise Manager for relational models, and the Analysis Manager for dimensional models. There are other tools that provide roughly the same capabilities, but these are the ones I prefer. Of course, once you understand the principles, you can use whichever tools best get the job done for you.

It's also possible to define the structure of your database using code, and we'll look at how you go about doing this, although under normal circumstances I don't recommend it. Unless for some reason you need to alter the structure of the data during the run-time use of your application (and with the possible exception of temporary tables, I'm highly suspicious of this practice—if the database schema isn't stable, you probably haven't understood the problem domain), the interactive tools are quicker, easier, and a lot more fun to use.

Front-End Development

Once the physical definition of your database is in place, you'll need tools to create the forms and reports your users will interact with. We'll draw our example from two of these: Access and Visual Studio .NET (specifically, Visual Basic .NET). Again, there are hundreds of front-end tools around, but the design principles remain the same, so you should be able to apply what you learn here to your front-end tool of choice. We'll take a quick look at Internet browsers in Chapter 10, but HTML itself is outside the scope of this book.

The Relational Model

The relational model is based on a collection of mathematical principles drawn primarily from set theory and predicate logic. These principles were first applied to the field of data modeling in the late 1960s by Dr. E. F. Codd, then a researcher at IBM, and first published in 1970.[1] The rules of the relational model define the way data can be represented (data structure), the way data can be protected (data integrity), and the operations that can be performed on data (data manipulation).

The relational model is not the only method available for storing and manipulating data. Alternatives include the hierarchical, network, and Object/Data models. Each of these models has its advocates, and each has its advantages for certain tasks. But because of its efficiency and flexibility, the relational model is by far the most popular database technique and is the one discussed in this book. Both the Microsoft Jet database engine and Microsoft SQL Server implement the relational model.

We'll also be discussing the dimensional model, a special kind of relational schema used for tracking historical data. We'll look at the dimensional model and its relationship to the relational model in detail in Part III.

---

1. Codd, E. F. "A Relational Model of Data for Large Shared Data Banks," Communications of the ACM, Vol. 13, No. 6 (June 1970).

In general terms, relational database systems have the following characteristics:

- All data is conceptually represented as an orderly arrangement of data into rows and columns, called a **relation**.
- All values are **scalar**. That is, at any given row/column position in the relation there is one and only one value.
- All operations are performed on an entire relation and result in an entire relation, a concept known as **closure**.

If you've worked with Microsoft Access databases at all, you'll recognize a "relation" as a "recordset" or, in SQL Server terms, as a "result set." Dr. Codd, when formulating the relational model, chose the term "relation" because it was comparatively free of connotations, unlike, for example, the word "table." It's a common misconception that the relational model is so called because relationships are established between tables. In fact, the name is derived from the relations on which it's based.

Notice that the model requires only that data be *conceptually* represented as a relation; it doesn't specify how the data should be physically stored. This separation of the conceptual and physical representations, although it seems obvious now, was a major innovation 30 years ago when database programming generally meant writing machine code to physically manipulate the data storage devices.

In fact, relations need not have a physical representation at all. A given relation might map to an actual physical table someplace on a disk, but it can just as well be based on columns drawn from half a dozen different tables, with a few calculated columns—which aren't physically stored anywhere—thrown in for good measure. A relation is a relation provided that it's arranged in row and column format and its values are scalar. Its existence is completely independent of any physical representation.

The requirement that all values in a relation be scalar can be somewhat treacherous. The concept of "one value" is necessarily subjective, based as it is on the semantics of the data model. To give a common example, a "Name" might be a single value in one model, but another environment might require that the value be split into "Title", "Given Name", and "Surname", and another might require the addition of "Middle Name" or "Title of Courtesy". None of these is more or less correct in absolute terms; it depends on the use to which the data will be put.

The principle of closure—that both base tables and the results of operations are represented conceptually as relations—enables the results of one operation to be used as the input to another operation. Thus, with both the

Jet database engine and SQL Server we can use the results of one query as the basis for another. This provides database designers with functionality similar to a subroutine in procedural development: the ability to encapsulate complex or commonly performed operations and reuse them whenever and wherever necessary.

For example, you might have created a query called FullNameQuery that concatenates the various attributes representing an individual's name into a single calculated field called FullName. You can create a second query using FullNameQuery as a source that uses the calculated FullName field just like any field that's actually present in the base table. There is no need to recalculate the name.

This is, of course, a simple example, and it's probably not immediately obvious that calling FullNameQuery provides any significant advantages over simply recalculating the full name. But as we'll see, the SQL language allows for the generation of extremely complex queries, and as the complexity increases, so do the benefits of using existing queries as input for new ones.

Relational Terminology

Figure 1–3 shows a relation with the formal names of the basic components marked. Those of you who know something about relational design will recognize that the relation is not in normal form. That's okay; it still qualifies as a relation because it's arranged in row and column format and its values are scalar.

The entire structure is, as we've said, a **relation**. Each row of data is a **tuple** (rhymes with "couple"). Technically, each row is an n-tuple, but the "n-" is usually dropped. The number of tuples in a relation determines its **cardinality**. In this case, the relation has a cardinality of 18. Each column in the tuple is called an **attribute**. The number of attributes in a relation determines its **degree**. The example relation has a degree of 3.

The relation is divided into two sections, the **heading** and the **body**. The tuples make up the body, while the heading is composed of, well, the heading. Note that in its relational representation the label for each attribute is composed of two terms separated by a colon—for example, UnitPrice:Currency. The first part of the label is the name of the attribute, while the second part is its domain. The **domain** of an attribute is the "kind" of data it represents—in this case, currency.

Figure 1–3 The Components of a Relation

A domain is *not* the same as a data type. We'll be discussing this issue in detail in the next section. The specification of domain is often dropped from the heading.

The body of the relation consists of an unordered set of zero or more tuples. There are some important concepts here. First, the relation is unordered. Think of a relation as a brown paper bag (or perhaps a Ming bowl if you're feeling poetic) containing all the tuples in no particular order. Record numbers, a common mechanism to access records in non-relational databases, do *not* apply to relations. Second, a relation with no tuples (an **empty relation**) still qualifies as a relation. Third, a relation is a set. The items in a set are, by definition, uniquely identifiable. Therefore, for a table to qualify as a relation, each record must be uniquely identifiable and the table must contain no duplicate records.

If you've read the Access or SQL Server documentation, you might be wondering why you've never seen any of these words before. They're the formal terminology used in the technical literature, not the terms used by Microsoft. I've included them just so you won't be embarrassed at cocktail parties (at least not about n-tuples of third degree, anyway).

Unfortunately, not only do Microsoft products not conform to formal terminology, they're not consistent. The terms used by the two products are shown in Table 1–1. I'll use the formal terminology in this book.

Table 1-1 The Relational Terminology Used by the Products Examined in this Book

Formal Terminology			
Conceptual	Physical	Microsoft Access	SQL Server
relation	table	table or recordset	table or result set
attribute	field	field	column
tuple	record	record	row

The Data Model

The most abstract level of a database design is the **data model**, the conceptual description of a problem space. Data models are expressed in terms of entities, attributes, domains, and relationships. The remainder of this chapter discusses each of these in turn.

Entities

It's difficult to provide a precise formal definition of the term entity, but the concept is intuitively quite straightforward: An entity is anything about which the system needs to store information.

When you begin to design your data model, compiling an initial list of entities isn't difficult. When you (or your clients) talk about the problem space, most of the nouns and verbs used will be candidate entities. "Customers buy products. Employees sell products. Suppliers sell us products." The nouns "Customers," "Products," "Employees," and "Suppliers" are all clearly entities.

The events represented by the verbs "buy" and "sell" are also entities, but a couple of traps exist here. First, the verb "sell" is used to represent two distinct events: the sale of a product to a customer (Salesman→Customer) and the purchase of a product by the organization (Supplier→Company). That's fairly obvious in this example, but it's an easy trap to fall into, particularly if you're not familiar with the problem space.

The second trap is the inverse of the first: two different verbs ("buy" in the first sentence and "sell" in the second) are used to describe the same event, the purchase of a product by a customer. Again, this isn't necessarily obvious unless you're familiar with the problem space. This problem is often trickier to track down than the first. If a client is using different verbs to describe what appears to be the same event, they might in fact be describing different kinds of events. If the client is a tailor, for example, "customer buys suit" and "customer orders suit" might both result in the sale of a suit, but in the first case it's a prêt-à-porter sale and in the second it's bespoke. These are very different processes that will probably need to be modeled differently.

In addition to interviewing clients to establish a list of entities, it's also useful to review any documents that exist in the problem space. Input forms, reports, and procedures manuals are all good sources of candidate entities. You must be careful with documents, however. Printed documents have a great deal of inertia—input forms particularly are expensive to print and frequently don't keep up with changes to policies and procedures. If you stumble across an entity that's never come up in an interview, don't assume the client just forgot to mention it. Chances are that it's a legacy item that's no longer pertinent to the organization. You'll need to check.

Most entities model objects or events in the physical world: customers, products, or sales calls. These are **concrete entities**. Entities can also model abstract concepts. The most common example of an **abstract entity** is one that models the relationship between other entities—for example, the fact that a certain sales representative is responsible for a certain client or that a certain student is enrolled in a certain class.

Sometimes all you need to model is the fact that a relationship exists. Other times you'll want to store additional information about the relationships, such as the date on which it was established or some characteristic of the relationship. The relationship between cougars and coyotes is competitive, that between cougars and rabbits is predatory, and it's useful to know this if you're planning an open-range zoo.

Whether relationships that do not have attributes ought to be modeled as separate entities is a matter of some discussion. I personally don't think anything is gained by doing so, and it complicates the process of deriving a database schema from the data model. However, understanding that relationships are as important as entities is crucial for designing an effective data model.

Attributes

Your system will need to keep track of certain facts about each entity. As we've seen, these facts are the entity's attributes. If your system includes a Customer entity, for example, you'll probably want to know the names and addresses of the customers and perhaps the businesses they're in. If you're modeling an event such as a ServiceCall, you'll probably want to know who the customer was, who made the call, when it was made, and whether the problem was resolved. All of these are attributes.

Determining the attributes to be included in your model is a semantic process. That is, you must make your decisions based on what the data means and how it will be used. Let's look at one common example: an address. Do you model the address as a single entity (the Address) or as a set of entities (HouseNumber, Street, City, State, ZipCode)? Most designers (myself included) would tend to automatically break the address up into a set of attributes on the general principle that structured data is easier to manipulate, but this is not necessarily correct and certainly not straightforward.

Let's take, for instance, a local amateur musical society. It will want to store the addresses of its members in order to print mailing labels. That's the only purpose to which the address will be put, so there is no reason to ever look at an address as anything other than a single, multi-line chunk of text that gets spat out on demand.

But what about a mail-order company that does all its business on the Internet? For sales tax purposes, the company needs to know the states in which its customers reside. While it's possible to extract the state from the single text field used by the musical society, it isn't easy; so it makes sense in this case to at least model the state as a separate attribute. What about the rest of the address? Should it be composed of multiple attributes, and if so, what are they? You might think that a set of attributes {HouseNumber, Street, City, State, ZipCode} might be adequate. But then you need to deal with apartment numbers and post office boxes and APO addresses. What do you do with an address to be sent in care of someone else? And of course the world is getting smaller but not less complex, so what happens when you get your first customer outside the United States? While addresses in the United States conform to a fairly standard pattern, that isn't true when you start dealing with international orders.

Not only do you need to know the country and adjust the format of the zip code (and possibly start calling it a "post code"), but the arrangement of the attributes might need to change. In most of Europe, for example, the house number follows the street name. That's not too bad, it's easy enough to map that when you're entering data, but how many of your American data entry operators are going to know that in the address 4/32 Griffen Avenue, Bondi Beach, Australia, 4/32 means Apartment 4, Number 32?

The point here is not so much that addresses are hard to model, although they are, but rather that you can't make any assumptions about how you should model any specific kind of data. The complex schema that you develop for handling international mail order is completely inappropriate for the local musical society.

Matisse is reputed to have said that a painting was finished when nothing could be either added or subtracted. Entity design is a bit like that. How do you know when you've reached that point? The unfortunate answer is that you can never know for certain (and even if you think you do, it'll probably change over time). At the current state of technology, there isn't any way to develop a provably correct database design. You can prove that some designs have flaws, but you can't prove that any given design doesn't. You can't, if you will, prove your innocence. How do you tackle this problem? There are no rules, but there are some strategies.

The first strategy: **Start with the result and don't make the design any more complex than it needs to be.** What questions does your database have to answer? In our first example, the musical society, the only question was "Where do I mail a letter to this person?" so a single-attribute model was sufficient. The second example, the mail order company, also had to answer "In what state does this person live?" so we needed a different structure to provide the results.

You need to be careful, of course, that you try to provide the flexibility to handle not just the questions your users are asking now but also the ones you can foresee them asking in the future. I'd be willing to bet, for instance, that within a year of implementing the musical society system the society will come back asking you to sort the addresses by zip code so that they can qualify for bulk mail discounts.

You should also be on the lookout for questions the users would ask if they only knew they could, particularly if you're automating a manual system. Imagine asking a head librarian how many of the four million books in the collection were published in Chicago before 1900. He or she would point you to the card file and tell you to have fun. Yet this is trivial information to request from a well-designed database system.

One of the hallmarks of good designers is the thoroughness and creativity with which they solicit potential questions. Inexperienced analysts are frequently heard to remark that the users don't know what they want. Of course they don't; it's *your* job to help them discover what they want.

You need to be careful here, however. The trade-off for flexibility is often increased complexity. As we saw with the address examples, the more ways you want to slice and dice the data, the more exceptions you have to handle, and you will reach a point of diminishing returns.

This leads me to strategy two: **Find the exceptions**. There are two sides to this strategy. First, that you must identify all the exceptions, and second, that you must design the system to handle as many exceptions as you can without confusing users. To illustrate what this means, let's walk through another example: personal names.

If your system will be used to produce correspondence, it's crucial that you get the name right. (Case in point: Unsolicited mail arriving at my house addressed to *Mr.* R. M. Riordan doesn't even get opened.) Most names are pretty straightforward. Ms. Jane Q. Public consists of the Title, FirstName, MiddleInitial, and LastName, right? Wrong. (You saw that coming, didn't you?) To start with, FirstName and LastName are culturally specific. It's safer (and more politically correct) to use GivenName and Surname. Next, what happens to Sir James Peddington Smythe, Lord Dunstable? Is Peddington Smythe his Surname or is Peddington his MiddleName, and what do you do about the "Lord Dunstable" part? And the singer Sting? Is that a GivenName or a Surname? And what will happen to The Artist Formerly Known as Prince? Do you really care?

That last question isn't as flippant as it sounds. A letter addressed to Sir James Peddington Smythe probably won't offend anyone. But the gentleman in question is not Sir Smythe; he's Sir James, or maybe Lord Dunstable. Realistically, though, how many of your clients are lords of the realm? The local musical society is not going to thank you for giving them a membership system with a screen like the one in Figure 1–4.

Remember that there's a trade-off between flexibility and complexity. While it's important to catch as many exceptions as possible, it's perfectly reasonable to eliminate some of them as too unlikely to be worth the cost of dealing with them.

Distinguishing between entities and attributes is sometimes difficult. Again, addresses are a good example, and again, your decision must be

Figure 1–4 An Overly Complex Address Screen

based on the problem space. Some designers advocate the creation of a single address entity used to store all the addresses modeled by the system. From an implementation viewpoint, this approach has certain advantages in terms of encapsulation and code reuse. From a design viewpoint, I have some reservations.

It's unlikely, for example, that addresses for employees and customers will be used in the same way. Mass mailings to employees, for example, are more likely to be done via internal mail than the postal service. This being the case, the rules and requirements are different. That awful data entry screen shown in Figure 1–4 or something very like it might very well be justified for customer addresses, but by using a single address entity you're forced to use it for employees as well, where it's unlikely to be either necessary or appreciated.

Domains

You might recall from the beginning of this chapter that a relation heading contains an AttributeName:DomainName pair for each attribute. I said then that a domain definition specifies the kind of data represented by the attribute. More particularly, a **domain** is the set of all possible values that an attribute may validly contain.

Domains are often confused with data types; they are not the same. Data type is a physical concept while domain is a logical one. "Number" is a data type; "Age" is a domain. To give another example, "StreetName" and "Surname" might both be represented as text fields, but they are obviously different *kinds* of text fields; they belong to different domains.

Domain is also a narrower concept than data type in that a domain definition includes a more specific description of the valid data. Take, for example, the domain DegreeAwarded, which represents the degrees awarded by a university. In the database schema, this attribute might be defined as Text[3], but it's not just any three-character string, it's a member of the set {BA, BS, MA, MS, PhD, LLD, MD}.

Of course, not all domains can be defined by simply listing their values. Age, for example, contains a hundred or so values if we're talking about people, but tens of thousands if we're talking about museum exhibits. In such instances it's easier to define the domain in terms of the rules that can be used to determine the membership of any specific value in the set of all valid values rather than listing the values. For example, PersonAge could be defined as "an integer in the range 0 to 120," whereas ExhibitAge might simply be "an integer equal to or greater than 0."

At this point you might be thinking that a domain is the combination of the data type and the validation rule. Well, if you think of it this way, you won't go too far wrong. But validation rules are strictly part of the data integrity, not part of the data description. For example, the validation rule for a zip code might refer to the State attribute, whereas the domain of Zip-Code is "a five-digit string" (or perhaps an eleven-character string, if you're using the Zip + 4 format.)

Note that each of these definitions makes some reference to the kind of data stored (number or string). This looks a whole lot like a data type, but it isn't really. Data types, as I've said, are physical; they're defined and implemented in terms of the database engine. It would be a mistake to define a domain as varchar(30) or Long Integer, which are engine-specific descriptions.

For any two domains, if it makes sense to compare attributes defined on them (and, by extension, to perform relational operations such as joins, which we'll discuss in Chapter 5), then the two domains are said to be **type-compatible**. For example, given the two relations in Figure 1–5, it would be perfectly sensible to link them on EmployeeID = SalespersonID. You might, for example, do this to obtain a list of invoices for a given employee. The domains EmployeeID and SalespersonID are type-compatible. Trying to combine the relations on EmployeeID = OrderDate, however, would probably not result in a meaningful answer, even if the two domains were defined on the same data type.

Unfortunately, neither the Jet database engine nor SQL Server provides strong intrinsic support for domains beyond data types. And even within

Order ID	Customer	Salesperson ID	Order Date
10643	Alfreds Futterkiste	6	25-Aug-1997
10692	Alfreds Futterkiste	4	03-Oct-1997
10702	Alfreds Futterkiste	4	13-Oct-1997
10835	Alfreds Futterkiste	1	15-Jan-1998
10952	Alfreds Futterkiste	1	16-Mar-1998

Employee ID	Title Of Courtesy	Given Name	Surname	Title
1	Ms.	Nancy	Davolio	Sales Representative
2	Dr.	Andrew	Fuller	Vice President, Sales
3	Ms.	Janet	Leverling	Sales Representative
4	Mrs.	Margaret	Peacock	Sales Representative
5	Mr.	Steven	Buchanan	Sales Manager
6	Mr.	Michael	Suyama	Sales Representative
7	Mr.	Robert	King	Sales Representative
8	Ms.	Laura	Callahan	Inside Sales Coordinator
9	Ms.	Anne	Dodsworth	Sales Representative

Figure 1–5 The Employees and Orders Relations

data types, neither engine performs strong checking; both will quietly convert data behind the scenes. For example, if you're using Microsoft Access and have defined EmployeeID as a long integer in the Employees table and InvoiceTotal as a currency value in the Invoices, you can create a query linking the two tables on EmployeeID = InvoiceTotal, and Microsoft Jet will quite happily give you a list of all employees who have an EmployeeID that matches the total value of an invoice. The two attributes are not type-compatible, but the Jet database engine doesn't know or care.

So why bother with domains at all? Because, as we'll see in Part III, they're extremely useful design tools. "Are these two attributes interchangeable?" "Are there any rules that apply to one but don't apply to the other?" These are important questions when you're designing a data model, and domain analysis helps you think about them.

Relationships

In addition to the attributes of each entity, a data model must specify the relationships between entities. At the conceptual level, **relationships** are simply associations between entities. The statement "Customers buy products" indicates that a relationship exists between the entities Customers and Products. The entities involved in a relationship are called its **participants**. The number of participants is the **degree** of the relationship. (The degree of a relationship is similar to, but not the same as, the degree of a relation, which is the number of attributes.)

The vast majority of relationships are binary, like the "Customers buy products" example, but this is not a requirement. Ternary relationships, those with three participants, are also common. Given the binary relationships "Employees sell products" and "Customers buy products," there is an implicit ternary relationship "Employees sell products to customers." However, specifying the two binary relationships does not allow us to identify which employees sold which products to which customers; only a ternary relationship can do that.

A special case of a binary relationship is an entity that participates in a relationship with itself. This is often called the bill of materials relationship and is most often used to represent hierarchical structures. A common example is the relationship between employees and managers: Any given employee might both *be* a manager and *have* a manager.

The relationship between any two entities can be one-to-one, one-to-many, or many-to-many. One-to-one relationships are rare, but can be useful in certain circumstances.

One-to-many relationships are probably the most common type. An invoice includes many products. A salesperson creates many invoices. These are both examples of one-to-many relationships.

Although not as common as one-to-many relationships, many-to-many relationships are also not unusual and examples abound. Customers buy many products, and products are bought by many customers. Teachers teach many students, and students are taught by many teachers. Many-to-many relationships can't be directly implemented in the relational model, but their indirect implementation is quite straightforward, as we'll see in Chapter 3.

The participation of any given entity in a relationship can be **partial** or **total**. If it is not possible for an entity to exist unless it participates in the relationship, the participation is total; otherwise, it is partial. For example, Salesperson details can't logically exist unless there is a corresponding Employee. The reverse is not true. An employee might be something other than a salesperson, so an Employee record can exist without a corresponding Salesperson record. Thus, the participation of Employee in the relationship is partial, while the participation of Salesperson is total.

The trick here is to ensure that the specification of partial or total participation holds true for all instances of the entity for all time. It's not unknown for companies to change suppliers for a product, for example. If the participation of Products in the "Suppliers provide products" relation has been defined as total, it won't be possible to delete the current supplier without deleting the product details.

Entity Relationship Diagrams

The Entity Relationship model, which describes data in terms of entities, attributes, and relations, was introduced by Peter Pin Shan Chen in 1976.[2] At the same time, he proposed a method of diagramming called Entity Relationship (E/R) diagrams, which has become widely accepted. E/R diagrams use rectangles to describe entities, ellipses for attributes, and diamonds to represent relationships, as shown in Figure 1–6.

The nature of the relationship between entities (one-to-one, one-to-many, or many-to-many) is represented in various ways. A number of people use 1 and M or 1 and ∞ (representing infinity) to represent one and many. I use the "crow's foot" technique shown in Figure 1–6, which I find more expressive.

---

2. Peter Pin Shan Chen, "The Entity Relationship Model—Toward a Unified View of Data?", ACM TODS 1, No. 1 (March 1976).

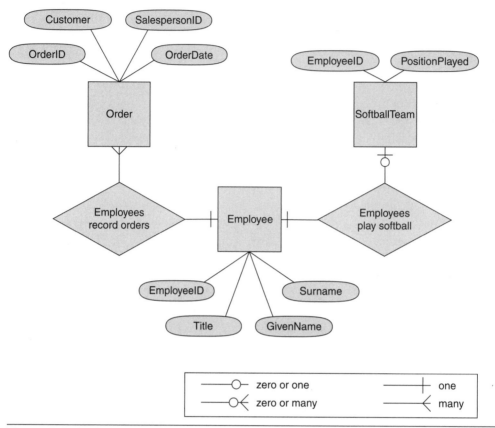

Figure 1–6 An E/R Diagram

The great advantage of E/R diagrams is that they're easy to draw and understand. In practice, though, I usually diagram the attributes separately, since they exist at a different level of detail. Generally, one is either thinking about the entities in the model and the relationships between them or thinking about the attributes of a given entity, but rarely thinking about both at the same time.

Summary

In this chapter, we've looked at the components of a database system and laid the foundations for the rest of the book. We began by describing the problem space as some well-defined part of the real world. The conceptual data model is a description of the problem space in terms of entities, attributes, and the domains on which they are defined. The physical layout of the data model is the database schema, which is instantiated as a database. Finally, the database engine handles the physical manipulation of the database on behalf of the application, which consists of the forms and reports with which users interact.

In the next chapter, we'll examine the structure of a database in more detail as we explore the principles of normalization.

CHAPTER 2

Database Structure

This chapter discusses the first facet of designing relational database models: the structure of the relations themselves. The primary goal of this design phase is simple: to ensure that the model is capable of answering every question that might reasonably be asked of it. The secondary goal is to minimize redundancy and the problems associated with it. We'll examine these two issues in reverse order.

Eliminating Redundancy

Redundancy wastes resources and, more importantly, it makes life a lot harder. Take, for example, the recordset shown in Figure 2–1, representing a company's invoices. (Assume, for the moment, that this recordset is a base table that is explicitly stored in the database, not the result of a query.)

Order ID	SalesPerson	Hire Date	Phone	Company Name	Product Name	Quantity
10871	Dodsworth, Anne	15-Nov-1994	452	Bon app'	Alice Mutton	16
10747	Suyama, Michael	17-Oct-1993	428	Piccolo und mehr	Gorgonzola Telino	8
10258	Davolio, Nancy	01-May-1992	5467	Ernst Handel	Chef Anton's Gumbo Mix	65
11007	Callahan, Laura	05-Mar-1994	2344	Princesa Isabel Vinhos	Thüringer Rostbratwurst	10
10421	Callahan, Laura	05-Mar-1994	2344	Que Delícia	Perth Pasties	15
10558	Davolio, Nancy	01-May-1992	5467	Around the Horn	Perth Pasties	18
10431	Peacock, Margaret	03-May-1993	5176	Bottom-Dollar Markets	Alice Mutton	50
10659	King, Robert	02-Jan-1994	465	Queen Cozinha	Gorgonzola Telino	20
10273	Leverling, Janet	01-Apr-1992	3355	QUICK-Stop	Gorgonzola Telino	15
10382	Peacock, Margaret	03-May-1993	5176	Ernst Handel	Chef Anton's Gumbo Mix	32
10949	Fuller, Andrew	14-Aug-1992	3457	Bottom-Dollar Markets	Alice Mutton	6
10285	Davolio, Nancy	01-May-1992	5467	QUICK-Stop	Perth Pasties	36
10867	Suyama, Michael	17-Oct-1993	428	Lonesome Pine Restaur	Perth Pasties	3
10691	Fuller, Andrew	14-Aug-1992	3457	QUICK-Stop	Thüringer Rostbratwurst	40
10354	Callahan, Laura	05-Mar-1994	2344	Pericles Comidas clásic	Thüringer Rostbratwurst	4
10698	Peacock, Margaret	03-May-1993	5176	Ernst Handel	Thüringer Rostbratwurst	12
10962	Callahan, Laura	05-Mar-1994	2344	QUICK-Stop	Perth Pasties	20
10465	Davolio, Nancy	01-May-1992	5467	Vaffeljernet	Thüringer Rostbratwurst	18
10549	Buchanan, Steven	17-Oct-1993	3453	QUICK-Stop	Gorgonzola Telino	55

Figure 2–1 This Recordset Has Redundant Data

You can see that HireDate and Phone values are listed several times for each employee. Now, this has a number of consequences. First, it means that every time you enter a new invoice you have to re-enter values into these fields. And, of course, every time you enter something you have another chance to get it wrong. For example, given the recordset shown in Figure 2–2, how do you know whether Nancy Davolio was hired in 1992 or 1999?

Second, the structure prevents you from storing the hire date or phone number for a new employee until that employee has made a sale. Third, if the invoices for a given year are archived and removed from the database, the hire date and phone number information will be lost.

These kinds of problems, usually called **update anomalies**, are even worse if the redundant data is stored in more than one relation. Consider the recordsets shown in Figure 2–3. (Again, assume that these are base tables, not query results.) If the phone number of Alfreds Futterkiste changes, it must be changed in seven different places—once in the Customer recordset, and six times in the Invoice recordset.

It's not so much that this is impossible or even particularly difficult to do. The problem is remembering to do it. And even if *you* never forget anything, how will you ensure that the maintenance programmer modifying your system six months from now will know there are redundancies of this kind, much less remember (or know how) to handle them appropriately? It's better, much better, to avoid the redundancies and the resulting problems altogether.

However, you need to make sure that the redundant attributes you're considering really are redundant. Consider the example in Figure 2–4. At first glance, you might think that the UnitPrice attributes in these two relations are redundant. But they actually represent two distinct values. The UnitPrice attribute in the Products relation represents the current selling price. The UnitPrice attribute in the Orders relation represents the price at the time the item was sold. Tofu, for example, is listed at a UnitPrice of $18.60 in the Orders relation and $23.25 in the Products relation. The fact

When was she hired?

Order ID	SalesPerson	Hire Date	Phone	Company Name	Product Name	Quantity
10871	Dodsworth, Anne	15-Nov-1994	452	Bon app'	Alice Mutton	16
10747	Suyama, Michael	17-Oct-1993	428	Piccolo und mehr	Gorgonzola Telino	8
10258	Davolio, Nancy	01-May-1992	5467	Ernst Handel	Chef Anton's Gumbo Mix	65
11007	Callahan, Laura	05-Mar-1994	2344	Princesa Isabel Vinhos	Thüringer Rostbratwurst	10
10421	Callahan, Laura	05-Mar-1994	2344	Que Delícia	Perth Pasties	15
10558	Davolio, Nancy	01-May-1999	5467	Around the Horn	Perth Pasties	18
10431	Peacock, Margaret	03-May-1993	5176	Bottom-Dollar Markets	Alice Mutton	50

Figure 2–2 Duplicate Data Can Result in Inconsistencies

Customers Relation

Customer ID	Company Name	Phone
ALFKI	Alfreds Futterkiste	030-0074321
ANATR	Ana Trujillo Emparedados y helados	(5) 555-4729
ANTON	Antonio Moreno Taquería	(5) 555-3932
AROUT	Around the Horn	(171) 555-7788
BERGS	Berglunds snabbköp	0921-12 34 65
BLAUS	Blauer See Delikatessen	0621-08460
BLONP	Blondel père et fils	88.60.15.31
BOLID	Bólido Comidas preparadas	(91) 555 22 82
BONAP	Bon app'	91.24.45.40
BOTTM	Bottom-Dollar Markets	(604) 555-4729
BSBEV	B's Beverages	(171) 555-1212
CACTU	Cactus Comidas para llevar	(1) 135-5555
CENTC	Centro comercial Moctezuma	(5) 555-3392

Invoices Relation

Order ID	Company Name	Phone
10643	Alfreds Futterkiste	030-0074321
10692	Alfreds Futterkiste	030-0074321
10702	Alfreds Futterkiste	030-0074321
10835	Alfreds Futterkiste	030-0074321
10952	Alfreds Futterkiste	030-0074321
11011	Alfreds Futterkiste	030-0074321
10308	Ana Trujillo Emparedados y helados	(5) 555-4729
10625	Ana Trujillo Emparedados y helados	(5) 555-4729
10759	Ana Trujillo Emparedados y helados	(5) 555-4729
10926	Ana Trujillo Emparedados y helados	(5) 555-4729
10365	Antonio Moreno Taquería	(5) 555-3932
10507	Antonio Moreno Taquería	(5) 555-3932
10535	Antonio Moreno Taquería	(5) 555-3932
10573	Antonio Moreno Taquería	(5) 555-3932
10677	Antonio Moreno Taquería	(5) 555-3932

Figure 2–3 The Same Duplicate Data Can Exist in Multiple Recordsets

that Tofu currently sells for $23.25 doesn't change the fact that it was sold for $18.60 at some point in the past. The two attributes are defined on the same domain, but they are logically distinct.

Ensuring Flexibility

The other goal of the design phase is to ensure that the database is flexible—that it can answer every question that might reasonably be asked of it. Flexibility is primarily determined by its completeness (obviously, no database system can provide data it doesn't contain) and only secondarily by its structure. But the *ease* with which questions can be answered is almost

Product ID	Product Name	Unit Price
1	Chai	$18.00
2	Chang	$19.00
3	Aniseed Syrup	$10.00
4	Chef Anton's Cajun Seasoning	$22.00
5	Chef Anton's Gumbo Mix	$21.35
6	Grandma's Boysenberry Spread	$25.00
7	Uncle Bob's Organic Dried Pears	$30.00
8	Northwoods Cranberry Sauce	$40.00
9	Mishi Kobe Niku	$97.00
10	Ikura	$31.00
11	Queso Cabrales	$21.00
12	Queso Manchego La Pastora	$38.00
13	Konbu	$6.00
14	Tofu	$23.25

These are not
the same value

Order ID	Product Name	Unit Price	Quantity	Unit Price
10248	Mozzarella di Giovanni	$34.80	5	$174.00
10248	Queso Cabrales	$21.00	12	$168.00
10248	Singaporean Hokkien Fried Mee	$14.00	10	$98.00
10249	Manjimup Dried Apples	$53.00	40	$1,696.00
10249	Tofu	$23.25	9	$167.40

Figure 2–4 Seemingly Identical Data Might Not Actually Be Redundant

exclusively the result of the structure. The principle here is that it is easy to combine attributes and relations, but very difficult to take them apart.

Employee ID	Title	Given Name	Surname	Title
1	Ms.	Nancy	Davolio	Sales Representative
2	Dr.	Andrew	Fuller	Vice President, Sales
3	Ms.	Janet	Leverling	Sales Representative
4	Mrs.	Margaret	Peacock	Sales Representative
5	Mr.	Steven	Buchanan	Sales Manager
6	Mr.	Michael	Suyama	Sales Representative
7	Mr.	Robert	King	Sales Representative
8	Ms.	Laura	Callahan	Inside Sales Coordinator
9	Ms.	Anne	Dodsworth	Sales Representative

Employee ID	FullName
1	Ms. Nancy Davolio, Sales Representative
2	Dr. Andrew Fuller, Vice President, Sales
3	Ms. Janet Leverling, Sales Representative
4	Mrs. Margaret Peacock, Sales Representative
5	Mr. Steven Buchanan, Sales Manager
6	Mr. Michael Suyama, Sales Representative
7	Mr. Robert King, Sales Representative
8	Ms. Laura Callahan, Inside Sales Coordinator
9	Ms. Anne Dodsworth, Sales Representative

Figure 2–5 Concatenating Information Is Easy, but Extracting It from Composite Fields Is Hard

For example, given the two relations shown in Figure 2–5, the FullName can be easily derived from the top relation with the statement:

```
TitleOfCourtesy & " " & GivenName & " " & Surname & _
   ", " & Title
```

But retrieving only the LastName from the FullName field shown in the bottom relation would require manipulating the string itself:

```
Function GetLastname(FullName) As String
   Dim lastname As String

   'strip off the Title
   lastname = Left(FullName, InStr(FullName, ",") - 1)
   'strip off the TitleOfCourtesy
   lastname = Right(lastname, Len(lastname) _ _
      InStr(lastname, " "))
   'strip off FirstName
   lastname = Right(lastname , Len(lastname ) - _
      InStr(lastname , " "))

   GetLastname = lastname

End Function
```

This technique is also vulnerable to variations in the contents of the FullName field. For example, the name "Billy Rae Jones" is going to return "Rae Jones", when what you probably wanted was "Jones". Producing a list in the format LastName, FirstName could get very ugly.

The second principle involved in creating a data model that can effectively answer the questions asked of it is to avoid situations where answering the question requires evaluating the same information from multiple fields. Take the relations shown in Figure 2–6, for example, both of which model student enrollments.

To answer the question "Which students are studying Biology this year?" using the first relation, you would have to search for the value "Biology" in three fields. The SQL SELECT statement[1] would look like this:

```
SELECT StudentID FROM Enrollments WHERE Period1 = "Biology"
   OR Period2 = "Biology" OR Period3 = "Biology"
```

---

1. Don't worry too much about the SQL syntax in these examples. We'll be examining the SQL language in detail in Chapter 5.

StudentID	GivenName	Surname	Period1	Period2	Period3
1	Nancy	Davolio	Biology	History	English
2	Andrew	Fuller	Physical Education	Biology	French
3	Janet	Levering	Physical Education	Biology	French
4	Margaret	Peacock	French	Physical Education	History
5	Steven	Buchanan	Biology	French	Physical Education
6	Michael	Suyama	French	Physical Education	Biology
7	Robert	King	History	French	English

StudentClassID	GivenName	Surname	Period	Class
10	Margaret	Peacock	1	French
19	Robert	King	1	History
4	Andrew	Fuller	1	Physical Education
16	Michael	Suyama	1	French
7	Janet	Leverling	1	Physical Education
13	Steven	Buchanan	1	Biology
1	Nancy	Davolio	1	Biology
2	Nancy	Davolio	2	French
5	Andrew	Fuller	2	Biology
8	Janet	Leverling	2	Biology
11	Margaret	Peacock	2	Physical Education
14	Steven	Buchanan	2	French
17	Michael	Suyama	2	Physical Education
20	Robert	King	2	French
21	Robert	King	3	Biology
9	Janet	Leverling	3	French
15	Steven	Buchanan	3	Physical Education
6	Andrew	Fuller	3	French
18	Michael	Suyama	3	Biology
3	Nancy	Davolio	3	English
12	Margaret	Peacock	3	History

Figure 2–6 These Two Recordsets Contain the Same Data

Using the second structure requires searching only a single field, Class:

```
SELECT StudentID FROM Enrollments WHERE Class = "Biology";
```

They both work, but the second one is obviously easier and less error-prone to code, not to mention easier to think about.

Avoiding redundancy and making it easy to retrieve the data are all you need to know about data modeling; the rest is just an attempt to formalize these two basic principles. But if you've ever done much (or any) data modeling, you'll know that, simple as they might be, these principles can be very slippery to apply. They're like a paper clip: The answer is perfectly obvious once you've seen it, but a little hard to come up with the first time you're faced with a bunch of loose paper and a bit of wire.

Basic Principles

The process of structuring the data in the problem space to achieve these two goals of eliminating redundancy and ensuring flexibility is called **normalization**. The principles of normalization discussed in the rest of this chapter are tools for controlling the structure of data in the same way that a paper clip controls sheets of paper. The **normal forms** (we'll discuss six) specify increasingly stringent rules for the structure of relations. Each form extends the previous one in such a way as to prevent certain kinds of update anomalies.

Bear in mind that the normal forms are not a prescription for creating a "correct" data model. A data model could be perfectly normalized and still fail to answer the questions asked of it; or, it might provide the answers, but so slowly and awkwardly that the database system built around it is unusable. But if your data model is normalized—that is, if it conforms to the rules of relational structure—the chances are high that the result will be an efficient, effective data model.

Before we turn to normalization, however, you should be familiar with a couple of underlying principles.

Lossless Decomposition

The relational model allows relations to be joined in various ways by linking attributes. The process of obtaining a fully normalized data model involves removing redundancy by dividing relations in such a way that the resultant relations can be recombined without losing any of the information. This is the principle of **lossless decomposition**. For example, given the relation shown in Figure 2–7, you can derive the two relations shown in Figure 2–8.

Order ID	Order Date	Required Date	Customer ID	Company Name	Address	City
10853	27-Jan-1998	24-Feb-1998	BLAUS	Blauer See Delikatessen	Forsterstr. 57	Mannheim
10905	24-Feb-1998	24-Mar-1998	WELLI	Wellington Importadora	Rua do Mercado, 12	Resende
10953	16-Mar-1998	30-Mar-1998	AROUT	Around the Horn	120 Hanover Sq.	London
11016	10-Apr-1998	08-May-1998	AROUT	Around the Horn	120 Hanover Sq.	London
10736	11-Nov-1997	09-Dec-1997	HUNGO	Hungry Owl All-Night Grocers	8 Johnstown Road	Cork
11022	14-Apr-1998	12-May-1998	HANAR	Hanari Carnes	Rua do Paço, 67	Rio de Janeiro
10577	23-Jun-1997	04-Aug-1997	TRAIH	Trail's Head Gourmet Provisione	722 DaVinci Blvd.	Kirkland
10750	21-Nov-1997	19-Dec-1997	WARTH	Wartian Herkku	Torikatu 38	Oulu
10324	08-Oct-1996	05-Nov-1996	SAVEA	Save-a-lot Markets	187 Suffolk Ln.	Boise

Figure 2–7 An Unnormalized Relation

Customer ID	Company Name	Address	City
ALFKI	Alfreds Futterkiste	Obere Str. 57	Berlin
ANATR	Ana Trujillo Emparedados y helados	Avda. de la Constitución 2222	México D.F.
ANTON	Antonio Moreno Taquería	Mataderos 2312	México D.F.
AROUT	Around the Horn	120 Hanover Sq.	London
BERGS	Berglunds snabbköp	Berguvsvägen 8	Luleå
BLAUS	Blauer See Delikatessen	Forsterstr. 57	Mannheim
BLONP	Blondel père et fils	24, place Kléber	Strasbourg
BOLID	Bólido Comidas preparadas	C/ Araquil, 67	Madrid

Order ID	Order Date	Required Date	Customer
11077	06-May-1998	03-Jun-1998	RATTC
11076	06-May-1998	03-Jun-1998	BONAP
11075	06-May-1998	03-Jun-1998	RICSU
11074	06-May-1998	03-Jun-1998	SIMOB
11073	05-May-1998	02-Jun-1998	PERIC
11072	05-May-1998	02-Jun-1998	ERNSH
11071	05-May-1998	02-Jun-1998	LILAS
11070	05-May-1998	02-Jun-1998	LEHMS
11069	04-May-1998	01-Jun-1998	TORTU

Figure 2–8 The Relation in Figure 2–8 Can Be Divided into These Two Relations without Losing Any Information

Candidate Keys and Primary Keys

In Chapter 1, I defined a relation body as an unordered set of zero or more tuples and pointed out that, by definition, each member of a set is unique. This being the case, for any relation there must be some combination of attributes that uniquely identifies each tuple. If the rows cannot be uniquely identified, they do not constitute tuples in relational theory. This set of one or more attributes is called a **candidate key**.

There might be more than one candidate key for any given relation, but it must always be the case that each candidate key uniquely identifies each tuple, not just for any specific set of tuples but for all possible tuples for all time. The inverse of this principle must also be true, by the way. Given any two tuples with the same candidate key, both tuples must represent the same entity.

Like so many things in relational design, the identification of a candidate key is semantic. You cannot do it by inspection. Just because some field or combination of attributes is unique for a given set of tuples, you cannot guarantee that it will be unique for *all* tuples, which it must be to qualify as a candidate key. Once again, you must understand the semantics—what the data means—of the data model, not what it *appears* to mean.

Consider the Orders relation shown at the bottom of Figure 2–8. The CustomerID is unique in the example, but it's extremely unlikely that it will remain that way. After all, most companies rely on repeat business. Despite appearances, the semantics of the model tell us that this field is *not* a candidate key.

By definition, all relations must have at least one candidate key: the set of all attributes comprising the tuple. Candidate keys can be composed of a single attribute (a **simple key**) or of multiple attributes (a **composite key**).

Some people are under the impression that composite keys are somehow incorrect, and that they must add an artificial identifier—either an identity or autonumber field—to their tables to avoid them. Nothing could be further from the truth. Artificial keys are often more convenient, as we'll see, but composite keys are perfectly acceptable.

However, an additional requirement of a candidate key is that it must be irreducible, so the set of all attributes is not *necessarily* a candidate key. In the relation shown in Figure 2–9, the attribute {CategoryName} is a candidate key, as is {Description}, but the set {CategoryName, Description}, although it is unique, is not a candidate key since the Description attribute is unnecessary.

It is sometimes the case—although it doesn't happen often—that there are multiple possible candidate keys for a relation. In this case, it is customary to designate one candidate key as a **primary key** and consider other candidate keys **alternate keys**. This is an arbitrary decision and isn't very useful at the logical level. (Remember that the data model is purely abstract.) To help maintain the distinction between the model and its physical implementation, I prefer to use the term "candidate key" at the data model level and reserve "primary key" for the implementation.

When the only possible candidate key is unwieldy—it requires too many attributes or is too large, for example—you can use an artificial unique field data type for creating artificial keys with values that will be generated by the system.

Category Name	Description
Beverages	Soft drinks, coffees, teas, beers, and ales
Condiments	Sweet and savory sauces, relishes, spreads, and seasonings
Confections	Desserts, candies, and sweet breads
Dairy Products	Cheeses
Grains/Cereals	Breads, crackers, pasta, and cereal
Meat/Poultry	Prepared meats
Produce	Dried fruit and bean curd
Seafood	Seaweed and fish

Figure 2–9 Candidate Keys Must Be Irreducible, so {CategoryName} Qualifies, but { CategoryName, Description} Does Not

Called AutoNumber fields in Microsoft Jet and Identity fields in SQL Server, fields based on this data type are terrifically useful tools, provided you don't try to make them mean anything. They're just tags. They aren't guaranteed to be sequential, you have very little control over how they're generated, and if you try to use them to mean anything you'll cause more problems than you solve.

Although choosing candidate keys is, as we've seen, a semantic process, don't assume that the attributes you use to identify an entity in the real world will make an appropriate candidate key. Individuals, for example, are usually referred to by their names, but a quick look at any phone book will establish that names are hardly unique.

Of course, the name must provide a candidate key when combined with some other set of attributes, but this can be awkward to determine. I once worked in an office with about 20 people, of whom two were named Larry Simon and one was named Lary Simon. All three were Vice Presidents. Amongst ourselves, they were "Short Lary," "German Larry," and "Blond Larry"; that's height, nationality, and hair color combined with name, hardly a viable candidate key.

In situations like this, it's probably best to use a system-generated ID number, such as an Autonumber or Identity field, but remember, don't try to make it *mean* anything. You need to be careful, of course, that your users are adding apparent duplicates intentionally, but as we'll see in Chapter 20, it's best to do this as part of the user interface rather than imposing artificial (and ultimately unnecessary) constraints on the data the system can maintain.

Functional Dependency

The concept of **functional dependency** is an extremely useful tool for thinking about data structures. Given any tuple T, with two sets of attributes $\{X_1...X_n\}$ and $\{Y_1...Y_n\}$ (the sets need not be mutually exclusive), then set Y is functionally dependent on set X if, for any legal value of X, there is only one legal value for Y.

For example, in the relation shown in Figure 2–9, every tuple that has the same values for {CategoryName} will have the same value for {Description}. We can therefore say that the attribute CategoryName *functionally determines* the attribute Description. Note that functional dependency doesn't necessarily work the other way: knowing a value for Description won't allow us to determine the corresponding value for CategoryID.

You can indicate the functional dependency between sets of attributes as shown in Figure 2–10. In text, you can express functional dependencies as X→Y, which reads "X functionally determines Y."

Figure 2–10 Functional Dependency Diagrams Are Largely Self-Explanatory

Functional dependency is interesting to academics because it provides a mechanism for developing something that starts to resemble a mathematics of data modeling. You can, for example, discuss the reflexivity and transitivity of a functional dependency if you are so inclined.

In practical application, functional dependency is a convenient way of expressing what is a fairly self-evident concept: Given any relation, there will be some set of attributes that is unique to each tuple, and knowing those, it is possible to determine those attributes that are not unique.

Thus, given the tuple {X, Y}, if {X} is a candidate key, then all attributes {Y} must necessarily be functionally dependent on {X}; this follows from the definition of candidate key. If {X} is not a candidate key and the functional dependency is not trivial (that is, {Y} is not a subset of {X}), then the relation will necessarily involve some redundancy, and further normalization will be required. To return to the example shown in Figure 2–9, by knowing the CategoryName, we can easily determine the CategoryDescription.

In a sense, data normalization is the process of ensuring that, as shown in Figure 2–10, all the arrows come *out* of candidate keys.

First Normal Form

A relation is in first normal form if the domains on which its attributes are defined are scalar. This is at once both the simplest and most difficult concept in data modeling. The principle is straightforward: Each attribute of a tuple must contain a single value. But what constitutes a single value? In the relation shown in Figure 2–11, the Items attribute obviously contains multiple values and is therefore not in first normal form. But the issue is not always so clear cut.

OrderID	CustomerID	OrderDate	Items	OrderTotal
1	CACTU	1/1/1999	3 Zaanse koeken, 1 Tarte au sucre	$89.70
2	BSBEV	1/5/1999	4 Mozzarella di Giovanni	$139.20
3	SUPRD	5/2/1999	3 Ravioli Angelo, 6 Tofu	$198.06

Figure 2–11 The Items Attribute in This Relation Is Not Scalar

We saw some of the problems involved in determining whether an attribute is scalar when we looked at the modeling of names and addresses in Chapter 1. Dates are another tricky domain. They consist of three distinct components: the day, the month, and the year. Ought they be stored as three attributes or as a composite? As always, the answer can be determined only by looking to the semantics of the problem space you're modeling.

If your system most often uses all three components of a date together, it is scalar. But if your system must frequently manipulate the individual components of the date, you might be better off storing them as separate attributes. You might not care about the day, for example, but only the month and year. Or you might care only about the month and day, but not the year. This isn't often the case, but it happens.

In the specific instance of dates, because date arithmetic is tedious to perform, it will often make your life easier if you use an attribute defined on the DateTime data type, which combines all three components of the date and the time. The DateTime data types allow you to offload the majority of the work involved in, for example, determining the date 37 days from today, to the development environment.

However, DateTime attributes can get you into trouble if you're doing comparisons on a single component. This is particularly true if you're ignoring the time component of a field. For example, if your application sets the value of a DateCreated field to the result of the VBA function Now, which returns both date and time, and then later attempts to compare it to the value returned by Date(), which returns the date only, you might get unexpected results. Even if you never display the time to users, it is being stored, and obviously "1/1/1999 12:30:19 AM" isn't the same as "1/1/1999".

Another place people frequently have problems with non-scalar values is with codes and flags. Many companies assign case numbers or reference numbers that are calculated values, usually something along the lines of REF0010398, which might indicate that this is the first case opened in March 1998. While it's unlikely that you'll be able to alter company policy, it's not a good idea to attempt to manipulate the individual components of the reference number in your data model.

It's far easier in the long run to store the values separately: {Reference#, Case#, Month, Year}. This way, determining the next case number or the number of cases opened in a given year becomes a simple query against an attribute and doesn't require additional manipulation. This has important performance implications, particularly in client/server environments, where extracting a value from the middle of an attribute might require that each individual record be examined locally (and transferred across the network) rather than by the database server.

Another type of non-scalar attribute that causes problems for people is the bit flag. In conventional programming environments, it's common practice to store sets of Boolean values as individual bits in a word, and then to use bitwise operations to check and test them. Windows API programming relies heavily on this technique, for example. In conventional programming environments, this is a perfectly sensible thing to do. In relational data models, it is not. Not only does the practice violate first normal form, but it's extraordinarily tedious and, as a general rule, inefficient.

Unfortunately, this is the kind of constraint that frequently gets imposed on you for historical reasons, but if you've any choice in the matter, don't encode more than one piece of information in a single attribute. If you're using legacy information, you can always unpack the data and store both versions in the recordset.

There's another kind of non-scalar value to be wary of when checking a relation for first normal form: the repeating group. Figure 2–12 shows an Invoice relation. Someone, at some point, decided that customers are not allowed to buy more than three items. I wonder if they checked that decision with the sales manager first? Seriously, this is almost certainly an artificial constraint imposed by the system, not the business. Artificial system constraints are evil, and in this case, just plain wrong as well.

Another example of a repeating group is shown in Figure 2–13. This isn't as obvious an error, and many successful systems have been implemented using a model similar to this. But this is really just a variation of the structure shown in Figure 2–12 and has the same problems. Imagine the query to determine which products exceeded target by more than 10 percent any time in the first quarter.

OrderID	CustomerID	Item1	Qty1	Item2	Qty2	Item3	Qty3
1	ANTON	Queso Cabrales	4	Tofu	3	Ravioli Angelo	1
2	BLAUS	Chai	2		0		

Figure 2–12 This Data Model Restricts the Number of Items a Customer Can Purchase

Product	Year	TargetJan	ActualJan	TargetFeb	ActualFeb
Aniseed Syrup	2004	$1,000.00	$1,300.00	$0.00	$0.00
Chai	2004	$4,000.00	$2,000.00	$0.00	$0.00
Chang	2004	$3,000.00	$8,022.00	$0.00	$0.00

Figure 2–13 This Is a Repeating Group

Second Normal Form

A relation is in second normal form if it is in first normal form and, in addition, all its attributes are dependent on the entire candidate key. The key in Figure 2–14, for example, is {ProductName, SupplierName}, but the SupplierPhoneNumber field is dependent only on the Supplier-Name, not on the full composite key.

We've already seen that this causes redundancy, and that the redundancy can, in turn, result in unpleasant maintenance problems. A better model would be that shown in Figure 2–15.

Logically, this is an issue of not trying to represent two distinct entities, Products and Suppliers, in a single relation. By separating the representation,

Product Name	SupplierName	Category Name	SupplierPhoneNumber
Chai	Exotic Liquids	Beverages	(171) 555-2222
Chang	Exotic Liquids	Beverages	(171) 555-2222
Guaraná Fantástica	Refrescos Americanas LTDA	Beverages	(11) 555 4640
Sasquatch Ale	Bigfoot Breweries	Beverages	(503) 555-9931
Steeleye Stout	Bigfoot Breweries	Beverages	(503) 555-9931
Côte de Blaye	Aux joyeux ecclésiastiques	Beverages	(1) 03.83.00.68
Chartreuse verte	Aux joyeux ecclésiastiques	Beverages	(1) 03.83.00.68
Ipoh Coffee	Leka Trading	Beverages	555-8787
Laughing Lumberjack Lager	Bigfoot Breweries	Beverages	(503) 555-9931
Outback Lager	Pavlova, Ltd.	Beverages	(03) 444-2343

Figure 2–14 All the Attributes in a Relation Should Depend on the Whole Key

Product ID	Product Name	Category
1	Chai	Beverages
2	Chang	Beverages
3	Aniseed Syrup	Condiments
4	Chef Anton's Cajun Seasoning	Condiments
5	Chef Anton's Gumbo Mix	Condiments
6	Grandma's Boysenberry Spread	Condiments
7	Uncle Bob's Organic Dried Pears	Produce

Supplier ID	SupplierName	SupplierPhoneNumber
1	Exotic Liquids	(171) 555-2222
2	New Orleans Cajun Delights	(100) 555-4822
3	Grandma Kelly's Homestead	(313) 555-5735
4	Tokyo Traders	(03) 3555-5011
5	Cooperativa de Quesos 'Las Cabras'	(98) 598 76 54
6	Mayumi's	(06) 431-7877
7	Pavlova, Ltd.	(03) 444-2343
8	Specialty Biscuits, Ltd.	(161) 555-4448
9	PB Knäckebröd AB	031-987 65 43

Figure 2–15 These Two Relations Are in Second Normal Form

Supplier ID	Address	City	Region	Postal Code
1	49 Gilbert St.	London		EC1 4SD
2	P.O. Box 78934	New Orleans	LA	70117
3	707 Oxford Rd.	Ann Arbor	MI	48104
4	9-8 Sekimai	Tokyo		100
5	Calle del Rosal 4	Oviedo	Asturias	33007
6	92 Setsuko	Osaka		545
7	74 Rose St.	Melbourne	Victoria	3058
8	29 King's Way	Manchester		M14 GSD
9	Kaloadagatan 13	Göteborg		S-345 67
10	Av. das Americanas 12.890	São Paulo		5442

Figure 2–16 Suppliers Might Have More Than One Address

you're not only eliminating the redundancy, you're also providing a mechanism for storing information that you couldn't otherwise capture. In the example in Figure 2–15, it becomes possible to capture information about Suppliers before obtaining any information regarding their products. That could not be done in the first relation, since neither component of a primary key can be empty.

The other way that people get into trouble with second normal form is in confusing constraints that happen to be true at any given moment with those that are true for all time. The relation shown in Figure 2–16, for example, assumes that a supplier has only one address, which might be true at the moment but will not necessarily remain true in the future.

Third Normal Form

A relation is in third normal form if it is in second normal form and in addition all non-key attributes are mutually independent. Let's take the example of a company that has a single salesperson in each state. Given the relation shown in Figure 2–17, there is a dependency between Region and

Order ID	Company Name	Region	Salesperson
11076	Bon app'	WA	Margaret Peacock
11077	Rattlesnake Canyon Grocery	WA	Nancy Davolio
11075	Richter Supermarkt	WA	Laura Callahan
11074	Simons bistro		Robert King
11071	LILA-Supermercado	WA	Nancy Davolio
11072	Ernst Handel	WA	Margaret Peacock

Figure 2–17 Although Mutually Dependent, neither Region nor Salesperson Should Be a Candidate Key

Salesperson, but neither of these attributes is reasonably a candidate key for the relation.

It's possible to get really pedantic about third normal form. In most places, for example, you can determine a PostalCode value based on the City and Region values, so the relation shown in Figure 2–18 is not strictly in third normal form.

The two relations shown in Figure 2–19 are technically more correct, but in reality the only benefit you're gaining is the ability to automatically look up the PostalCode when you're entering new records, saving users a few keystrokes. This isn't a trivial benefit, but there are probably better ways to implement this functionality, ones that don't incur the overhead of a relation join every time the address is referenced.

As with every other decision in the data modeling process, when and how to implement third normal form can only be determined by considering the

Company Name	Address	City	Region	Postal Code
Exotic Liquids	49 Gilbert St.	London		EC1 4SD
New Orleans Cajun Delights	P.O. Box 78934	New Orleans	LA	70117
Grandma Kelly's Homestead	707 Oxford Rd.	Ann Arbor	MI	48104
Tokyo Traders	9-8 Sekimai	Tokyo		100
Cooperativa de Quesos 'Las Cabras'	Calle del Rosal 4	Oviedo	Asturias	33007
Mayumi's	92 Setsuko	Osaka		545
Pavlova, Ltd.	74 Rose St.	Melbourne	Victoria	3058

Figure 2–18 This Relation Is Not in Strict Third Normal Form

Company Name	Address	City	Region
Exotic Liquids	49 Gilbert St.	London	
New Orleans Cajun Delights	P.O. Box 78934	New Orleans	LA
Grandma Kelly's Homestead	707 Oxford Rd.	Ann Arbor	MI
Tokyo Traders	9-8 Sekimai	Tokyo	
Cooperativa de Quesos 'Las Cabras'	Calle del Rosal 4	Oviedo	Asturias
Mayumi's	92 Setsuko	Osaka	
Pavlova, Ltd.	74 Rose St.	Melbourne	Victoria

City	Region	Postal Code
Melbourne	Victoria	3058
Ste-Hyacinthe	Québec	J2S 7S8
Montréal	Québec	H1J 1C3
Bend	OR	97101
Sydney	NSW	2042
Ann Arbor	MI	48104
Boston	MA	02134
New Orleans	LA	70117
Oviedo	Asturias	33007

Figure 2–19 These Two Relations Are in Third Normal Form

semantics of the model. It's impossible to give fixed rules, but there are some guidelines: You should create a separate relation only when

- The entity is important to the model, or
- The data changes frequently, or
- You're certain there are technical implementation advantages

Postal codes do change, but not often; and they aren't intrinsically important in most systems. In addition, a separate postal code table is impractical in most real-world applications because of the varying rules for how postal codes are defined.

Further Normalization

The first three normal forms were included in Codd's original formulation of relational theory, and in the vast majority of cases they're all you'll need to worry about. Just remember the jingle I learned in grad school: "The key, the whole key, and nothing but the key, so help me Codd."

The further normal forms—Boyce/Codd, fourth, and fifth—have been developed to handle special cases, most of which are rare.

Boyce/Codd Normal Form

Boyce/Codd normal form, which is considered a variation of third normal form, handles the special case of relations with multiple candidate keys. In fact, for Boyce/Codd normal form to apply, the following conditions must hold true:

- The relation must have two or more candidate keys.
- At least two of the candidate keys must be composite.
- The candidate keys must have overlapping attributes.

The easiest way to understand Boyce/Codd normal form is to use functional dependencies. Boyce/Codd normal form states, essentially, that there must be no functional dependencies *between* candidate keys. Take, for example, the relation shown in Figure 2–20. The relation is in third normal form (assuming supplier names are unique), but it still contains significant redundancy.

Supplier ID	SupplierName	Product	Quantity	Unit Price
5	Cooperativa de Quesos 'Las Cabras'	Queso Cabrales	12	$14.00
20	Leka Trading	Singaporean Hokkien Fried Mee	10	$9.80
14	Formaggi Fortini s.r.l.	Mozzarella di Giovanni	5	$34.80
24	G'day, Mate	Manjimup Dried Apples	40	$42.40
6	Mayumi's	Tofu	9	$18.60
24	G'day, Mate	Manjimup Dried Apples	35	$42.40
19	New England Seafood Cannery	Jack's New England Clam Chowder	10	$7.70
2	New Orleans Cajun Delights	Louisiana Fiery Hot Pepper Sauce	15	$16.80

Figure 2–20 This Relation Is in Third Normal Form but Not in Boyce/Codd Normal Form

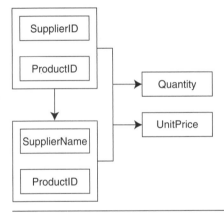

Figure 2–21 This Is the Functional Dependency Diagram of the Relation in Figure 2–20

The two candidate keys in this case are {SupplierID, ProductID} and {SupplierName, ProductID}, and the functional dependency diagram is shown in Figure 2–21.

As you can see, there is a functional dependency {SupplierID}→ {SupplierName}, which is in violation of Boyce/Codd normal form. A correct model is shown in Figure 2–22.

Fourth Normal Form

Fourth normal form provides a theoretical foundation for a principle that is intuitively obvious: Independent repeating groups should not be combined in a single relation. By way of example, let's assume that the own-brand products sold by Northwind Traders come in multiple package sizes, that they are sourced from multiple suppliers, and that all suppliers provide all pack sizes. A completely unnormalized version of the Products relation might look like Figure 2–23.

Supplier ID	SupplierName
1	Exotic Liquids
2	New Orleans Cajun Delights
3	Grandma Kelly's Homestead
4	Tokyo Traders
5	Cooperativa de Quesos 'Las Cabras'
6	Mayumi's

SupplierID	ProductID	Quantity	UnitPrice
2	65	15	$21.05
24	53	15	$32.80
8	20	40	$81.00
22	47	16	$9.50
6	14	9	$23.25
28	59	30	$55.00
28	60	40	$34.00
21	46	15	$12.00

Figure 2–22 This Model Is a Full Normalized Version of Figure 2–21

ProductName	SupplierName	PackSize
Chai	Exotic Liquids	8 oz., 16 oz., 32 oz.
Chef Anton's Cajun Seasoning	New Orleans Cajun Delights	8 oz., 16 oz., 32 oz.
Pavlova	Pavlova, Ltd.	8", 10"

Figure 2–23 This Is the Unnormalized Relation

Now, the first step in normalizing this relation is to eliminate the non-scalar PackSize attribute, resulting in the relation shown in Figure 2–24.

Surprisingly, Figure 2–24 is in Boyce/Codd normal form, since it is "all key." But there are clearly redundancy problems, and maintaining data integrity could be a nightmare. The resolution to these problems lies in the concept of **multi-valued dependency pairs** and fourth normal form.

A multi-valued dependency pair is two mutually-independent sets of attributes. In Figure 2–23, the multi-valued dependency is {Product-Name}→{PackSize}| {SupplierName}, which is read "Product multi-

ProductName	SupplierName	PackSize
Chai	Exotic Liquids	8 oz.
Chai	Exotic Liquids	16 oz.
Chai	Exotic Liquids	32 oz
Chef Anton's Cajun Seasoning	New Orleans Cajun Delights	8 oz.
Chef Anton's Cajun Seasoning	New Orleans Cajun Delights	16 oz.
Chef Anton's Cajun Seasoning	New Orleans Cajun Delights	32 oz.
Pavlova	Pavlova, Ltd.	8"
Pavlova	Pavlova, Ltd.	10"

Figure 2–24 This Version of the Relation Shown in Figure 2–23 Is in Boyce/Codd Normal Form

ProductName	PackSize
Chai	32 oz
Chef Anton's Cajun Seasoning	32 oz.
Chai	16 oz.
Chef Anton's Cajun Seasoning	16 oz.
Pavlova	10"
Chai	8 oz.
Chef Anton's Cajun Seasoning	8 oz.
Pavlova	8"

ProductName	SupplierName
Chai	Exotic Liquids
Chai	Exotic Liquids
Chai	Exotic Liquids
Chef Anton's Cajun Seasoning	New Orleans Cajun Delights
Chef Anton's Cajun Seasoning	New Orleans Cajun Delights
Chef Anton's Cajun Seasoning	New Orleans Cajun Delights
Pavlova	Pavlova, Ltd.
Pavlova	Pavlova, Ltd.

Figure 2–25 Relations Containing Multi-Valued Dependencies Should Be Decomposed

determines PackSize and Supplier." Fourth normal form states, informally, that multi-valued dependencies must be divided into separate relations, as shown in Figure 2–25. Formally, a relation is in fourth normal form if it is in Boyce/Codd normal form, and in addition, all the multi-valued dependencies are also functional dependencies out of the candidate keys.

Fifth Normal Form

Fifth normal form addresses the extremely rare case of **join dependencies**. A join dependency expresses the cyclical constraint "if Entity1 is linked to Entity2, and Entity2 is linked to Entity3, and Entity3 is linked back to Entity1, then all three entities must *necessarily* coexist in the same tuple."

To translate this into something resembling English, it would mean that if {Supplier} supplies {Product}, and {Customer} ordered {Product}, and {Supplier} supplied *something* to {Customer}, then {Supplier} supplied {Product} to {Customer}. Now, in the real world this is not a valid deduction. {Supplier} could have supplied anything to {Customer}, not necessarily {Product}. A join dependency exists only if there is an additional constraint that states that the deduction is valid.

It is not sufficient, in this situation, to use a single relation with the attributes {Supplier, Product, Customer} because of the resulting update problems. Given the relationship shown in Figure 2–26, for example, inserting the tuple {"Ma Maison", "Aniseed Syrup", "Berglunds snabbkop"}

Supplier	Product	Customer
Exotic Liquids	Aniseed Syrup	Alfreds Futterkiste
Exotic Liquids	Chef Anton's Cajun Seasoning	Berglunds snabbkop

Figure 2–26 This Relation Is Not in Fifth Normal Form

requires the insertion of a second tuple, {"Exotic Liquids", "Aniseed Syrup", "Berglunds snabbkop"}, since a new link, "Aniseed Syrup" to "Berglunds snabbkop", has been added to the model.

Decomposing the relation into three distinct relations (SupplierProduct, ProductCustomer, and SupplierCustomer) eliminates this problem but causes problems of its own; in re-creating the original relation, all three relations must be joined. Interim joins of only two relations will result in invalid information.

From a system designer's point of view, this is a terrifying situation, since there's no intrinsic method for enforcing the three-table join except through security restrictions. Further, if a user should create an interim result set, the results will *seem* perfectly reasonable, and it's unlikely that the user will be able to detect the error by inspection.

Fortunately, this cyclical join dependency is so rare that the complications can be safely ignored in most situations. Where they can't, your only resource is to build the database system in such a way as to ensure the integrity of the multi-relation join.

Summary

In this chapter, we've examined the structure of databases in terms of the normalization process. The basic principle underlying normalization is the elimination of redundancy by way of lossless decomposition—the ability to split relations apart without losing information. This principle is formalized in the concept of normal forms. The first three normal forms, which are the ones most commonly applied, are encapsulated in the jingle "The key, the whole key, and nothing but the key, so help me Codd." The remaining three normal forms are used only in exceptional cases.

In the next chapter, we'll examine how relations are logically linked when we explore the modeling of the relationships between entities.

CHAPTER 3

Relationships

Chapter 2 explored the design of the database structure, the process of analyzing the entities in the problem space and developing a set of relations that capture all the relevant data efficiently and effectively. But the relations are only one part of the data model. The associations between relations and the constraints on those associations are just as important. In this chapter, we'll look at modeling **relationships**, the representation of associations in the relational model. As with defining relations, the basic principles are straightforward once you understand the semantics of the data model. Certain special cases don't fit neatly into the model of relationships, however, and we'll look at some of these later.

Terminology

Some basic terminology applies to relationships. The entities that are related are called **participants**, and the number of participants in a relationship is its **degree**. The vast majority of relationships are **binary**, having two participants, but **unary relationships** (a relation that is related to itself) are also common, while **ternary relationships** (with three participants) are not unknown. The examples throughout most of this chapter are binary. We'll examine unary and ternary relationships as special cases later in the chapter.

The participation of an entity in a relationship can be classified as **total** or **partial**, depending on whether the entity can exist independently of the relationship. For example, given the two entities Customer and Order, the participation of Customer in the relationship is partial since Customer details might be entered before the customer has placed any orders. Order, on the other hand, has total participation, since an order can't be placed except by a Customer.

The same principle is sometimes used to classify the entities themselves as either **weak** (having total participation) or **regular** (having partial participation). Weak entities can exist only in relationships with other entities, while regular entities can exist in isolation. This classification is part of the Entity Relationship (E/R) diagramming method as originally described by Chen. You can use the notation shown in Figure 3–1 in E/R diagrams to show whether an entity is weak or regular.

The classification of participation in a relationship is also an indication of the **optionality** of the relationship: whether or not an entity is required to participate in a given relationship. This is a rather tricky area because implementation by the database engines doesn't match the problem space, as we'll see when we discuss the implementation of data integrity in Chapter 4.

It's occasionally useful to divide relationships into "IsA" and "HasA" types. The concept is straightforward: entity X either *IsA* Y or *HasA* Y. For example, an Employee IsA SoftballTeam member; the same Employee HasA(n) Address. Of course, "is" and "has" are not always very good English terms to describe a relationship. An Employee doesn't "have" a SalesOrder, he "creates" one; but as it's clearly not the case that the Employee *is* a Sales-Order, the intellectual stretch isn't too great.

The maximum number of instances of one entity that can be associated with an instance of another entity is what I refer to as the **cardinality** of a relationship. (Note that both degree and cardinality have slightly different meanings when applied to relationships than when applied to relations.) There are three generic flavors of relationship cardinality: one-to-one, one-to-many, and many-to-many.

I use the notation shown in Figure 3–2 to indicate the cardinality and optionality of relationships. I find the crow's foot notation introduced in Chapter 1 to be the most expressive and the simplest to explain to clients. Obviously, alternative techniques are available, and you must use the one that works best for you.

Figure 3–1 This Notation Can Be Used to Distinguish between Weak and Regular Entities

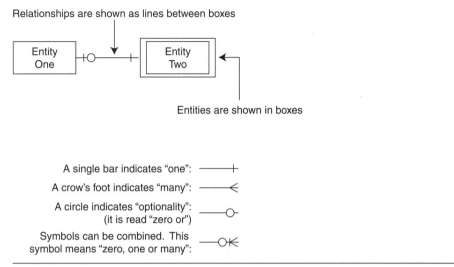

Figure 3–2 This Notation Will Be Used to Indicate Optionality and Cardinality

Modeling Relationships

Once you've determined that a relationship exists, you must model it by including attributes from one relation (the *primary relation*) in the other (the *foreign relation*), as shown in Figure 3–3.

The choice of primary and foreign relations isn't arbitrary. It is determined first by the cardinality of the relationship and second—in the rare situation where there is any doubt—by the semantics of the data model. For example, given two relations that have a one-to-many relationship, the relation on the one side is always the primary relation, while the relation on the

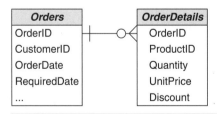

Figure 3–3 A Relationship Is Modeled by Including Attributes from the Primary Relation (Orders) in the Foreign Relation (OrderDetails)

many side is always the foreign relation. That is, a candidate key from the relation on the one side is added (as a foreign key) to the relation on the many side. We'll be looking at this issue as we examine each type of relationship in the rest of this chapter.

And, of course, you don't just copy *any* attributes from the primary relation to the foreign relation; you must choose attributes that uniquely identify the primary entity. In other words, you add the attributes that make up the candidate key in the primary relation to the foreign relation. Not surprisingly, the duplicated attributes become known as the **foreign key** in the foreign

On Diagramming Relationships

You'll notice some differences between Figure 3–3 and the formal E/R diagram shown in Figure 1–6 on page 22. First, the attributes are not shown as separate objects. At this level of design, you're primarily interested in the relationships between entities, not their composition. I find showing the attributes separately to be distracting, and it clutters up the diagram.

Second, the relationships are not labeled. Some analysts (and some diagramming tools) add a descriptive label to each relationship. In our example, the label might be something along the lines of "Orders consist of OrderDetails". I find labeling unnecessary, and because the description of the relationship changes depending on which direction you're reading it (teachers *teach* students, but students *learn from* teachers), labels can sometimes be confusing.

As I said, I've found this style of diagram useful when working with clients, and it's easy to draw by hand or by using a diagramming tool such as Microsoft Visio. But Microsoft Access, Microsoft SQL Server, and Microsoft Visual Studio all provide diagramming tools that have their own conventions, and you may decide to use them in preference to, or in addition to, the technique I've shown.

The advantage of using either the Access relationships window (for a Jet database engine ".mdb" file) or database diagrams (for a database implemented using SQL Server) is that the diagrams become part of the database and automatically reflect changes to it. Unfortunately, this is also the greatest disadvantage of these tools. You can't build abstract diagrams; you must build the physical tables. There is always a danger in jumping into anything that even *looks* like implementation too early in the design process, before the implementation model has been finalized.

In my own work, I often use both abstract diagrams and ones that are embedded in the database. I create abstract diagrams in the early stages of the design process, and use one of the Microsoft tools once the conceptual design has been finalized and I'm documenting the physical database schema.

relations. In the example shown in Figure 3–3, OrderID—the candidate key of the Orders relation—has been added to the OrderDetails relation. Orders is the primary relation, and OrderDetails is the foreign relation.

Note that the candidate key/foreign key pair that models the relationship need not be the primary key of the primary table; any candidate key will serve. You should use the candidate key that makes the most sense semantically.

Sometimes you'll want to model not only the fact that a relationship exists, but also certain properties of the relationship—its duration or its commencement date, for example. In this case, it's useful to create an abstract relation representing the relationship. The Positions relation, shown in Figure 3–4, is an example of a "relationship relation".

NOTE: Some theoreticians argue that all relationships should be modeled separately, but it has always seemed to me that their argument is with the relational model itself, not the conventional methods for modeling a problem space.

Separate relations representing relationships complicate the data model somewhat, and one might be tempted to simply include the relationship attributes in one of the participating relations. This approach isn't necessarily disastrous, but if there are a lot of attributes or a lot of relations with attributes, it can get unwieldy. More importantly, a distinct relationship entity allows you to track the history of a relationship. The model shown in Figure 3–4, for example, allows you to determine an individual's employment history, which would not have been possible had Position been made an attribute of the Employees relation.

Abstract relationship entities are also useful when you need to track the way a relationship changes over time. Figure 3–5, for example, is a State Transition diagram describing the possible legal changes in an individual's marital status.

Figure 3–4 Abstract Relations Can Model the Properties of Relationships

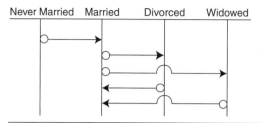

Figure 3–5 State Transition Diagrams Plot the Valid Changes in an Entity's Status, in This Case an Individual's Marital Status

State Transition diagrams are not difficult to understand. Each vertical line indicates a valid state, while a horizontal line represents a change from one state to another. For example, an individual can go from "married" to "divorced", and vice versa, but not from "divorced" to "never married".

Now, if all you need to model is an individual's current marital status, you don't need to implement an abstract relationship entity to make sure only valid changes are made. But if you ever need to know that John and Mary Smith were married in 1953 and divorced in 1972, and that Mary remarried in 1975 but was widowed in 1986, then you'll need an abstract relationship entity to track that.

One-to-One Relationships

Perhaps the simplest type of relationship is the one-to-one relationship. If it's true that any instance of entity X can be associated with only one instance of entity Y, then the relationship is one-to-one. Most IsA relationships will be one-to-one, but otherwise, it's fairly unusual to find one in the problem domain.

One thing to be careful of: When choosing a one-to-one relationship between entities, you need to be sure that the relationship is either true for all time or, if it does change, that you don't care about past values. For example, say you're modeling the office space in a building. Assuming that there is one person to an office, there's a one-to-one relationship between the Office and Employee relations, as shown in Figure 3–6.

Figure 3–6 There Is a One-to-One Relationship between Office and Employee

But the relationship between an employee and an office is true only at a specific moment in time. Over time, different employees will be assigned to the office. (The arrangement of offices in the building might change as well, but that's a different problem.) If you use the one-to-one relationship shown in Figure 3–6, you will have a simple, clean model of the building, but you'll have no way of determining the history of occupancy.

You might not care. If you're building a system for a mail room, you need to know where to send Jane Doe's mail today, not where it would have been sent three months ago. But if you're designing a system for a property manager, you can't lose this historical information—the system will be asked to determine, for example, how often tenants change.

Although one-to-one relationships are rare in the real world, they're very common abstract constructs, and extremely useful ones. They're most often used in two situations: when you want (or need) to reduce the number of attributes in a relation or to model entity sub-classes.

There is a physical limitation of 255 fields per table if you're using the Jet database engine, and 1024 fields per table if you're using SQL Server. I'm suspicious—*very* suspicious—of any data model that exceeds these limitations. But I have occasionally seen systems, usually in science and medicine, where the entities genuinely had more than 255 attributes. In these cases, you have no choice but to create a new relation with some arbitrary subset of attributes and to create a one-to-one relationship between it and the original, controlling relation.

A problem domain that often *appears* to require that the physical limitations on table size be exceeded is the modeling of tests and questionnaires. Given a test with an arbitrary number of questions, you might be tempted to model an individual's responses as shown in Figure 3–7.

This structure is easy to implement, particularly if the database will only be used for this test, and this test only. But it is not the best solution, and will fail if you ever have a test with a different number of questions. The

Figure 3–7 This Structure Is Sometimes Used to Model Tests and Questionnaires, but It Is Not Ideal

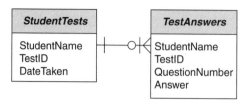

Figure 3–8 Although More Difficult to Implement, This Structure Is Preferable for Modeling Tests and Questionnaires

answer attributes are a repeating group, and the relationship is therefore not in first normal form. A better model is shown in Figure 3–8.

Sub-Classing Entities

A more interesting use of one-to-one relationships is for entity sub-classing, a concept borrowed from object-oriented programming. To see some of the benefits of sub-classing entities, let's first look at a more traditional implementation. In the Microsoft Access Northwind sample database, each product is assigned to a product category, as shown in Figure 3–9.

Having a Categories relation allows the products to be grouped for reporting purposes and might be all that is required by your problem space. But with this design, you can treat a product only as a product, not as an instance of its specific category. Any attributes defined for Products are stored for *all* products, whatever their type. This isn't a very close match to the problem domain—Beverages intrinsically have different attributes than Condiments.

You might be tempted to model the Northwind product list as shown in Figure 3–10. This model allows us to store all the information specific to each product type since each relation can have a different set of

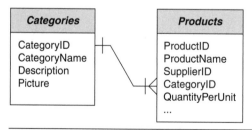

Figure 3–9 Each Product in the Northwind Database Is Assigned to a Product Category

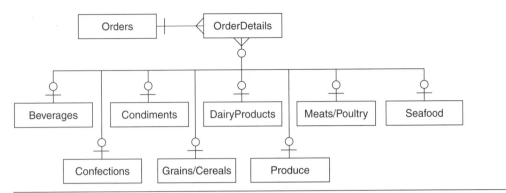

Figure 3–10 This Model Allows Category-Specific Attributes to Be Captured

attributes. The problem with this schema is that it makes it difficult to treat a product *as* a product.

Imagine, for example, the process of checking that a product code entered by a user is correct: "if the code exists in the x relation, or the y relation, or...". This is as ugly as the repeating group query in Chapter 2. Also, you might run into integrity problems with this structure if you have certain attributes that apply only to one product category (UnitsPerPackage, for example, might pertain to Beverages but not DairyProducts) and the category of a particular product changes. What do you do in these circumstances? Throw away the old values? But what if the change was accidental and the user immediately changes it back?

Sub-classing the product entity provides the best of both worlds. You can capture information specific to certain product categories without losing the ability to treat the products simply as products when that's appropriate, and you can defer the deletion of the no-longer-applicable information until you're certain it really *is* no longer applicable. Figure 3–11 shows a model developed using entity sub-classes.

It must be said that while entity sub-classing is an elegant solution to certain types of data modeling problems, it can be an awkward beast to implement. To take just one example, a report containing Product details would need to include conditional processing to display only the fields appropriate to the current sub-class. This isn't an insurmountable task by any means, but it *is* a consideration. Under most circumstances, I wouldn't recommend that you compromise the data model to make life easier for the programmers. But there's certainly no point in adding the complexity of sub-classing to the model if all you need is the ability to group or categorize entities for

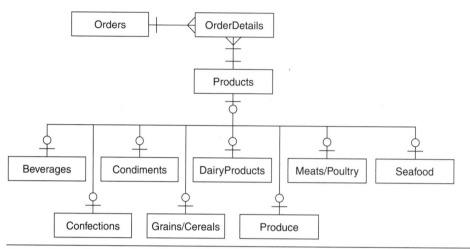

Figure 3–11 This Model uses Sub-Classing to Provide the Capabilities of Figures 3–9 and 3–10

reporting purposes; in this situation, the structure shown in Figure 3–9 is perfectly adequate and far more sensible.

Identifying the primary and foreign relations in a one-to-one relationship can sometimes be tricky. As always, you must base the decision on the semantics of the data model. If you've chosen this structure in order to subclass the entity, the generic entity becomes the primary relation and each of the sub-classes becomes a foreign relation.

NOTE: In this situation, the foreign key that the sub-classes acquire is often also the candidate key of the subclasses. There is rarely a reason for subclasses to have their own identifiers.

If, on the other hand, you're using one-to-one relationships to avoid field limitations, or the entities have a genuine one-to-one relationship in the problem space, the choice will be somewhat arbitrary. You must choose the primary relation based on your understanding of the problem space.

One thing that can help in this situation is the optionality of the relationship. If the relationship is optional on one side only (and I've never seen a model where a one-to-one relationship was optional on both sides), the relation on the optional side is the foreign relation. In other words, if only one of the entities is weak and the other regular, the regular entity is the primary relation and the weak entity is the foreign relation.

One-to-Many Relationships

The most common type of relationship between entities is one-to-many, wherein a single instance of one entity can be associated with zero, one, or many instances of another entity. The majority of the normalization techniques discussed in Chapter 2 result in relations with one-to-many relationships between them.

One-to-many relationships present few problems once they've been identified. However, it's important to be careful in specifying the optionality on each side of the relationship. It's commonly thought that only the many side of the relationship can be optional, but this isn't the case. Take, for example, the relationship shown in Figure 3–12.

The relationship between Client and CustomerServiceRep is optional in both directions. In English, this would be expressed as a "CustomerServiceRep can have zero or more clients. A client's CustomerServiceRep, *if one has been assigned,* must be present in the CustomerServiceRep relation." Specifying optionality on the one side of a one-to-many relationship has important implications for both the implementation and usability of the system. We'll discuss these issues in detail in later chapters, but understand here that relational theory does *not* require that the one side of a one-to-many relationship be mandatory.

Identifying the primary and foreign relations in a one-to-many relationship is easy. The entity on the one side of the relationship is always the primary relation; its candidate key is copied to the relation on the many side, which becomes the foreign relation. The candidate key of the primary relation often forms part of the candidate key for the relation on the many side, but it can never uniquely identify the tuples of foreign relation by itself. It must be combined with one or more other attributes to form a candidate key.

Many-to-Many Relationships

Many-to-many relationships exist aplenty in the real world. Students take many courses; any given course is attended by many students. Customers

Figure 3–12 This Relationship Is Optional in Both Directions

This many-to-many relationship:

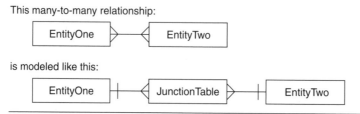

is modeled like this:

Figure 3–13 An Intermediary Table Called a Junction Table Is Used to Resolve Many-to-Many Relationships

shop in many stores; a store has many customers, or so one hopes! But many-to-many relationships can't be directly represented in a relational database. Instead, they are modeled using an intermediary relation that has a one-to-many relationship with each of the original participants, as shown in Figure 3–13. Such an intermediary relation is usually called a **junction table,** even when working at the data model level, where of course we're talking about relations, not tables.

Since a many-to-many relationship is modeled as two one-to-many relationships, determining the primary and foreign relations is straightforward. As we've seen, the relation on the one side of a one-to-many relationship is always the primary relation. This means that each of the original entities will become a primary relation, and the junction table will be the foreign relation, receiving the candidate keys of the relations on each side of it.

Junction tables most often contain only the candidate keys of the two original participants, but they are really just a special case of the abstract relationship entities discussed earlier. As such, they can contain whatever additional attributes are appropriate. The junction table that resolves a many-to-many relationship between "Courses" and "Students", for example, might include an attribute indicating the Term in which a specific student enrolled in a specific course. (And the Term attribute could, in turn, participate in a one-to-many relationship with a Term entity. The schema can be as simple or complex as required.)

Unary Relationships

All the relationships discussed so far have been binary relationships having two participants. Unary relationships have only one participant—the relation is associated with itself. The classic example of a unary relationship is

Employee to Manager. One's manager is, in most cases, also an employee with a manager of his or her own.

Unary relationships can be of any cardinality. One-to-many unary relationships are used to implement hierarchies, such as the organizational hierarchy implicit in the Employee-Manager relationship. Many-to-many unary relationships, like their binary counterparts, must be modeled with a junction table. Unary relationships can also be optional on the one side, as shown in Figure 3–14. The CEOs of most organizations do not have a manager. (The stockholders don't count unless they're an independent part of the data model.)

Unary relationships are modeled in the same way as binary relationships—the candidate key of the primary relation is added to the foreign relation. The only difference is that the primary and foreign relations are the same. Thus, if the candidate key of the Employee relation is EmployeeID, declared on the EmployeeID domain, then you'd add an attribute to the relation called perhaps ManagerID, also declared on the EmployeeID domain, as shown in Figure 3–14

Which raises an interesting issue: For reasons that are probably obvious, no two fields in a table can have the same name. (You shouldn't have two attributes in a single relation with the same name either, but "name" is a slightly slippery concept at the abstract level.) You must, therefore, rename either the primary or foreign key in a unary relationship. Most often, you'll re-name the foreign key. In our example, you would probably call the foreign key "ManagerID".

In fact, you can re-name the foreign key attribute in any relation, and it often makes sense, semantically, to do so. The EmployeeID of the Employee relation, for example, would become CustomerServiceRepID in the Customer relation. The fact that the development environment can make some smart guesses about combining tables based on fields of the same name should *not* be construed as a recommendation to blindly copy names from one relation to another.

Figure 3–14 A Unary Relationship Exists When a Relation Is Linked to Itself

Ternary Relationships

Ternary relationships are usually in the form *X does Y to Z*, and like many-to-many relationships they can't be directly modeled in a relational database. Unlike many-to-many relationships, however, there isn't a single recipe for modeling them.

In Figure 3–15, we can see that the Mozzarella di Giovanni purchased by Vins et alcools Chevalier is supplied by both Formaggi Fortini s.r.l. and Forets d'erables, but there is no way to determine which of them supplied the specific cheese that was shipped to Vins et alcools Chevalier. A ternary relationship has been lost in the data model. Suppliers don't merely supply products; they supply products that are purchased by specific customers.

To understand the problem, it's useful to first examine the relationships in a more typical problem space, as shown in Figure 3–16.

In Figure 3–16, each product is provided by only a single supplier and the ternary relationship is maintained—if you know the product, you know who supplied it. In Figure 3–17, however, each product is provided by multiple suppliers and the ternary relationship has been lost.

The key to resolving the problem is to examine the direction of the one-to-many relationships. Given any entity on the many side, you can determine the corresponding entity on the one side. Thus, given a specific OrderDetails item in Figure 3–16, you can determine the Orders item to which it belongs, and knowing the Orders item, you can determine the Customers. The process

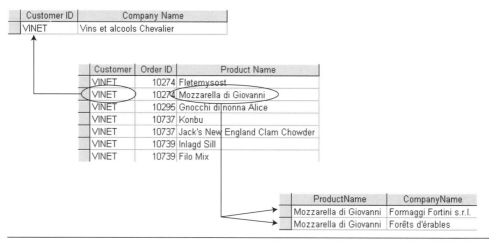

Figure 3–15 These Relations Don't Indicate Which Supplier's Cheese Was Purchased by Vins et alcools Chevalier

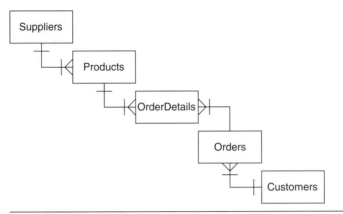

Figure 3–16 This Is the Typical Relationship Chain for the Entities Participating in an Order

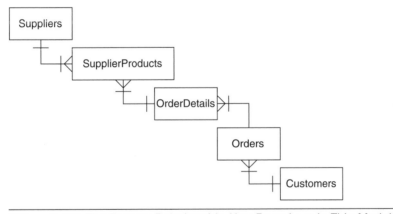

Figure 3–17 The Ternary Relationship Has Been Lost in This Model

works in the other direction as well, of course: Knowing the OrderDetails item, you can determine the product and then the supplier.

But the reverse is not true. Having identified an entity on the one side of the relationship, you can't select a single entity on the many side. This is the problem with Figure 3–17. Knowing an OrderDetails item, you can determine the product, but knowing the product, you can't determine to which SupplierProducts entity it's linked.

An easy way to think of this is that you can't change direction from one-to-many to many-to-one more than once in a relationship chain. The chain in Figure 3–16 changes direction only once, at OrderDetails. The chain in

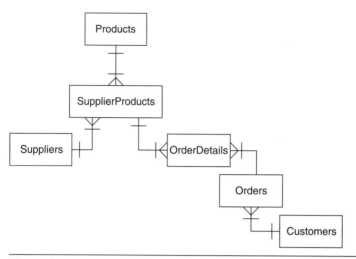

Figure 3–18 This Model Preserves the Ternary Relationship

Figure 3–17 changes direction twice, at OrderDetails and again at Supplier-Products.

The solution is to eliminate the Products entity from the chain, as shown in Figure 3–18.

The chain now changes direction only once, at OrderDetails, and the relationship has been maintained. Notice, however, that the Products entity hasn't been eliminated. Chances are good that orders will still be placed for Products rather than for SupplierProducts, and maintaining the Products entity allows the user interface to accommodate this.

Of course, you might not care about the ternary relationships in your problem space, or there may be some other way of tracing the relationship when necessary, such as a lot number on the packaging. In this case, there is absolutely no need to model it. It's important to understand that the model in Figure 3–18 isn't intrinsically better or more correct than that in Figure 3–17. You must choose the model that best reflects the semantics of your problem space.

Relationships of Known Cardinality

Occasionally the minimum, absolute, or maximum number of tuples on the many side of a one-to-many relationship will be known in advance. There

StudentNumber	GivenName	Surname	Period1	Period2	Period3
1	Nancy	Davolio	Biology	French	English
2	Andrew	Fuller	Physical Education	Biology	French
3	Janet	Levering	Physical Education	Biology	French

Figure 3–19 It's Tempting, but Unwise, to Model Known Cardinality Like This

are five periods in the school day, there are 200 bones in the adult skeleton, and a golfer is allowed to carry only 14 clubs during tournament play.

It's always tempting to model this situation by including the candidate key of each tuple as an attribute in the relation on the one side, as shown in Figure 3–19, but there are two major problems with this approach. First, it's a repeating group, and second, it's unreliable.

The repeating nature of the attributes is disguised in Figure 3–19 by the attribute names, but they're all defined on the same domain, ClassPeriod. Whenever you have multiple attributes defined on the same domain, chances are good that you have category or type values masquerading as attribute names.

In addition to this theoretical problem, structures like this are unreliable. It might very well be company policy, for example, that managers have a maximum of five employees reporting directly to them, but policy isn't reality. By embedding the policy in the data model, you're implementing it as a non-negotiable system constraint. I'd be willing to bet that you'll discover during initial data entry that at least one manager has six direct reports. What happens then? Will somebody suddenly have a new boss? Will the manager get entered (and maybe paid) twice? Or will the programmer who implemented your design, and then got a support call at 3. A.M., say some *very* uncharitable things about you?

Limitations on cardinality such as these must be implemented as system constraints; they shouldn't be embedded in the structure of the relations themselves. Furthermore, as we'll discuss in Chapter 19, you should think long and hard about the impact on usability before implementing limitations on cardinality at all.

Summary

In this chapter, we've examined the relationships between entities in detail. We've looked at each type of binary relationship—one-to-one, one-to-many, and many-to-many—and seen how to represent them in the data model by establishing a primary relation and including its candidate key in the other relationship participant, the foreign relation. In addition, we've examined the special cases of unary and ternary relationships and seen how they can also be represented in the data model.

You've now seen all the basic components of a data model: the entities, their attributes, and the relationships between them. In Chapter 4, we'll turn to data integrity and the mechanisms available to you to maintain the consistency of the database.

Data Integrity

Creating a model of the entities in the problem space and the relationships between them is only part of the data modeling process. You must also capture the rules that the database system will use to ensure that the actual physical data stored in it is, if not correct, at least plausible. In other words, you must model the **data integrity**.

It's important to understand that the chances of being able to guarantee the literal *correctness* of the data are diminishingly small. Take, for example, an order record showing that Mary Smith purchased 17 hacksaws on July 15, 1999. The database system can ensure that Mary Smith is a customer known to the system, that the company does indeed sell hacksaws, and that it was taking orders on July 15, 1999. It can even check that Mary Smith has sufficient credit to pay for the 17 hacksaws. What it can't do is verify that Ms. Smith actually ordered 17 hacksaws and not 7 or 1, or 17 screwdrivers instead. The best the system might do is notice that 17 is rather a lot of hacksaws for an individual to purchase and notify the person entering the order to that effect. Even having the system do this much is likely to be expensive to implement, probably more expensive than its value warrants.

My point is that the system can never verify that Mary Smith did place the order as it's recorded; it can verify only that she *could have done so*. Of course, that's all any record-keeping system can do, and a well-designed database system can certainly do a better job than the average manual system, if for no other reason than its consistency in applying the rules. But no database system, and no database system designer, can guarantee that the data in the database *is* true, only that it *could* be true. It does this by ensuring that the data complies with the **integrity constraints** that have been defined for it.

Integrity Constraints

Some people refer to integrity constraints as business rules. However, the concept of business rules is much broader; it includes all of the constraints on the system rather than just the constraints concerning the integrity of the data. In particular, system security—the definition of which users can do what and under what circumstances they can do it—is part of system administration, not data integrity. But certainly security is a business requirement and will constitute one or more business rules. We'll look at database security issues in Chapter 13 when we discuss system administration.

Data integrity is implemented at several levels of granularity. Domain, transition, and entity constraints define the rules for maintaining the integrity of the individual relations. Referential integrity constraints ensure that necessary relationships between relations are maintained. Database integrity constraints govern the database as a whole, and transaction integrity constraints control the way data is manipulated either within a single database or between multiple databases.

Domain Integrity

As we discussed in Chapter 1, a domain is the set of all possible values for a given attribute. A domain integrity constraint—usually just called a **domain constraint**—is a rule that defines these legal values. It might be necessary to define more than one domain constraint to describe a domain completely.

A domain isn't the same thing as a data type, and defining domains in terms of physical data types is a tempting (and common) practice, but it can backfire. The danger is that you will unnecessarily constrain the values—for example, by choosing an Integer data type because you think it will be big enough in practice, rather than because 255 is the largest permitted value for the domain.

That being said, however, data type *can* be a convenient shorthand in the data model, and for this reason choosing a logical data type is often the first step in determining the domain constraints in a system. By **logical data type**, I mean "date," "string," or "image," nothing more specific than that. Dates are probably the best example of the benefits of this approach. I'd recommend against defining the domain TransactionDate as "DateTime", which is a physical representation. But defining it as "a date" allows you to concentrate on it being "between the commencement of business and the present date, inclusive" and ignore all those rather tedious rules about leap years.

Having chosen a logical data type, it might be appropriate to narrow the definition by, for example, indicating the scale and precision of a numeric type, or the maximum length of string values. This is very close to specifying a physical data type, but you should still be working at the logical level.

Obviously, you will not be hit by lightning if your particular shorthand for "a string value of no more than 30 characters" is char[30]. But the more abstract you keep the description in the data model, the more room you'll have to maneuver later, and the less likely you'll be to impose accidental constraints on the system.

The next aspect of domain integrity to consider is whether a domain is permitted to contain unknown or nonexistent values. The handling of these values is contentious, and we'll be discussing them repeatedly as we examine various aspects of database system design. For now, it's necessary to understand only that there is a difference between an unknown value and a nonexistent value, and that it is often (although not always) possible to specify whether either or both of these is permitted for the domain.

The first point here, that "unknown" and "nonexistent" are different, doesn't present too many problems at the logical level. (And please remember, always, that a data model is a *logical* construct.) My father does not have a middle name; I do not know my neighbor's. These are quite different issues. There are implementation issues that need not yet concern us, but the logical distinction is quite straightforward.

The second point is that, having determined whether a domain is allowed to include unknown or nonexistent values, you'll need to decide whether either of these can be accepted by the system. To return to our TransactionDate example, it's certainly possible for the date of a transaction to be unknown, but if it occurred at all it occurred at some fixed point in time and therefore cannot be nonexistent. In other words, there must *be* a transaction date; we just might not *know* it.

Now, obviously, we can be ignorant of anything, so any value can be unknown. That's not a useful distinction. What we're actually defining here is not so much whether a value can be unknown as whether an entity with an unknown value in this attribute should be stored. It might be that it's not worth storing data unless the value is known, or it might be that we can't identify an entity without knowing the value. In either case, you would prevent a record containing an unknown value in the specified field from being added to the database.

This decision can't always be made at the domain level, but it's always worth considering since doing so can make the job a little easier down the line. To some extent, your decision depends on how generic your domains are. As an example, say that you have defined a Name domain and declared the attributes GivenName, MiddleName, Surname, and CompanyName against it. You might just as well have defined these attributes as separate domains, but there are some advantages to using the more general domain definition because doing so allows you to capture the overlapping rules (and in this case, there are probably a lot of them) in a single place. However, in this case you won't be able to determine whether empty or unknown values are acceptable at the domain level; you will have to define these properties at the entity level.

The final aspect of domain integrity is that you'll want to define the set of values represented by a domain as specifically as possible. Our Transaction Date domain, for example, isn't just the set of all dates; it's the set of dates from the day the company began trading until the current date. It might be further restricted to eliminate Sundays, public holidays, and any other days on which the company does not trade, although you need to be careful here. It's not unknown for employees to be in the office even though business is officially "closed," and absolutely no reason to restrict them from answering the phone to take an order when they are.

Sometimes the easiest way to describe a domain is to simply list the domain values. The domain of Weekends is completely described by the set {"Saturday", "Sunday"}. Sometimes it will be easier to list one or more rules for determining membership, as we did for TransactionDate. Both techniques are perfectly acceptable, although a specific design methodology might dictate a particular method of documenting constraints. The important thing is that the constraints be captured as carefully and completely as possible.

Transition Integrity

Transition integrity constraints define the states through which a tuple can validly pass. The State-Transition diagram in Figure 4–1, for example, shows the states through which an order can pass.

You would use transitional integrity constraints, for instance, to ensure that the status of a given order never changed from "Entered" to

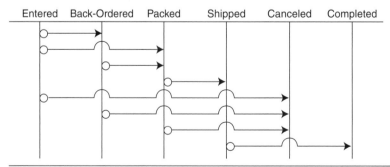

Figure 4–1 This Diagram Shows the States through Which an Order Can Pass

"Completed" without passing through the interim states, or to prevent a canceled order from changing status at all.

The status of an entity is usually controlled by a single attribute. In this case, transition integrity can be considered a special type of domain integrity. Sometimes, however, the valid transitions are controlled by multiple attributes or even multiple relations. Because transition constraints can exist at any level of granularity, it's useful to consider them a separate type of constraint during preparation of the data model.

For example, the status of a customer might only be permitted to change from "Normal" to "Preferred" if the customer's credit limit is above a specified value and he or she has been doing business with the company for at least a year. The credit limit requirement would most likely be controlled by an attribute of the Customers relation, but the length of time the customer has been doing business with the company might not be explicitly stored anywhere. It might be necessary to calculate the value based on the oldest record for the customer in the Orders relation.

Entity Integrity

Entity constraints ensure the integrity of the entities being modeled by the system. At the simplest level, the existence of a primary key is an entity constraint that enforces the rule "every entity must be uniquely identifiable."

In a sense, this is *the* entity integrity constraint; all others are technically entity-level integrity constraints. The constraints defined at the entity level can govern a single attribute, multiple attributes, or the relation as a whole.

The integrity of an individual attribute is modeled first and foremost by defining the attribute against a specific domain. An attribute within a relation inherits the integrity constraints defined for its domain. At the entity level, these inherited constraints can properly be made more rigorous, but they cannot be relaxed. Another way of thinking about this is that the entity constraint can specify a subset of the domain constraints but not a superset. For example, an OrderDate attribute defined against the TransactionDate domain might specify that the date must be in the current year, whereas the TransactionDate domain allows any date between the date business commenced and the current date. An entity constraint cannot, however, allow OrderDate to contain dates in the future, since the attribute's domain prohibits these.

Similarly, a CompanyName attribute defined against the Name domain might prohibit empty values, even though the Name domain permits them. Again, this is a narrower, more rigorous definition of permissible values than that specified in the domain.

NOTE: Designers often specify the validity of empty and unknown values at the entity level rather than the domain level. In fact, some designers would argue that these constraints apply only at the entity level. There is some justification for this position, but I recommend making the domain definition as inclusive as possible. Certainly, *considering* empty and unknown values at the domain level does no harm and can make the process of specification (and implementation) simpler.

In addition to narrowing the range of values for a single attribute, entity constraints can also affect multiple attributes. A requirement that ShippingDate be on or after OrderDate is an example of such a constraint. Entity constraints can't reference other relations, however. It wouldn't be appropriate, for example, to define an entity constraint that sets a customer DiscountRate (an attribute of the Customer relation) based on the customer's TotalSales (which is based on multiple records in the OrderItems relation). Constraints that depend on multiple relations are database-level constraints; we'll discuss them later in this chapter.

Be careful of multiple-attribute constraints; they often indicate that your data model isn't fully normalized. If you are restricting or calculating the value of one attribute based on another, you're probably OK. An entity constraint that says "Status is not allowed to be 'Preferred' unless the Customer record is at least one year old" would be fine. But if the value of one attribute *determines* the value of another—for example, "If the customer record is older than one year, then Status = 'Preferred'"—then you have a functional dependency and you're in violation of third normal form.

Referential Integrity

In Chapter 3, we looked at the decomposition of relations to minimize redundancy and at foreign keys to implement the links between relations. If these links are ever broken, the system will be unreliable at best and unusable at worst. **Referential integrity constraints** maintain and protect these links.

There is really only one referential integrity constraint: Foreign keys cannot become orphans. In other words, no record in the foreign table can contain a foreign key that doesn't match a record in the primary table. Tuples that contain foreign keys that don't have a corresponding candidate key in the primary relation are called **orphan entities**. There are four ways orphan entities can be created:

1. A tuple is added to the foreign table with a key that does not match a candidate key in the primary table.
2. The foreign key is changed to a value not in the primary table.
3. The candidate key in the primary table is changed.
4. The referenced record in the primary table is deleted.

All four of these cases must be handled if the integrity of a relationship is to be maintained. The first case, the addition of an unmatched foreign key, is usually simply prohibited. But note that unknown and nonexistent values don't count—that's a separate rule. If the relationship is declared as optional, any number of unknown and nonexistent values can be entered without compromising referential integrity.

The second and third causes of orphaned entities—changing the candidate key value in the referenced table—shouldn't occur very often. In fact, I would strongly recommend that changes to candidate and foreign keys be prohibited altogether wherever possible. (This would be an entity constraint, by the way: "Candidate keys are not allowed to change.")

If your model does allow candidate keys to be changed, you must ensure that these changes are made in the foreign keys as well. This is known as a **cascading update**. Both Microsoft Jet and Microsoft SQL Server provide mechanisms for easily implementing cascading updates.

If your model allows foreign keys to change, in effect allowing the entity to be re-assigned, you must ensure that the new value is valid. Again, Microsoft Jet and Microsoft SQL Server both allow this constraint to be easily implemented, even though it doesn't have a specific name.

The final cause of orphan foreign keys is the deletion of the record containing the primary entity. If one deletes a Customer record, for example, what becomes of that customer's orders? As with candidate key changes, you can simply prohibit the deletion of tuples in the primary relation if they are referenced in a foreign relation. This is certainly the cleanest solution if it is a reasonable restriction for your system. When it's not, both the Jet database engine and SQL Server provide a simple means of cascading the operation, known as a **cascading delete**.

But in this case, you also have a third option that's a little harder to implement because it can't be implemented automatically. You might want to re-assign the dependent records. This isn't often appropriate, but it is sometimes necessary. Say, for example, that CustomerA purchases CustomerB. It might make sense to delete CustomerB and reassign all of CustomerB's orders to CustomerA.

A special kind of referential integrity constraint is the maximum cardinality issue discussed in Chapter 3. In the data model, rules such as

"Managers are allowed to have a maximum of five individuals reporting to them" are defined as referential constraints.

Database Integrity

The most general form of integrity constraint is the **database constraint**. Database constraints reference more than one relation: "All Products sold to Customers with the status of 'Government' must have more than one Supplier." The majority of database constraints take this form, and, like this one, may require calculations against multiple relations.

You should be careful not to confuse a database constraint with the specification of a work process. A **work process** is something that is done with the database, such as adding an order, whereas an integrity constraint is a rule about the contents of the database. The rules that define the tasks that are performed using the database are part of the work process, not database constraints. Work processes, as we'll see in Chapter 11, can have a major impact on the data model, but they shouldn't be made a part of it.

It isn't always clear whether a given business rule is an integrity constraint or a work process (or something else entirely). The difference might not be desperately important. All else being equal, implement the rule where it's most convenient to do so. If it's a straightforward process to express a rule as a database constraint, do so. If that gets tricky (as it often can, even when the rule is clearly an integrity constraint), move it to the middle tier or the front end, where it can be implemented procedurally.

Transaction Integrity

The final form of database integrity is **transaction integrity**. Transaction integrity constraints govern the ways in which the database can be manipulated. Unlike other constraints, transaction constraints are procedural and thus are not part of the data model *per se.*

Transactions are closely related to work processes. The concepts are, in fact, orthogonal, inasmuch as a given work process might consist of one or more transactions and vice versa. It isn't quite correct, but it's useful to think of a work process as an abstract construct ("add an order") and a transaction as a physical one ("update the OrderDetail table").

A transaction is usually defined as a "logical unit of work," which I've always found to be a particularly unhelpful bit of rhetoric. Essentially, a transaction is a group of actions, all of which (or none of which) must be completed. The database must comply with all of the defined integrity constraints before the transaction commences and after it's completed, but might be temporarily in violation of one or more constraints *during* the transaction.

The classic example of a transaction is the transfer of money from one bank account to another. If funds are debited from Account A but the system fails to credit them to Account B, money has been lost. Clearly, if the second command fails, the first must be undone. In database parlance, it must be "rolled back." Transactions can involve multiple records, multiple relations, and even multiple databases.

To be precise, all operations against a database are transactions. Even updating a single existing record is a transaction. Fortunately, these low-level transactions are implemented transparently by the database engine, and you can generally ignore this level of detail.

Both the Jet database engine and SQL Server provide a means of maintaining transactional integrity by way of the BEGIN TRANSACTION, COMMIT TRANSACTION, and ROLLBACK TRANSACTION statements. As might be expected, SQL Server's implementation is more robust and better able to recover from hardware failure as well as certain kinds of software failure. However, these are implementation issues and are outside the scope of this book. What is important from a design point of view is to capture and specify transaction dependencies, those infamous "logical units of work."

Implementing Data Integrity

Up until now, we've concentrated on capturing the problem space at an abstract level in the conceptual data model. In this section, we'll look at a few of the issues involved in creating the physical model of the problem space: the database schema. Moving from one level to another is primarily a change in terminology—relations become tables and attributes become fields—except for issues of data integrity. These never map quite as cleanly as one wants.

Unknown and Nonexistent Values (Again)

Earlier in this chapter, I somewhat blithely declared that domains and attributes should be examined to determine whether they are permitted to be empty or unknown. I didn't, then, discuss how these constraints might be implemented. The implementation issue (and it *is* an issue) can't be avoided once we turn to the database schema.

The so-called "missing information problem" has been acknowledged since the relational model was first proposed. How does one indicate that any given bit of information is either missing (the customer does have a surname, we just don't know what it is) or nonexistent (the customer doesn't have a middle name)? Most relational databases, including Microsoft Jet databases and SQL Server databases, have incorporated the Null as a way of handling missing and nonexistent values.

To call the Null a solution to the issue is probably excessive, as it has numerous problems. Some database experts reject Nulls entirely. C. J. Date declares that they "wreck the model,"[1] and I've lost track of how many times I've heard them declared "evil." Any remarks about the complexity of handling Nulls or rueful admissions to having been caught out by them will result in remarks along the lines of "Good. You shouldn't be using them. They *should* hurt."

As an alternative, the "Nulls are evil" school recommends the use of specific values of the appropriate domain to indicate unknown or nonexistent values, or both. I think of this as the **conventional value** approach. The conventional value approach has several problems. First, in many instances the chosen value *is* only conventional. A date of 9/9/1900 doesn't *really* mean the date is unknown, we just agree that's what we'll interpret it to mean. And it's one of those "you only know if somebody tells you" situations that place an unfair burden on the system and the user alike.

I fail to see that this approach is an improvement over the Null. A Null is a conventional value as well, of course, but it can't be confused with anything else, and it has the advantage of being supported by the relational model and most relational database engines.

The second, and to my mind disqualifying, problem with the conventional value approach is its impact on referential integrity. Take, for example, an optional relationship between a Customer and a Customer Service Representative (CSR), such that the CSR, if one is assigned, must be listed in the CSR table. The conventional value approach requires that a record be added to the CSR table to match the conventional value chosen to indicate that no CSR is assigned, as shown in Figure 4–2.

Now, how many CSRs does the company employ? One less than the number of CSRs listed in the table, since one of them is a dummy record. Eek. What's the average number of customers per CSR? The number of records in the Customer table minus the number of records that match the

---

1. Date, C.J. *An Introduction to Database Systems*. 6th edition. Reading: Addison-Wesley, 1995, 129.

CustomerID	CompanyName	CSR
ANATR	Ana Trujillo Emparedados y helados	Andrew Fuller
ANTON	Antonio Moreno Taquería	Anne Dodsworth
AROUT	Around the Horn	Steven Buchanan
BERGS	Berglunds snabbköp	Margaret Peacock
BLAUS	Blauer See Delikatessen	UNASSIGNED
BLONP	Blondel père et fils	Steven Buchanan
BOLID	Bólido Comidas preparadas	Nancy Davolio
BONAP	Bon app'	UNASSIGNED
BOTTM	Bottom-Dollar Markets	Janet Leverling
BSBEV	B's Beverages	Margaret Peacock
CACTU	Cactus Comidas para llevar	Michael Suyama
CENTC	Centro comercial Moctezuma	UNASSIGNED

EmployeeID	Surname	GivenName
1	Davolio	Nancy
2	Fuller	Andrew
3	Leverling	Janet
4	Peacock	Margaret
5	Buchanan	Steven
6	Suyama	Michael
7	King	Robert
8	Callahan	Laura
9	Dodsworth	Anne
10	UNASSIGNED	

Figure 4–2 Conventional Values Require the Addition of "Dummy" Records to Maintain Referential Integrity

"UNASSIGNED" CSR, divided by one less than the number of records in the CSR table. Double eek.

Conventional values *are* useful when you're producing reports. For example, you might want to substitute "Unknown" for Null values and "Not Applicable" for empty values. But that is a very different proposition from storing these conventional values in the database, where they interfere with data manipulation, as we've seen.

Evil the Null might be, and ugly it most assuredly is, but it's the best tool we have for handling unknown and nonexistent values. Just think the issue through, find alternatives where that's reasonable, and allow for the difficulties of using Nulls where alternatives are *not* reasonable.

One of the problems with Nulls is that, with the exception of domains declared to be string or text data types, they might be forced to do double duty. A field declared as a DateTime data type can accept only dates or Nulls. If the corresponding attribute is defined as allowing both unknown and nonexistent values, and both are represented by Null, there is no way to determine whether a Null in any specific record represents "unknown" or "nonexistent." This problem doesn't arise for string or text data types, since you can use an empty, zero-length string for the empty value, leaving Null to represent the unknown value.

In practice, this problem doesn't occur as often as one might expect. Few non-text domains permit the nonexistent value, so in these domains a Null can always be interpreted as meaning unknown. For those domains that do accept a nonexistent value, a sensible alternative can often be chosen to represent it. Note that I'm recommending an actual value here, not a conventional one. For example, even though a Product relation has a Weight attribute, a Service Call, which obviously doesn't have a weight, can use the value zero. (Zero is a good choice to represent empty for many, but not all, numeric fields.)

The second and far more serious problem with Nulls is that they complicate data manipulation. Logical comparisons become more complex, and posing certain kinds of questions can get a bit hairy. We'll look at this in detail in Chapter 5.

I don't take Nulls lightly, and when there's a reasonable alternative, I'd recommend taking it. But as I've said elsewhere, don't dent the data model just to make life easier for the programmers. Think it through, but if the system requires Nulls, use them.

Violation Responses

When defining the database schema, you must not only determine how a given integrity constraint might most effectively be implemented, you must also decide what action the database engine should take if the constraint is violated. In most cases, of course, the database will simply reject the offending command, returning an error in whatever using whatever method is appropriate. Sometimes, however, the database can take corrective action that makes the requested change acceptable. Examples of this include the provision of a default value for attributes that do not allow empty values, or performing a cascading update or cascading delete to preserve referential integrity. We'll discuss violation responses in detail in Part IV.

Declarative and Procedural Integrity

Relational database engines provide integrity support in two ways: declarative and procedural. **Declarative integrity** support is explicitly defined ("declared") as part of the database schema. Both the Jet database engine and SQL Server provide some declarative integrity support. Declarative integrity is the preferred method for implementing data integrity. You should use it wherever possible.

SQL Server implements **procedural integrity** support by way of **trigger** procedures that are executed ("triggered") when a record is inserted, updated, or deleted. The Jet database engine does not support procedural integrity. When an integrity constraint cannot be implemented using declarative integrity, and the system is using the Jet engine, the constraint must be implemented in the front end.

Domain Integrity

SQL Server provides a limited kind of support for domains in the form of user-defined data types (UDDTs). Fields defined against a UDDT will inherit the data type declaration as well as domain constraints defined for the UDDT.

Equally importantly, SQL Server will prohibit comparison between fields declared against different UDDTs, even when the UDDTs in question are based on the same system data type. For example, even though the CityName domain and the CompanyName domain are both defined as being char(30), SQL Server would reject the expression CityName = CompanyName. This can be explicitly overridden by using the convert function CityName = CONVERT(char(30), CompanyName), but the restriction forces you to think about it before comparing fields declared against different domains. This is a good thing, since these comparisons don't often make sense.

UDDTs can be created either through the SQL Server Enterprise Manager or through the system stored procedure sp_addtype. Either way, UDDTs are initially declared with a name or a data type and by whether they are allowed to accept Nulls. Once a UDDT has been created, default values and validation rules can be defined for it. A SQL Server rule is a logical expression that defines the acceptable values for the UDDT (or for a field, if it is bound to a field rather than a UDDT). A default is simply that—a default value to be inserted by the system into a field that would otherwise be Null because the user did not provide a value.

Binding a rule or default to a UDDT is a two-step procedure. First you must create the rule or default, and then bind it to the UDDT (or field). The "it's not a bug, it's a feature" justification for this two-step procedure is that, once defined, the rule or default can be reused elsewhere. I find this tedious since in my experience these objects are reused only rarely. When defining a table, SQL Server provides the ability to declare defaults and CHECK constraints directly, as part of the table definition.

(CHECK constraints are similar to rules, but more powerful.) Unfortunately this one-step declaration is not available when declaring UDDTs, which must use the older "create-and-then-bind" methodology. It is heartily to be wished that Microsoft add support for default and CHECK constraint declarations to UDDTs in a future release of SQL Server.

A second way of implementing a kind of deferred domain integrity is to use lookup tables. This technique can be used in both Microsoft Jet and SQL Server. As an example, take the domain of USStates. Now, theoretically, you can create a rule listing all 50 states. In reality, this would be a painful process, particularly with the Jet database engine, where the rule would have to be retyped for every field declared against the domain. It's much, much easier to create a USStates lookup table and use referential integrity to ensure that the field values are restricted to the values stored in the table.

Entity Integrity

In the database schema, entity constraints can govern individual fields, multiple fields, or the table as a whole. Both the Jet database engine and SQL Server provide mechanisms for ensuring integrity at the entity level. Not surprisingly, SQL Server provides a richer set of capabilities, but the gap is not as great as one might expect.

At the level of individual fields, the most fundamental integrity constraint is of course the data type. Both the Jet database engine and SQL Server provide a rich set of data types, as shown in Table 4–1.

As we saw in the previous section, SQL Server also allows fields to be declared against UDDTs. A UDDT field inherits the nullability, defaults, and rules that were defined for the type, but these can be overridden by the field definition. Logically, the field definition should only narrow UDDT constraints, but in fact SQL Server simply replaces the UDDT definition in the field description. It is thus possible to allow a field to accept Nulls even though the UDDT against which it is declared does not. (Even after all these years, I've never been able to determine whether SQL Server lacks rigor, or I'm just stuffy.)

Both SQL Server and the Jet database engine provide control over whether a field is allowed to contain Nulls. When defining a column in SQL Server, one simply specifies NULL or NOT NULL or clicks the appropriate box in the Enterprise Manager.

The Jet database engine equivalent of the Null flag is the Required field. In addition, the Jet database engine provides the AllowZeroLength flag, which determines whether empty strings ("") are permitted in Text and Memo fields. This constraint can be implemented in SQL Server using a CHECK constraint.

Table 4–1 The Physical Data Types Supported by Microsoft Jet and SQL Server

Logical Data Type	SQL Server Data Type	Microsoft Jet Data Type	Value Range	Storage Size
Integer	Int	Long integer	Whole numbers from −2,147,483,648 to 2,147,483,647	4 bytes
	Smallint		Whole numbers from −32,768 to 32,767	2 bytes
	Tinyint		Whole numbers from 0 to 255	1 byte
Packed decimal (exact numeric)	Decimal	Number (type varies)	Whole or fractional numbers from −10^{38}−1 to 10^{38}−1	2–17 bytes
Floating point (approx. numeric)	Float (15-digit precision)	Double	Approximations of numbers from −1.79E^{308} to 1.79E^{308} Positive range: 2.23E^{-308} to 1.79E^{308} Negative range: −2.23E^{-308} to −1.79E^{308}	8 bytes
	Real	Single	Approximations of numbers from −3.40E^{38} to 3.40E^{38} Positive range: 1.18E^{-38} to 3.40E^{38} Negative range: −1.18E^{-38} to −3.40E^{38}	4 bytes
Character (fixed length)	Char	N/A	Maximum of 255 characters in Jet; 8000 characters in SQL Server 7.0 (255 in previous versions)	1 byte per character declared
Character (variable length)	Varchar	Text	Maximum of 255 characters in Jet; 8000 characters in SQL Server 7.0 (255 in previous versions)	1 byte per character stored
Monetary	Money	Currency	Numbers accurate to four decimal places, from −922,337,208,685,477.5808 to 922,337,208,685,477.5807	8 bytes

Table 4–1 The Physical Data Types Supported by Microsoft Jet and SQL Server (Continued)

Logical Data Type	SQL Server Data Type	Microsoft Jet Data Type	Value Range	Storage Size
	Smallmoney	N/A	Numbers accurate to four decimal places, from –214,748.3648 to 214,748.3647	4 bytes
Date and Time	Datetime	Date/Time	1 January 1753 to 31 December 9999 in SQL Server; 1 January 100 to 31 December 9999 in Jet	8 bytes
	Smalldatetime	N/A	1 January 1900 to 6 June 2079	4 bytes
Binary (fixed length)	Binary	N/A	Maximum of 8000 bytes	Number of bytes declared plus 4 bytes
Binary (variable length)	Varbinary	(Supported only for linked tables)	Maximum of 8000 bytes	Number of bytes actually stored plus 4 bytes
Long Text/Binary Long OBject	Text	Memo	Character data up to 2 GB in SQL Server, or 1 GB in a Microsoft Jet database	Amount of data stored plus 16 bytes
(BLOB)	Image	OLE Object	Binary data up to 2 GB in SQL Server, or 1 GB in a Microsoft Jet database	Amount of data stored plus 16 bytes
Boolean	Bit	Yes/No	0 or 1	1 byte, but bit columns in a table are combined in SQL Server; thus 8 or fewer columns will take 1 byte in total

Simply setting the appropriate property when defining the field sets default values in the Jet database engine. In SQL Server, you can set the Default property when creating the field, or you can bind a system default to the field as described for UDDTs. Declaring the default as part of the table definition is certainly cleaner and the option I would generally recommend if you do not (or cannot) declare the default at the domain level.

Finally, both the Jet database engine and SQL Server allow specific entity constraints to be established. The Jet database engine provides two field properties: ValidationRule and ValidationText. SQL Server allows CHECK constraints to be declared when the field is defined or system rules to be bound to the field afterwards. CHECK constraints are the preferred method.

At first glance, the Jet database engine validation rules and SQL Server CHECK constraints appear to be identical, but there are some important differences. Both take the form of a logical expression, and neither is allowed to reference other tables or columns. However, a Jet database engine validation rule must evaluate to True for the value to be accepted. A SQL Server CHECK constraint must not evaluate to False. This is a subtle point: both True and Null are acceptable values for a CHECK constraint; only a True value is acceptable for a validation rule.

In addition, multiple CHECK constraints can be defined for one SQL Server field. In fact, one rule and any number of CHECK constraints can be applied to a single SQL Server field, whereas a Jet database engine field has a single ValidationRule property. The Jet database engine Validation-Text property setting, by the way, is returned to the front end as an error message. Microsoft Access displays the text in a message box; it is available to Visual Basic and other programming environments as the text of the Errors collection.

Entity constraints that reference multiple fields in a single table are implemented as table validation rules in the Jet database engine and table CHECK constraints in SQL Server. Other than being declared in a different place, these table-level constraints function in precisely the same way as their corresponding field-level constraints.

The most fundamental entity integrity constraint is the requirement that each instance of an entity be uniquely identifiable. Remember that this is *the* entity integrity rule; all others are more properly referred to as entity-level integrity constraints. The Jet database engine and SQL Server support uniqueness constraints in pretty much the same way, but the support looks quite different. Both engines implement the constraints using indices, but SQL Server hides this from the user. Whether one explicitly creates an index (Jet database engine) or declares a constraint (SQL Server) is largely a mechanical detail.

Both the Jet database engine and SQL Server support the definition of sets of fields as being unique. Both also support the definition of a set of one or more fields as being the primary key, which implies uniqueness. There can be only one primary key for a table, although it can consist of multiple fields. There can be any number of unique constraints.

The other important difference between unique constraints and primary keys is that unique indices can contain Nulls; primary keys cannot. There are some differences in the way the two engines treat Nulls in unique indices. The Jet database engine provides a property, IgnoreNulls, which prevents records containing Null values in the indexed columns from being added to the index. The records are added to the table but not included in the index. This capability is not available in SQL Server.

In addition, SQL Server allows only a single record containing NULL in the index. This is logically incorrect. It treats records with NULL values as being equal, which of course they are not. A Null is not equal to anything, including another Null.

Interestingly, neither the Jet database engine nor SQL Server requires that a primary key be defined for a table or even that it have a unique constraint. In other words, it is possible to create tables that are not relations, since tuples in relations must be uniquely identifiable but records in tables need not be. Why one would want to do this escapes me, but I suppose it's nice to know that the possibility is there if you should ever need it.

SQL Server also provides a procedural mechanism for providing entity-level integrity that the Jet database engine does not provide. **Triggers** are little bits of code that are automatically executed when a specific event occurs. In the current version of SQL Server, the code must be Transaction SQL. The next version, codenamed "Yukon," will allow triggers to be written in any .NET language. Multiple triggers can be defined for each INSERT, UPDATE, or DELETE event, as well as the new INSTEAD OF event, and a given trigger can be defined for multiple events.

Referential Integrity

While their support for entity integrity is substantively the same, the Jet database engine and SQL Server implement different paradigms for supporting referential integrity. SQL Server allows foreign key constraints to be declared as part of the table definition. A **foreign key constraint** establishes a reference to a candidate key in another table, the primary table. Once the reference is established, SQL Server prevents the creation of orphan records by rejecting any insertions that do not have a matching record in the primary table. Nulls are not prohibited in foreign key columns, although they can be prevented if the column participates in the primary key of the table, which is usually the case. SQL Server also prohibits the deletion of records in the primary table if they have any matching foreign key values.

The Jet database engine supports referential integrity through a Relation object within the database. Microsoft's terminology is unfortunate here—the Jet database engine Relation object is a physical representation of the relationship between two entities. Don't confuse the Relation object with the logical relations that are defined in the data model.

The simplest way of creating Relation objects is in the Access user interface (using the Relationships command on the Tools menu), but they can also be created in code. The Data Access Object (DAO) Relation object's Table and ForeignTable properties define the two tables participating in the relationship, while the Fields collection defines the linked fields in each table.

The manner in which the Jet database engine will maintain referential integrity for the relation is governed by the Attributes property of the relation, as shown in Table 4–2.

Note the attribute flags dbRelationUpdateCascade and dbRelation-DeleteCascade. If the update flag is set and a referenced field is changed, the Jet database engine will automatically update the matching fields in the foreign table. Similarly, the delete flag will cause the matching records to be automatically deleted from the foreign table. SQL Server 2000 introduced comparable automatic flags, and the more complex cascading behavior can easily be implemented using triggers.

Table 4–2 The Constants Used When Defining Relations in the Jet Database

Attribute Constant	Description
dbRelationUnique	The relationship is one-to-one.
dbRelationDontEnforce	The relationship isn't enforced. (There is no referential integrity.)
dbRelationInherited	The relationship exists in a noncurrent database that contains the two linked tables.
dbRelationUpdateCascade	Updates will cascade.
dbRelationDeleteCascade	Deletes will cascade.

Other Kinds of Integrity

In the data model, we define three additional kinds of integrity: database, transition, and transaction. Some transition constraints are simple enough to be declared as validation rules. Most, however, including all database and transaction constraints, must be implemented procedurally. For SQL Server databases, this means using triggers. Since the Jet database engine does not support triggers, these constraints must be implemented in the front end.

Summary

In this chapter, we've looked at modeling and implementing data integrity. Three kinds of integrity constraints—domain, transition, and entity—control individual relations, while referential integrity constraints ensure that the relations between relations are maintained. Finally, database constraints and transaction constraints control the database as a whole.

Data integrity is implemented in the database schema using a combination of declarative and procedural integrity. Declarative integrity is explicitly declared as part of the schema and is the preferred method of implementation. However, not all constraints can be implemented using declarative integrity, and where they cannot, procedural integrity must be used.

In Chapter 5, we'll examine relational algebra and the operations that can be performed on the relations in the database.

Relational Algebra

In the previous chapters, we have looked at defining a particular kind of relation, called a **base relation**, which will be given a physical representation in the database. The relational model also supports the creation of several kinds of derived relations. A **derived relation** is a relation that is defined in terms of other relations rather than in terms of attributes. These named relations can be base relations or other derived relations, in any combination.

In the database schema, a base relation is represented by a table. Derived relations are represented by **views** in Microsoft SQL Server and **queries** in the Microsoft Jet database engine. For the sake of linguistic simplicity, I'll use the term "view," since it's the standard relational term and avoids any possible confusion with the process of querying, which is just close enough to be confusing. I'll also use the term "recordset" generically when I mean either a table (base relation) or a view (derived relation).

Views are defined in terms of the relational operations that are the subject of this chapter. Microsoft Access and the SQL Server Enterprise Manager provide a graphical interface for defining views, which are more commonly defined in terms of SQL SELECT statements.

SQL (usually pronounced "sequel") stands for **S**tructured **Q**uery **L**anguage. It is a standard language for expressing relational operations. Both the Jet database engine and SQL Server support a dialect of SQL. Not, of course, the same dialect—that would be entirely too easy. Fortunately, the differences between the two implementations don't often affect the relational algebra that we'll be discussing in this chapter. Where the syntax differs, I'll give examples from both dialects.

The SQL SELECT statement is extremely powerful and more than a little complex, and a detailed examination of it is outside the scope of this book. There are some general references listed in the Bibliography. For our purposes, we can restrict ourselves to the basic structure, which has the following syntax:

```
SELECT <fieldList>
FROM <recordsetList>
    <joinType> JOIN <joinCondition>
WHERE <selectionCriteria>
GROUP BY <groupByFieldList>
HAVING <selectionCriteria>
ORDER BY <orderByFieldList>
```

The <fieldList> in the SELECT clause is a list of one or more fields to be included in the recordset resulting from the statement. The fields can be physically present in the underlying recordsets, or they can be calculated based on other fields. The <recordsetList> in the FROM clause is, as one might expect, a list of tables and views on which the SELECT statement is based. These are the only two clauses of the SELECT statement that must be included; all others are optional.

The JOIN clause defines the relationship between the recordsets listed in <recordsetList>. We'll be looking at joins in detail later in this chapter. The WHERE clause defines a logical expression, <selectionCriteria>, that restricts the data to be included in the resulting recordset. We'll look at restriction in detail later, as well.

The GROUP BY clause combines records having the same values in the specified list of fields to be combined into a single record. The HAVING clause is used to further restrict the rows returned after they've been combined by the GROUP BY clause. Finally, the ORDER BY clause causes the recordset to be sorted according to the fields listed in <orderByFieldList>.

Nulls and Three-Valued Logic (One More Time)

Most of the operations of relational algebra involve the use of **logical operators**, operators that usually return a **Boolean result**—that is, True or False. I say "usually" because, with the addition of Nulls to the relational model, things get a little more complicated.

Nulls add a third value to the set of Boolean values; you must then work with True, False, and Null. Not surprisingly, these operators become known as **three-valued logic**. The three-valued truth tables for the standard logical operators are shown in Figure 5–1.

As you can see, Null *op* anything, where *op* is a logical operator, results in Null. This is generally also true of the logical comparison operators, as shown in Figure 5–2.

AND	True	False	Null
True	True	False	Null
False	False	False	Null
Null	Null	Null	Null

OR	True	False	Null
True	True	True	Null
False	True	False	Null
Null	Null	Null	Null

XOR	True	False	Null
True	False	True	Null
False	True	False	Null
Null	Null	Null	Null

Figure 5–1 The Three-Valued And, Or, and XOr Truth Tables

=	True	False	Null
True	True	False	Null
False	False	True	Null
Null	Null	Null	Null

≠	True	False	Null
True	False	True	Null
False	True	False	Null
Null	Null	Null	Null

Figure 5–2 The Three-Valued Equal and Not Equal Truth Tables

There are two exceptions to this. Microsoft Jet returns True instead of Null as the result of "True Xor Null" (which kind of makes sense), and SQL Server, for reasons that I'm sure make sense to its designers, adds an

	Is Null	Is Not Null
\<value\>	False	True
True	False	True
False	False	True
Null	True	False

Figure 5–3 The IS NULL and IS NOT NULL Truth Tables

"extension" to normal logical operations. If the option ANSI_NULLS is turned off, Null = Null evaluates to True, and Null = \<value\>, where \<value\> is anything except Null (including the Boolean values True and False), evaluates to False. Frankly, I can't imagine why anyone would want to break the rules of relational algebra in this way—working with Nulls is complicated enough without adding uncertainty about how operators will behave.

SQL provides two unary operators—IS NULL and IS NOT NULL—to specifically handle Null values. They work exactly as one might expect. The truth tables for IS NULL and IS NOT NULL are shown in Figure 5–3. Again, \<value\> indicates anything except Null.

Relational Operations

We'll begin our examination of relational algebra with the four types of relational operations: restriction, projection, join, and divide. The first two affect a single recordset, although that recordset can, of course, be a view based on any number of other recordsets. The join operator is perhaps the most fundamental to the relational model and defines how two recordsets are to be combined. The final operator, divide, is a rarely used but occasionally handy method of determining which records in one recordset match all the records in a second recordset.

All of these operators are implemented using some form of the SQL SELECT statement. They can be combined in any way you want, subject to the system constraints regarding maximum length and complexity for the statement.

Restriction

The restriction operator returns only those records that meet the specified selection criteria. It is implemented using the WHERE clause of the SELECT statement, as follows:

```
SELECT *
FROM Employees
WHERE LastName = "Davolio";
```

In the Northwind database, this statement returns Nancy Davolio's employee record, since she's the only person in the table with that last name. (The * in the <fieldList> section of the statement is special shorthand for "all fields.")

The selection criteria specified in the WHERE clause can be of arbitrary complexity. Logical expressions can be combined with AND and OR. The expression will be evaluated for each record in the recordset, and if it returns True, that record will be included in the result. If the expression returns either False or Null for the record, it will not be included.

Projection

While restriction takes a horizontal slice of a recordset, projection takes a vertical slice; it returns only a subset of the fields in the original recordset.

SQL performs this simple operation using the <fieldList> section of the SELECT statement by only including the fields that you list. For example, you could use the following statement to create an employee phone list:

```
SELECT LastName, FirstName, Extension
FROM Employees
ORDER BY LastName, FirstName;
```

Remember that the ORDER BY clause does just that, it sorts the data, and as such really has nothing to do with the projection itself. In this case, the list will be sorted alphabetically by the LastName field and then by the FirstName field.

Join

Join operations are probably the most common relational operations. Certainly they are fundamental to the model—it would not be feasible to decompose data into multiple relations were it not possible to recombine them as necessary. This is precisely what a join operator does; it combines recordsets based on the comparison of one or more common fields.

Joins are implemented using the JOIN clause of the SELECT statement. They are categorized based on the type of comparison between the fields involved and the way the results of the comparison are treated. We'll look at each of these in turn.

Equi-Joins

When the join comparison is made on the basis of equality, the join is an **equi-join**. In an equi-join operation, only those records that have matching values in the specified fields will be returned.

Take, for example, the relations in Figure 5–4. This is a typical case of related tables resulting from the normalization process. OrderID is the primary key of the Orders table and a foreign key in the Order Details table.

To recombine (and consequently denormalize) the tables, you would use the following SELECT statement:

```
SELECT Orders.OrderID, Orders.CustomerID, [Order Details].ProductID
FROM Orders
INNER JOIN [Order Details] ON Orders.OrderID = [Order Details].OrderID
WHERE Orders.OrderID=10248;
```

This statement would result in the recordset shown in Figure 5–5.

Figure 5–4 These Tables Can Be Recombined Using the JOIN Operator

Order ID	Customer	Product
10248	WILMK	11
10248	WILMK	42
10248	WILMK	72

Figure 5–5 This Recordset Is the Result of Joining the Orders and Order Details Tables

NOTE: If you run this query in Access 2000 using the Northwind database, the result set will show the customer name rather than the CustomerID. This is because Access allows fields to display something *other* than what's actually stored in them when you declare a lookup control in the table definition. This can be convenient when Access is used interactively, but wreaks havoc on authors trying to provide examples.

Natural Joins

A special case of the equi-join is the **natural join**. To qualify as a natural join, a join operation must meet the following conditions:

- The comparison operator must be equality.
- All common fields must participate in the join.
- Only one set of common fields must be included in the resulting recordset.

There's nothing intrinsically magical about natural joins. They don't behave in a special manner, nor does the database engine provide special support for them. They are merely the most common form of join, so common that they've been given their own name.

The Jet database engine does do something particularly magical if you create a natural join that meets some additional conditions. If a one-to-many relationship has been established between the two tables, and the common fields included in the view are from the many-side of the relationship, then the Jet database engine will perform something called **Row Fix-Up** or **AutoLookup**. When the user enters a value in a control on an Access form that is bound to the fields used in the join criteria, the Jet database engine will automatically provide the data for controls bound to fields on the many-side, a spectacular bit of sleight of hand that makes the programmer's life much simpler.

Theta-Joins

A join based on any comparison operator other than equals (<>, >, >=, <, <=) is a **theta-join**. (Technically, all joins are theta-joins, but by custom, if the comparison operator is equality, the join is always referred to as an equi-join or just as a join.)

Theta-joins are extremely rare in practice, but they can be handy in solving certain kinds of problems. These problems mostly involve finding records that have a value greater than an average or total, or records that fall within a certain range.

Let's say, for example, that you've created two views, one containing the average number of units sold for each product category and a second containing the total units sold by product, as shown in Figure 5–6. (We'll look at how to create these views later in this chapter. For now, just assume their existence.)

The following SELECT statement, based on the comparison operator >, will produce a list of the best-selling products within each category:

```
SELECT DISTINCTROW ProductCategoryAverages.CategoryName,
  ProductTotals.ProductName
FROM ProductCategoryAverages
INNER JOIN ProductTotals
  ON ProductCategoryAverages.CategoryID = ProductTotals.CategoryID
  AND ProductTotals.TotalSold > [ProductCategoryAverages].[AverageSold];
```

The results are shown in Figure 5–7.

In this example, the view could also have been defined using a WHERE clause restriction. In fact, Access will rewrite the query when you leave SQL view to look like the following:

```
SELECT DISTINCTROW ProductCategoryAverages.CategoryName,
  ProductTotals.ProductName
FROM ProductCategoryAverages
INNER JOIN ProductTotals
ON ProductCategoryAverages.CategoryID = ProductTotals.CategoryID
WHERE ProductTotals.TotalSold>ProductCategoryAverages.AverageSold;
```

Technically, all joins, including equi-joins and natural joins, can be expressed using a restriction. In the case of theta-joins, this formulation using a restriction is almost always to be preferred since the database engines are better able to optimize its execution.

Category ID	Category Name	AverageSold
1	Beverages	24
2	Condiments	25
3	Confections	24
4	Dairy Products	25
5	Grains/Cereals	23
6	Meat/Poultry	24
7	Produce	22
8	Seafood	23

Category ID	Product ID	Product Name	TotalSold
1	1	Chai	828
1	2	Chang	1057
1	24	Guaraná Fantástica	1125
1	34	Sasquatch Ale	506
1	35	Steeleye Stout	883
1	38	Côte de Blaye	623
1	39	Chartreuse verte	793
1	43	Ipoh Coffee	580
1	67	Laughing Lumberjack Lager	184
1	70	Outback Lager	817
1	75	Rhönbräu Klosterbier	1155
1	76	Lakkalikööri	981
2	3	Aniseed Syrup	328

Figure 5–6 These Views Can Be Joined Using a Theta-Join

Category Name	Product Name
Beverages	Chai
Beverages	Chang
Beverages	Guaraná Fantástica
Beverages	Sasquatch Ale
Beverages	Steeleye Stout
Beverages	Côte de Blaye
Beverages	Chartreuse verte
Beverages	Ipoh Coffee
Beverages	Laughing Lumberjack Lager
Beverages	Outback Lager
Beverages	Rhönbräu Klosterbier
Beverages	Lakkalikööri
Condiments	Aniseed Syrup
Condiments	Chef Anton's Cajun Seasoning

Figure 5–7 This Recordset Is the Result of a Theta-Join

Outer Joins

All of the joins we've examined so far have been **inner joins**, joins that return only those records where the join condition evaluates as True. Note that this isn't exactly the same as returning only the records where the specified fields match, although this is how an inner join is usually described. "Match" implies equality, and as we know, not all joins are based on equality.

Relational algebra also supports another kind of join, the **outer join**. An outer join returns all the records returned by an inner join, *plus* all the records from either or both of the other recordsets. The missing ("unmatched") values will be Null.

Outer joins are categorized as being left, right, or full, depending on which additional records are to be included. Now, when I was in grad school, a **left outer join** returned all the records from the recordset on the one side of a one-to-many relationship, while a **right outer join** returned all the records from the many side. For both the Jet database engine and SQL Server, however, the distinction is based on the order in which the recordsets are listed in the SELECT statement. Thus the following two statements both return all the records from X and only those records from Y where the <condition> evaluates to True:

```
SELECT * FROM X LEFT OUTER JOIN Y ON <condition>
SELECT * FROM Y RIGHT OUTER JOIN X ON <condition>
```

A **full outer join** returns all records from both recordsets, combining those where the condition evaluates as True. SQL Server supports full outer joins with the FULL OUTER JOIN condition:

```
SELECT * FROM X FULL OUTER JOIN Y ON <condition>
```

The Jet database engine does not directly support full outer joins, but performing a union of a left outer join and a right outer join can duplicate them. We'll discuss unions in the next section.

Divide

The final relational operation is division. The **relational divide** operator (so called to distinguish it from mathematical division) returns the records in one recordset that have values that match all the corresponding values in the second recordset. For example, given a recordset that shows the categories of products purchased from each supplier, a relational division will produce a list of the suppliers that provide products in all categories.

This is not an uncommon situation, but the solution is not straightforward since the SQL SELECT statement does not directly support relational division. There are numerous ways to achieve the same results as a relational division, however. The easiest method is to rephrase the request.

Instead of "list the suppliers who provide all product categories," which is difficult to process, try "list all suppliers where the count of their product categories is equal to the count of all product categories." This is an example of the extension operation that we'll discuss later in this chapter. It won't always work, and in situations where it doesn't, you can implement division using correlated queries. Correlated queries are, however, outside the scope of this book. Please refer to one of the references listed in the Bibliography.

Set Operators

The next four operations of relational algebra are based on traditional set theory. They have, however, been modified slightly to account for the fact that we're dealing with relations, not undifferentiated sets.

Union

Conceptually, a **relational union** is the concatenation of two recordsets. It's more or less the relational version of addition. The result of the union of recordset A with recordset B is the same as actually adding all the records in A to B.

As an example, say you need a list of all the names and addresses known to the database for a mass mailing. The Northwind database Customers and Employees recordsets both have addresses and so can easily be combined in a union operation. In this case, we'd use the UNION statement, as follows:

```
SELECT CompanyName AS FullName, Address, City, PostalCode
FROM Customers
UNION SELECT [FirstName] & " " & [LastName] AS FullName,
   Address, City, PostalCode
FROM Employees
ORDER BY FullName;
```

Note that the CompanyName field is renamed "FullName" and the FirstName and LastName fields from the Employees table are concatenated. The resulting field is also "FullName." The union query doesn't require that the fields in the <fieldList> of each SELECT statement have the same name, but there must be the same number of them and they must have the same (or compatible) types. The results of this statement in Access are shown in Figure 5–8.

Name	Address	City	PostalCode
Alfreds Futterkiste	Obere Str. 57	Berlin	12209
Ana Trujillo Emparedados y helados	Avda. de la Constitución 2222	México D.F.	05021
Andrew Fuller	908 W. Capital Way	Tacoma	98401
Anne Dodsworth	7 Houndstooth Rd.	London	WG2 7LT
Antonio Moreno Taquería	Mataderos 2312	México D.F.	05023
Around the Horn	120 Hanover Sq.	London	WA1 1DP
Berglunds snabbköp	Berguvsvägen 8	Luleå	S-958 22
Blauer See Delikatessen	Forsterstr. 57	Mannheim	68306
Blondel père et fils	24, place Kléber	Strasbourg	67000
Bólido Comidas preparadas	C/ Araquil, 67	Madrid	28023
Bon app'	12, rue des Bouchers	Marseille	13008
Bottom-Dollar Markets	23 Tsawassen Blvd.	Tsawassen	T2F 8M4

Figure 5–8 The UNION Statement Combines the Records from Two Tables

Intersection

The **relational intersection** operator returns the records that two record-sets have in common. It is, in essence, a "find the duplicates" operation, and that's the way it is most often used.

An intersection is implemented using outer joins. As an example, suppose that you have inherited client lists from several legacy systems, as shown in Figure 5–9.

CustomerID	CompanyName
ALFKI	Alfreds Futterkiste
ANATR	Ana Trujillo Emparedados y helados
ANTON	Antonio Moreno Taquería
AROUT	Around the Horn
BERGS	Berglunds snabbköp
BLAUS	Blauer See Delikatessen
BLONP	Blondel père et fils
BOLID	Bólido Comidas preparadas

CustomerID	CompanyName
ALFKI	Alfreds Futterkiste
ANATR	Ana Trujillo Emparedados y helados
ANTON	Antonio Moreno Taquería
AROUT	Around the Horn
FAMIA	Familia Arquibaldo
FISSA	FISSA Fabrica Inter. Salchichas S.A.
FOLIG	Folies gourmandes
FOLKO	Folk och fä HB
FRANK	Frankenversand

Figure 5–9 Legacy Tables Often Have Duplicate Data

CustomerID	CompanyName
ALFKI	Alfreds Futterkiste
ANATR	Ana Trujillo Emparedados y helados
ANTON	Antonio Moreno Taquería
▶ AROUT	Around the Horn

Figure 5–10 An Outer Join Combined with the IS NOT NULL Operator Performs an Intersection

The following SELECT statement will return the duplicate records:

```
SELECT DuplicateCustomers1.*
FROM DuplicateCustomers1
LEFT JOIN DuplicateCustomers2
  ON DuplicateCustomers1.CustomerID = DuplicateCustomers2.CustomerID
WHERE DuplicateCustomers2.CustomerID IS NOT NULL;
```

The results of this statement are shown in Figure 5–10.

Difference

While the intersection of two recordsets is used to "find the duplicates," the difference operator will "find the orphans." The **relational difference** of two recordsets is the records that belong to one recordset but not the other.

As an example, given the same two recordsets shown in Figure 5–9, the following SELECT statement will return the *unmatched* records:

```
SELECT DuplicateCustomers1.*
FROM DuplicateCustomers1
LEFT JOIN DuplicateCustomers2
  ON DuplicateCustomers1.CustomerID = DuplicateCustomers2.CustomerID
WHERE DuplicateCustomers2.CustomerID IS NULL;
```

The outer join operation in this statement returns all the records from the two lists. As you will recall, an outer join supplies Null for the fields that do not have a match in the other table. The WHERE clause uses the IS NULL operator to restrict the records returned to only those (unmatched) records.

If this all seems as clear as mud, try performing the operation in two discrete steps: First create the outer join as a view, and then restrict the view with the WHERE statement. This process is shown in Figure 5–11.

Step 1: Create the outer join

```
SELECT DuplicateCustomers1.*
FROM DuplicateCustomers1
LEFT JOIN DuplicateCustomers2
ON DuplicateCustomers1.CustomerID = DuplicateCustomers2.CustomerID
```

05_09a.Custom	CompanyName	05_09b.Custom
ALFKI	Alfreds Futterkiste	ALFKI
ANATR	Ana Trujillo Emparedados y helados	ANATR
ANTON	Antonio Moreno Taquería	ANTON
AROUT	Around the Horn	AROUT
BERGS	Berglunds snabbköp	
BLAUS	Blauer See Delikatessen	
BLONP	Blondel père et fils	
▶ BOLID	Bólido Comidas preparadas	

Step 2: Select for CustomerID = Null

```
SELECT DuplicateCustomers1.*
FROM DuplicateCustomers1
LEFT JOIN DuplicateCustomers2
ON DuplicateCustomers1.CustomerID = DuplicateCustomers2.CustomerID
WHERE DuplicateCustomers2.CustomerID is Null
```

05_09a.Custom	CompanyName	05_09b.Custom
BERGS	Berglunds snabbköp	
BLAUS	Blauer See Delikatessen	
▶ BLONP	Blondel père et fils	
BOLID	Bólido Comidas preparadas	

Figure 5–11 The Difference Operation Is Performed in Two Steps

Cartesian Product

The final set operator is the Cartesian product. Like its counterpart in traditional set theory, the **Cartesian product** of two recordsets combines every record in one set with every record in the other.

The Cartesian product (or just "product") of two recordsets is returned by a SELECT statement that specifies two (or more) recordsets but no JOIN clause. The following statement will return every customer combined with every customer service representative:

```
SELECT CustomerName, CSRName FROM Customer, CSRs;
```

Cartesian products are occasionally useful either for analysis purposes or as interim results for further manipulation. Most often, though, they're produced by accident. Forget to drag the join line in the Access query designer and bingo, you've got a Cartesian product. It's amazingly easy to do, so don't be embarrassed the first (dozen) times it happens to you.

Special Relational Operators

Various extensions to relational algebra have been proposed since the relational model was first formulated. We'll look at three that have been generally accepted: summarize, extend, and rename. We'll also look at three extensions provided by Microsoft: transform, rollup, and cube.

Summarize

The summarize operator does precisely what one would expect it to do: It produces records containing summary data grouped according to the specified fields. Summarization is extremely useful in any number of situations in which you want to examine data at a higher level of abstraction than is stored in the database.

The summarize operation is implemented using the GROUP BY clause of the SELECT statement. There will be one record returned for each distinct value in the specified field or fields. If more than one field is listed, groups will be nested. For example, consider the following statement:

```
SELECT Categories.CategoryName, Products.ProductName,
  SUM([Order Details].Quantity) AS SumOfQuantity
FROM Categories
INNER JOIN Products
  ON Categories.CategoryID = Products.CategoryID)
INNER JOIN [Order Details]
  ON Products.ProductID = [Order Details].ProductID
GROUP BY Categories.CategoryName, Products.ProductName;
```

This statement will return one record for each product in the Northwind database, grouped by category and containing three fields: CategoryName, ProductName, and SumOfQuantity—the total number of each product sold—as shown in Figure 5–12.

The fields listed in <fieldList> in the SELECT statement must be either part of the <groupFieldList> or an argument to a SQL aggregate function. **SQL aggregate functions** calculate summary values for each

Category Name	Product Name	SumOfQuantity
Beverages	Chai	828
Beverages	Chang	1057
Beverages	Chartreuse verte	793
Beverages	Côte de Blaye	623
Beverages	Guaraná Fantástica	1125
Beverages	Ipoh Coffee	580
Beverages	Lakkalikööri	981
Beverages	Laughing Lumberjack Lager	184
Beverages	Outback Lager	817
Beverages	Rhönbräu Klosterbier	1155
Beverages	Sasquatch Ale	506
Beverages	Steeleye Stout	883

Figure 5–12 The GROUP BY Clause Returns Summary Data

record. The most common aggregate functions are AVERAGE, COUNT, SUM, MAXIMUM, and MINIMUM.

Aggregates are another place where Nulls can bite you. Null values are included in the summarize operation—they form a group. They are, however, ignored by aggregate functions. This is usually only a problem if you're using one of the fields in the <groupFieldList> as the parameter to an aggregate function.

Extend

The extend operator allows you to define virtual fields that are calculated based on constants and values stored in the database. You create virtual fields simply by defining them in the <fieldList> of the SELECT statement, as follows:

```
SELECT [UnitPrice]*[Qty] AS ExtendedPrice
FROM [Order Details];
```

The calculations defining the virtual fields can be of arbitrary complexity. This process is so simple and fast, that there is rarely any justification for storing a calculated field in a table.

Rename

The final common operator is rename. The rename operation can be performed on either a recordset in <recordsetList> or on individual fields in <fieldList>. In the Jet database engine, a recordset renaming uses the following syntax:

```
SELECT <fieldName> AS <fieldAlias>
FROM <tableName> AS <tableAlias>
```

In SQL Server, the "AS" keyword is not necessary, as shown here:

```
SELECT <fieldName> <fieldAlias> FROM <recordsetName> <recordsetAlias>
```

Renaming is particularly useful when you're defining a view with a self-join, as shown in the following code:

```
SELECT Manager.Name, Employee.Name
FROM Employees AS Employee
INNER JOIN Employees AS Manager
  ON Employee.EmployeeID = Manager.EmployeeID;
```

This syntax allows you to keep each usage logically distinct.

Transform

The TRANSFORM statement is the first of the Microsoft extensions to the relational algebra that we'll examine. TRANSFORM takes the results of a summarize (GROUP BY) operation and rotates them 90 degrees. More often referred to as a **crosstab query**, this incredibly useful operation is only supported by the Jet database engine; it has not (yet) been implemented in SQL Server.

YUKON NOTE: Transact-SQL, the dialect supported by SQL Server, has been extended to support a version of the transform operation in Yukon.

The TRANSFORM statement has the following basic syntax:

```
TRANSFORM <aggregateFunction>
SELECT <fieldList>
FROM <recordsetList>
GROUP BY <groupByList>
PIVOT <columnHeading> [IN (<valueList>)]
```

The TRANSFORM <aggregateFunction> clause defines the summary data that will populate the recordset. The SELECT statement must include a GROUP BY clause and cannot include a HAVING clause. As with any

GROUP BY clause, the <groupByList> can contain multiple fields. (In a TRANSFORM statement, the <fieldList> and <groupByList> expressions are almost always identical.)

The PIVOT clause identifies the field whose values will be used as column headings. By default, the Jet database engine will include the columns in the recordset alphabetically from left to right. The optional IN statement, however, allows you to specify column names, which will be listed in the order in which they're included in <valueList>.

The following TRANSFORM statement provides essentially the same information as the summarize example given previously, the results of which are shown in Figure 5–12.

```
TRANSFORM Count(Products.ProductID) AS CountOfProductID
SELECT Suppliers.CompanyName
FROM Suppliers
INNER JOIN (Categories INNER JOIN Products
    ON Categories.CategoryID = Products.CategoryID)
ON Suppliers.SupplierID = Products.SupplierID
GROUP BY Suppliers.CompanyName
PIVOT Categories.CategoryName;
```

The results of this TRANSFORM operation are shown in Figure 5–13.

Rollup

The summarize operator implemented using the GROUP BY clause generates records containing summary data. The ROLLUP clause, supported only by SQL Server, provides a logical extension to this operation by providing total values.

Company Name	Beverages	Condiments	Confections	Dairy	Grains/Cereals	Meat/Poultry	Produce	Seafood
Aux joyeux ecclésiasti	2							
Bigfoot Breweries	3							
Cooperativa de Quesos				2				
Escargots Nouveaux								1
Exotic Liquids	2	1						
Forêts d'érables		1	1					
Formaggi Fortini s.r.l.				3				
Gai pâturage				2				
G'day, Mate						1	1	1
Grandma Kelly's Home		2					1	
Heli Süßwaren GmbH			3					
Karkki Oy	1		2					
Leka Trading	1	1				1		
Lyngbysild								2

Figure 5–13 The TRANSFORM Statement Rotates Results by 90 Degrees

The ROLLUP clause is only available in SQL Server. It is implemented as an extension to the GROUP BY clause:

```
SELECT Categories.CategoryName, Products.ProductName,
  SUM([Order Details].Quantity) AS SumOfQuantity
FROM (Categories INNER JOIN Products
  ON Categories.CategoryID = Products.CategoryID)
INNER JOIN [Order Details]
  ON Products.ProductID = [Order Details].ProductID
GROUP BY Categories.CategoryName, Products.ProductName WITH ROLLUP;
```

Cube

The CUBE operator is also available only in SQL Server and is implemented as an extension to the GROUP BY clause. Essentially, the CUBE clause summarizes every column in the <groupByList> by every other column. It is conceptually similar to the ROLLUP operator, but whereas ROLLUP produces totals for each column specified in the <groupByList>, CUBE creates summary data for additional groups.

For example, if you have three fields in the <groupByList>—A, B, and C—the CUBE operator will return the following seven aggregates:

1. The total number of Cs.
2. The total number of Cs, grouped by A.
3. The total number of Cs, grouped by C within A.
4. The total number of Cs, grouped by B within A.
5. The total number of Cs, grouped by B.
6. The total number of Cs, grouped by A within B.
7. The total number of Cs, grouped by C within B.

Summary

In this chapter, we've looked at manipulating base relations using various relational operators and seen some examples implemented in the SQL language. We've also had yet another look at the issue of Nulls and three-valued logic.

Of the standard relational operators, the restriction and projection operators select subsets of a single recordset. The join, union, intersection, difference, and Cartesian product operators control the way two recordsets are combined. All of these operators, with the exception of difference, can be implemented using a SQL SELECT statement. Difference can sometimes be implemented using SELECT and sometimes requires other techniques that are outside the scope of this book.

We've also looked at a few special operators. The summarize and extend operators perform calculations on the data. The rename operator controls the column headings that are displayed for the view. TRANSFORM, ROLLUP, and CUBE are special extensions to the SQL language implemented by Microsoft, each of which also provides a special way of summarizing and viewing data.

With this overview of relational algebra, we've completed Part I. Relational database theory is complex, and of course, there are issues and subtleties that I haven't been able to cover in the scope of an introductory book. But you've now seen all the major components of the theory. In the next section, we'll turn to the other type of modeling employed with relational databases: dimensional modeling.

Dimensional Database Theory

Basic Dimensional Concepts

In Part I, we looked at the fundamental principles of traditional relational theory and the entity-relationship model. The majority of database applications are built using these principles, and for good reason. If applied consistently, they ensure data integrity, resilience, and scalability in applications that involve frequent changes to data.

But not all database applications involve frequent changes to the data. There exists another entire class of database applications with very different purposes and requirements. These applications must store large (sometimes vast) amounts of historical data, but that data, once loaded, is only rarely changed. These applications rarely support more than a few dozen users, but those users must be able to produce reports on the data effectively. "Effectively" in this case means two things: Ad hoc queries must return results quickly, and the structure of the database schema must be easily comprehensible to the end user.

Database schemas produced using the normalization rules we examined in Part II rarely meet these requirements. Even when the databases are small enough to respond quickly, and few are, handling historical data can be clumsy using the relational model. Further, fully-normalized schemas hardly qualify as "easily comprehensible to the end user."

The dimensional database rules that we'll examine in this section, on the other hand, were developed to address just these needs. In this brief chapter, we'll look at the basic structure of a dimensional database.

The Dimensional Database Model

Relational databases based on the entity-relationship model often support the operational aspects of an organization, such as order processing or payroll management. They answer questions such as "how many screwdrivers did Mary Smith order on the 5th of June?" or "How much did we pay Jimmy Jones in January 2003?" The "grain" of the data in these databases is a single transaction—a single order line item (the number of screwdrivers), or a pay stub (Jimmy Jones' pay in January)—and the systems are thus often called *On-Line Transaction Processing* (OLTP) systems.

This label can be useful, but it's also inaccurate, since schemas based on the entity-relationship model are also the best structure for storing static data—the current holdings of a library (the "card catalog") or a mailing list, for example.

Database schemas based on the dimensional model, on the other hand, are almost always used for analyzing the state of an organization. They answer questions such as "What product groups are most profitable?" or "How do sales vary with the season?" For this reason, they are often called **O**n-**L**ine **A**nalytical **P**rocessing (OLAP) systems.

Again, OLAP is a useful but slightly inaccurate term. While OLAP systems are rarely used for anything other than analysis, OLTP systems can be, and often are, used for analysis as well. Thus the two types of system are not mutually-exclusive. Further, in the same way that it's important to keep the logical and physical design of a database distinct, it seems to me more than a little muddled to use functional terminology to make structural distinctions.

For these reasons, I'm going to use the terms "normalized" and "dimensional" to distinguish between schemas developed using the two sets of rules. But be aware that these are my terms. In the literature, the two types of database schemas are rarely discussed together, so the distinction simply isn't made. What I call normalized databases are simply referred to as "databases," while dimensional databases are called either "dimensional databases" or "OLAP databases."

For the purposes of this book, however, we do need to distinguish between the two types. So I'll use the term **normalized database** to refer to the traditional relational structures we examined in Part I, defined in terms of entities, attributes and relationships, as shown in Figure 6–1.

Note that the two entities shown in Figure 6–1 are not a complete schema; the Customer and Employee and Product entities are missing. This makes the diagram easier to understand than the complete database is likely to be. (I once worked with an analyst who created her initial schemas using little yellow sticky notes and string. One of her schemas took up the better part of a 12-foot-long hallway. Try teaching *that* to the Vice President of Marketing!)

Figure 6–2 shows a **dimensional database** equivalent to Figure 6–1 defined in terms of facts tables, facts and dimensions. As you can see, there is some overlap between the two models. We are, after all, still dealing with

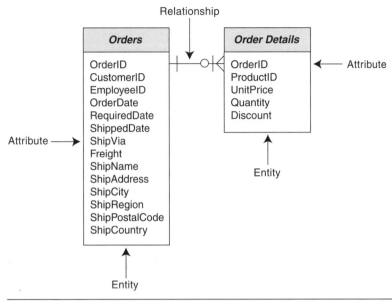

Figure 6-1 Two Tables from a Normalized Database Schema

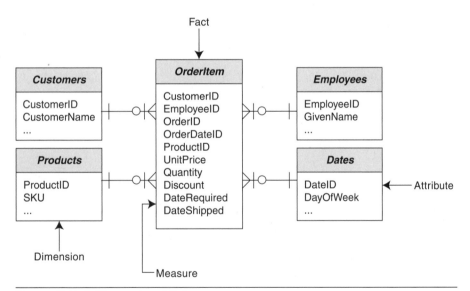

Figure 6-2 A Dimensional Schema

relational databases. The schema still consists of logical relations (although they're universally called "tables" in dimensional design), but the relations are divided into two quite distinct types: a single fact table, and multiple dimension tables.

Notice that, unlike the normalized version, Figure 6–2 contains all the relations in the schema. For readability, the dimension tables don't show all of their attributes, but all of the dimensions are shown. This structure is far simpler for an end user to understand than the equivalent normalized schema.

The single **fact table** models the data being used for reporting. It contains two distinct types of attributes: **key attributes**, all of which are foreign keys relating the fact table to the dimension tables, and **facts**, the attributes that contain the actual data being measured.

Notice that the fact table is placed in the center of the diagram with the dimension tables arranged around it. This is the conventional arrangement of these schemas. Someone, somewhere, decided this arrangement looks like a star and so these are called **star schemas**.

I confess that I do not see any great resemblance here, but perhaps I leave my poetry at home when I do database design (and perhaps I would be a better analyst if I didn't). In any event, these are called star schemas, whether or not the diagram is arranged in this fashion.

Are dimensional databases really relational?

Not always. There are three physical methods for storing dimensional databases: ROLAP, MOLAP and HOLAP. ROLAP stands for Relational OLAP. Dimensional databases that use the ROLAP model store their data in a relational database engine such as SQL Server, and thus qualify for the "relational database" label.

MOLAP stands for Multidimensional OLAP. These structures aren't relational. SQL Server Analysis Services, for example, uses a distinct physical storage structure for MOLAP databases. Finally HOLAP stands for Hybrid **OLAP**. These databases use a combination of relational and multidimensional storage.

In reality, not all normalized databases use a relational engine for physical storage, either. The vast majority of database schemas developed using the entity-relationship model will be implemented using a relational database engine, but not all of them. Increasingly, XML is used as the data storage mechanism for these databases. (XML is hierarchical, not relational.)

The entity-relationship model is still inherently relational. The dimensional model is also inherently relational, despite the fact that the physical implementation of dimensional databases may not be.

Remember when I said that it was important to keep the logical design and physical design separate? And you thought I was kidding...

The technical definition of a star schema is that it consists of a single fact table and multiple dimension tables, all of which are related directly to the fact table, and not, as a general rule, to other dimensions. However, there are some relatively rare situations in which it's appropriate to split the dimensions into multiple relations as shown in Figure 6–3.

This structure is known as a **snowflake schema.** The snowflake schema in effect normalizes the dimensions. As a general rule, normalization simply doesn't apply to dimensional databases, but there are a few exceptions that we'll discuss in Chapter 8.

Another way of conceiving the data stored in a dimensional database is as a **cube**, as shown in Figure 6–4. Indeed, many people refer to the dimensional database as "the cube." In fact, this is the term used by Microsoft in its documentation and products, and the one I will use to refer to the physical data store.

Technically, it's an "N-Cube" because it can have more than three dimensions, but the "N" is typically dropped. (You probably recall that the same is true of n-tuples, which are usually referred to simply as tuples.)

Using the term "cube" doesn't imply a different database schema—the schema is still defined by the rules we'll examine in the next few chapters—it merely reflects a different way of thinking about the data.

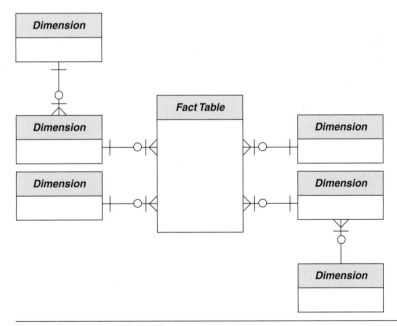

Figure 6–3 A Snowflake Schema

Figure 6–4 A Dimensional Cube

Terminology

A set of application architectures and analysis processes are clustered around the technique of dimensional design. Most of these are outside the scope of this book, but we will discuss them briefly in order to put dimensional analysis in context.

Unfortunately, the field is new and terminology hasn't yet settled—at one time or another most of the terms we'll discuss in this section have been used to describe the entire field. As always, I've picked a set of terms to use in the context of this book based on what seems sensible (to me) and in common use, but please be aware that other sources may not mean exactly the same thing—be sure to check.

For example, Microsoft uses the term "business intelligence" to describe the field in general, and "data warehousing" to describe—well, actually they use it to describe several things. Other authors use "data warehousing" as a generic term and "business intelligence" not at all. In the context of this book, I'll use **business intelligence** to refer to the field as a whole.

I'll use **data warehouse** to refer to the physical data structures, and **OLAP** to refer to the applications. I'll call the individual data cubes **data marts**. Using this definition, a data warehouse can be thought of as the set of individual data marts used by an organization. Be aware that other authors use these terms differently. Data warehouse is sometimes used to describe the source data for the data cubes.

In the literature, the term **data mining** is generally restricted to the application of specific statistical techniques to the transactional data in order to extract predictive rules. Data mining is a precise mathematical field. (SQL Server 2000 provides support for some specific techniques.) It does not by any means include all of the analytical tasks for which data warehouses are used. I'll use **business analysis** as the generic term. (I'm sorry if you were hoping for a more exotic term, but I've never seen any benefit in neologisms when there's already a perfectly good term available.)

YUKON NOTE: SQL Server Yukon adds some significant new data mining functionality to the product and a new interface for analysis services. You can expect the information in this chapter to still apply, but it will be extended in the new version.

In order to obtain a complete picture of the organization, it is usually necessary to extract data from multiple OLTP systems. Say, for example, that an organization uses two primary OLTP systems, one for manufacturing and the other for order processing. The most practical solution is to build two separate data cubes, one from each system.

A Potted History of Business Intelligence

All of these techniques and procedures, including dimensional design, grew out of a need. This is appropriate, of course, but surprisingly rare in our industry—more often, perceived need lags technical capability. At any rate, once the majority of operational systems had been computerized, people realized that the data stored in OLTP systems would be useful in the managerial decision-making process, but the data wasn't accessible.

Printed reports are the traditional method of providing information based on OLTP data. Unfortunately, it's difficult to predict the parameters of analysis reports in advance. Ad hoc reporting is problematic, the problem being that most reporting tools are not really intended for end users. I don't want to be in the room when you suggest that the Marketing Manager of a major corporation learn Crystal Reports or the Microsoft Access report writer, and as report writers go, these two are wonderfully intuitive.

Of course, there's always Microsoft Excel. I'd be prepared to bet that at least 90 percent of business analysis is done using Microsoft Excel, simply because it's the only game in town. It works, but not as effectively as one would hope. (I will admit to a certain prejudice here. Excel is a mathematical tool, not a data tool, and I rather resent the amount of my life I've had to spend explaining that to people.)

In the first place, we still have the problem of normalized schemas. If you restrict business analysts and managers to pre-defined queries, you may be restricting the analysis process unacceptably. But if you let these users have full access to the raw data, you risk kneecapping the system.

Remember that the OLTP systems in question are in use for transaction processing. That means that one analyst running a Cartesian product of three tables can bring the organization to a complete halt. Even in the best of circumstances, many of the questions analysts and managers want answered require large (slow) joins that place an unacceptable burden on the system.

It's obviously unacceptable to prevent users in the Southwest region from entering orders because the system is busy answering questions about orders in the Southwest region.

Data warehouses were designed to address these problems. In a data warehouse, data from multiple OLTP systems is extracted, "scrubbed," and made available to analysts and managers in an easily-understandable form. Dimensional design represents the current thinking regarding the best method for presenting that data.

Until the advent of SQL Server 2000, data warehouses were obscure, expensive, and usually restricted to large corporations. Dimensional analysis was not considered part of the mainstream of relational database design, despite the fact that the majority of data warehouses were implemented on relational databases.

But as has always been the case, now that business intelligence is available on the desktop, it is becoming integrated into mainstream application design. I urge you to consider it where appropriate—even small organizations can benefit from a better understanding of their operations.

And I promise that I am not employed by Microsoft's Marketing department. It's simply that I'm old enough to understand just how revolutionary this is…rather like replacing typewriters with word processors. (And I'm old enough to remember that, too!)

Summary

In this chapter, we took a high-level look at dimensional databases. We saw that, while the traditional normalized databases we examined in the last section are designed for handling frequent additions and updates to the data, dimensional databases are intended primarily for ad hoc querying by end users. The data, once uploaded to the dimensional database, is rarely updated. The star and snowflake schemas are the dimensional equivalent of the entity-relationship diagrams used to define normalized databases. Star schemas define relations in terms of fact and dimension tables. Fact tables consist of two types of attributes: key attributes, which are foreign to the dimension tables, and facts, the actual data being stored.

The relations defined by a star schema can also be conceived of as a cube (technically an "n-cube"). Data cubes and star schemas are largely interchangeable; they simply represent different ways of presenting the same concepts.

Dimensional design is the analytical component of a general field known as business intelligence (also called "data warehousing" by some authors). The applications built using these techniques are sometimes called OLAP ("on-line analytical processing") applications to distinguish them from the OLTP applications built using entity-relationship techniques.

OLAP applications often use data mining techniques for determining trends in the underlying data. Data mining, however, is only one component of the business analysis performed using these applications.

In Chapter 7, we'll begin a more detailed examination of dimensional databases with the definition of fact tables.

Fact Tables

In the last chapter, we looked at the big picture of dimensional design—what the bits are, and how they fit together, if you will. In this chapter, we'll begin examining the subject in detail with a closer look at fact tables. As you'll no doubt recall, fact tables are one of the two types of relations in the dimensional model (the other being dimension tables, which we'll examine in Chapter 8).

The Structure of a Fact Table

Figure 7–1 shows a fairly simple example of a fact table associated with a customer order. The basic structure is the same as a table developed using the relational model—the relation consists of a set. The attributes in a fact table can be divided into two types: **dimension keys**, which link the fact table to the dimension tables we'll discuss in the next chapter; and **facts**, which are the actual values to be measured.

Like dimensional sets, the set of attributes in a fact table can, in theory, be empty. In practice, however, it will almost always contain at least two attributes: either the combination of a dimension key and a fact, or, in some rare cases, two dimension keys.

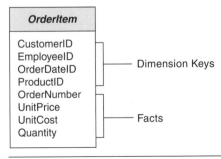

Figure 7–1 A Simple Fact Table

117

Dimension keys are essentially the same as foreign keys in the relational model in that they are used to relate the fact table to dimensional tables, but their primary purpose is somewhat different. As we saw in Part I, one of the primary goals of relational design is to eliminate redundant data and the update anomalies that it causes.

But this requirement simply doesn't apply to dimensional databases because they are rarely updated. Dimensional tables *do* reduce redundancy in the fact table, but that's a side effect; their primary purpose is to provide as many descriptive attributes as possible to the user, who will use them as selection criteria when analyzing the data.

This "irrelevant redundancy" principle applies to fact attributes as well. Note that the OrderNumber attribute is a fact, not a dimension key. In a normalized database, the attributes shown in this single fact table would be split into two separate tables, one representing the order itself, and a separate table representing each line item. In a typical implementation, there would be a single row in the order table for each order, and a row in the line item table for each product that was part of the order. The CustomerID, EmployeeID and OrderDate attributes would be part of the order table, and would thus only be recorded once for each order. In the example fact table, each of these will be repeated for each product ordered as part of the order. (Note, by the way, that the OrderDate of the normalized database has become a dimensional key in the fact table. We'll examine this issue in more detail in the next chapter.)

It is typical of fact tables to collapse normalized tables in this way, and doesn't represent a design flaw. Remember that the tables in a dimensional database are rarely updated, so the issue of changing a particular data item in multiple places simply doesn't apply. There is some storage overhead—in this example, the size of a date field times the average number of products per order—but that's far less important than the cost of doing an extra table join if the user wants to specify a date or date range as a reporting criterion.

The Characteristics of a Fact Attribute

In addition to dimension keys, fact tables contain fact attributes. (There is one exception to this rule; we'll examine it later in this chapter.) An ideal fact should have two characteristics: It should be both numeric and fully additive.

Remember that dimensional databases are used for analysis. As a result, users will rarely be examining rows in the fact table individually. If a fact is not numeric—if it is a date or a text field, for example—it becomes more difficult to combine records. Non-numeric attributes can be counted or listed, but they cannot be totaled or averaged.

For example, it's possible to determine the total number of blue size 13 widgets sold on the 1st of October by simply returning the SQL Sum of the Quantity fact. But if the value returned were CustomerName, you could only reasonably return a count: 325 customers placed orders on the 1st of October. In theory, you could return a list of all 325 of them, but since in a non-trivial application the number returned could just as easily be 325,000 or even 325,000,000, lists of facts are not likely to be useful.

Textual facts are an example of non-additive facts—the values cannot be added together. Obviously, non-numeric attributes are, by definition, also non-additive. This doesn't mean that they should never be included in fact tables, but it does mean that you should do so with caution. Before you add a non-additive attribute to a fact table, be very sure that you can't more effectively treat it as a dimension.

I've never run across a non-additive numeric fact, but I'm not pre-pared to say they don't exist. (I've been in this business too long to make that particular mistake!) It's not at all unusual, however, for numeric facts to be semi-additive. A **semi-additive** fact is additive across some, but not all, dimensions.

The classic example of a semi-additive fact is a daily account balance. It's perfectly legitimate to add the balances of every account on a specific day—the fact is additive across the Account dimension—but the end-of-month bal-ance of my savings account is not (unfortunately) the sum of the balances for the past month—the fact is non-additive across the dimension of time.

Semi-additive facts are less likely to be dimensions in disguise than non-additive facts, but they're not without problems. They don't impose any par-ticular constraints on the schema design of database implementation, but the front end should warn the user who tries to perform operations that require summarizing data across a semi-additive dimension.

One of the things we haven't yet discussed about dimensional databases is that, unlike normalized databases, their structures are always remarkably similar. The number of dimensions and the facts and attributes vary, of course, but the overall structure is always a single fact table surrounded by its dimensions.

This makes it possible to build generic front ends to dimensional data-bases. Of course, it's possible to build generic front ends to normalized data-bases as well; Microsoft Access is one. What I mean to say is that it's possible to build generic front ends to dimensional databases that are far less complicated for end users. The Analysis Manager that is part of SQL Server Analysis Services is a good example.

The problem here, of course, is that while it's possible for the front end to predict the general structure of the database in advance and to determine the specific schema at runtime, it isn't possible for the front end (or anyone or anything else, for that matter) to determine whether a numeric fact is semi- or fully additive by inspection. This information must be stored as meta-data. The growth of XML notwithstanding, meta-data formats remain largely proprietary.

What this means, ultimately, is that if you include semi-additive facts in a dimensional database, you should ideally use a customer front end that can read the meta-data and warn users if they attempt to summarize across a semi-additive dimension. You should also warn users that if they use a third-party front end (and there's no particular reason to prevent them from doing so) they're on their own in this regard.

Notice, by the way, that I said your front end should *warn* the user about summarizing data across a nonadditive dimension. I didn't say "prevent." If someone wants to divide the sum of the daily balances for the month of January 1953 by the inches of rain in Tashkent, Uzbekistan in March 2003, you can only assume the person has a perfectly rational reason for doing so.

The results might not make much sense, of course, and it's okay to point that out. It's not okay for the front end to prevent somebody doing it. After all, for many years the strongest indicator for the trend of the U.S. stock market was the length of women's skirts. No, that doesn't make sense. Yes, it was a fact. Might still be, for all I know.

Grain

The facts about an organization's operations can be measured at many levels of detail. At the lowest level of a sales organization, for example, is the individual line item on a sales order. At the highest level is the net operating profit of the organization as a whole. All of the facts in a fact table must be at the same level of detail, known as the fact table's **grain**.

As a general rule, you should build the fact table at the lowest level of detail for which data is available. For the majority of organizations, this will be at the level of an individual transaction: the line item of a sales order or an individual deposit into or withdrawal from an account—whatever is the smallest action for which information is available. The reason for this is probably obvious: You can always summarize data, but it's almost impossible to go the other direction and allocate already summarized data into more discrete units.

Retail operations are a good example of the problem. Until quite recently, most point-of-sale systems sent summary data to head office after the close of business each day: "We sold 16 green widgets, 36 blue widgets, 42 large gadgets, and 1 partridge in a pear tree." This is useful information, as far as it goes, but it doesn't really go far enough.

If the only sales information available is by-product-by-day, you can't perform what's generally called "market basket analysis"—answering questions like "how many of the people who bought milk also bought bread?", which is terribly important to marketing types.

Incidentally, the answer to that particular question is the reason your local grocery store places milk and bread as far apart as it's physically possible to get them. Since most people who buy one also buy the other, the store separates them so that you'll walk past as many other items as possible. The theory being that the more you see, the more likely you are to make an impulse purchase. (And honestly, grocery shopping was much more fun before I did those projects for one of Australia's largest grocery chains.)

But back to the subject. The principle is that the greater the detail, the more ways it can be analyzed, and thus the more useful it is. But that said, you can only capture detail that exists somewhere. In our example, the information required for market basket analysis simply isn't possible—unfortunate, but not negotiable. This may seem obvious to the point of banality, but if you do enough of this, I can almost guarantee that at some point some Marketing exec for whom it's *not* obvious is going to hold you personally responsible.

Grain can also become an issue when you're drawing facts from multiple systems, a common situation. Say, for example, that you're building a fact table at the grain of the individual order line item, and that the item selling price and order discount are available from the order entry system. So so good, but wouldn't it be useful to include the cost of each item, so that analysts can perform net profit calculations?

Great idea, but take my word for it: You will never be able to obtain a complete picture of costs at the item level. After all, a *complete* picture would have to include things like the CEO's expense account, and even if that information were available, it would be all but impossible to allocate it sensibly.

Given that a complete picture is impossible, you'll have to decide (in conjunction with your end users, of course) on a *reasonable* picture. Most sales organizations have some method of determining Cost of Goods Sold (COGS) for accounting purposes, and that's a good place to start. But you'll probably find that COGS is calculated at the order level, and it won't be acceptable to simply allocate the costs by dividing total COGS by the number of items.

Sometimes you get lucky, of course. I once worked with an organization that calculated COGS as 50 percent of the sale price. They weren't in business long, but it was pleasant relief to build simple (sloppy) systems for them.

You'll probably also find that the end users want to include (and allocate) costs beyond those included in COGS—shipping and advertising costs, for example. As an analyst, you must be very clear about your position: In order for a fact to be included in the dimensional database, the formula for allocating it at the necessary grain must be agreed upon by all interested parties. If it can't be agreed upon, it can't be included. End of discussion.

I recommend that you stay as far away as possible from the allocation discussions. I find it truly astonishing how emotional people get over these things. I was actually present at a meeting during which the VP of Sales threatened to throw the VP of Marketing out a 15th floor window over how to amortize the cost of an advertising campaign over time. (It was the only time in my career that a coffee break became a matter of self-defense.) Fortunately, the arguments don't often go to such ridiculous extremes, but do be prepared for the occasional, shall we say, "heated discussion"?

Once the users have agreed on an allocation formula (or thrown the fact out on the basis of intractability), it's important that the formula be fully documented, either in meta-data or (preferably) as an attribute of the relevant dimension.

This is particularly true if you're working with multiple data marts. Remember that I define a data mart as a single dimension database, and that it's common for multiple dimensional databases to be used together. For this to work, the same allocation formulas *must* be applied throughout, and that's only going to happen if they're documented within the data marts themselves.

Types of Fact Tables

So far we've concentrated on the most common type of fact table, one that models a transaction. Generically, we'll call this structure a **transaction table**. But there are a few other important types of which you should be aware.

Earlier I mentioned daily account balances as an example of semi-additive facts. Facts that represent balances are almost always part of the second important type of fact table: a **snapshot table**. Snapshot tables represent, as you might expect, periodic snapshots of the state of the organization.

This type of table is used whenever you are measuring a single value that varies over time. In addition to account balances, you would use a snapshot table to measure, for example, inventory levels, stock selling prices, student enrollments, even the temperature of a room.

Notice that some, but not all, of these facts are affected by transactions—inventory levels are, temperatures are not. When they are, it is customary for the data warehouse to include both a snapshot table and a transaction table.

You could, of course, calculate the balance based on a starting balance and recorded transactions; this is what accounting systems do. Maintaining balance snapshots uses storage, potentially quite a lot of it, but calculating can be a complicated and time-consuming process, requiring hundreds—potentially millions—of individual operations. Remember, storage is cheap; *time* is expensive.

A special type of transaction/snapshot pair is used to model accrual operations such as magazines, insurance, the operations of a cable television, or certain types of financial transactions such as loans. It is customary for these businesses to receive payment for their services in advance, but they don't actually accrue the revenue until the month the service (or product) is rendered.

So, for example, if I subscribe to a magazine, 12 issues for $24.00, the publishing company receives $24.00 of revenue when I subscribe, but can only book $2.00 of income as they send me each issue. Until that time, the subscription revenue is accounted as a liability, not an asset. (Isn't that fun? No, I don't think so either.)

In situations like this, you really don't want to try to perform income calculations at runtime. Even if you're working with a comparatively small number of rows in the dataset, the calculations require date arithmetic, which is notoriously slow and error-prone. And if you're working with an international company, things can get positively scary. If the client is in California, but the home office is in New South Wales, Australia, on the far side of the International Date Line, is the income accrued on the first of the month in California or in New South Wales (the previous day)? Better by far to let the Accounting department deal with this stuff. It is, after all, their job.

In addition to snapshot and transaction tables, there is one final type of fact table that you're likely to run across: the **coverage table**. Sometimes the mere existence of a row with a particular set of dimension identifiers tells you everything you need to know, or even everything you *can* know—there simply are no other facts.

Coverage tables, sometimes called "factless fact tables," are most often used to indicate that something occurred. The various dimension identifiers fully define the event, and the existence of the row is sufficient to indicate that the event occurred.

For example, the fact table shown in Figure 7–2 could be used to model class attendance.

Some analysts add an additional Boolean fact, always True, to the canonical structure, as shown in Figure 7–3. The theory here is that the fact makes the table easier for users to understand and manipulate.

Attendance

DateID
ClassID
TeacherID
StudentID

Figure 7–2 A Coverage Table that Models Class Attendance

Attendance

DateID
ClassID
TeacherID
StudentID
Present

Figure 7–3 A Coverage Table with an Artificial Boolean Fact

Personally I'm not a great fan of the practice. In the first place, a Boolean is neither numeric nor fully additive. In fact, it's not additive at all, which makes it a fairly ugly fact. In the second place, the existence of a True value implies that a value of False is possible, which is not the case. Remember that fact tables are always sparse. You should never add a row to indicate that something *didn't* happen. It's like trying to prove a negative proposition, and that way lies madness.

The judgment is, admittedly, subjective and somewhat aesthetic, however. Best practice is probably to check with your end users. After all, what's important is that the schema make sense to *them*, not to you. But I'll warn you, you may find it somewhat difficult to explain the issue.

Heterogeneous Facts

In Chapter 3, we talked about sub-classing entities in a normalized database as a method for modeling entities that must be handled both generically and as distinct types. The same issue arises in dimensional databases, of course, and the solution is similar, but not precisely the same. By convention, in dimensional database design these are referred to as **heterogeneous facts**.

Figure 7–4, adapted from our example in Chapter 3, shows the general approach in a normalized database. The Products entity contains all of the attributes common to every product, while the individual product type entities—Beverages, Condiments, and so forth—contain the attributes specific

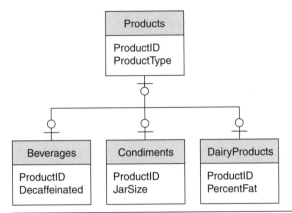

Figure 7–4 A Sub-Classed Entity from a Normalized Database

to that type. Including a ProductType attribute at the Product level makes it a fairly simple matter to treat any specific record, or group of records, as either a generic Product or an instance of a specific class.

The applications supported by normalized databases often treat entities at both levels simultaneously in this way. A product detail screen, for example, would need to display generic and category-specific fields for each record in the Products table. This requirement is rare in dimensional databases. In practice, users will be analyzing data *either* at the generic level or at the category level, but not both. To continue our product example, the analyst would want to be able to analyze sales of all products by product type, but that analysis would not require any product-specific details. Similarly, an analyst exploring sales of products in the Condiments category would be concentrating on that category and not require details about Beverages or DairyProducts.

Because of this different pattern of use, it's better to avoid table joins by creating separate fact tables for the generic type and for each category, as shown in Figure 7–5.

There are two things to notice here. First, the facts most likely to be used in analysis are repeated in both the generic and category-specific fact tables. Duplicating these facts requires some additional storage space, but it avoids the necessity of joining the tables, which generally results in a large improvement in performance.

The second thing to notice is that there are separate tables not just for facts, but also for the dimensions. This isn't strictly necessary. It is sometimes the case that there are no dimensional attributes specific to the category dimensions, and all the dimensional attributes can reasonably exist at the generic level. In this case, there is no value in duplicating the dimension.

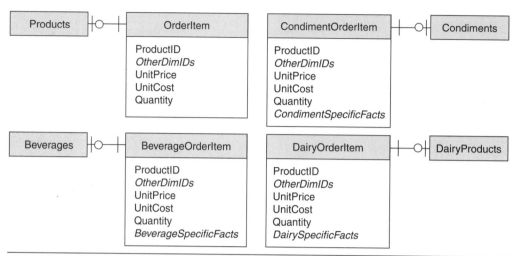

Figure 7–5 A Set of Fact Tables Representing a Heterogeneous Fact

More often, however, each category does have dimensional attributes that are not shared by the other categories. In this case, multiple tables are more efficient because they avoid wide, largely empty, dimensional records.

Whatever you do, avoid trying to define attributes at runtime, such that "If ProductType = 'Beverage', then Att1 = Decaffeinated; if ProductType = 'Condiment' then Att1 = JarSize" and so forth. I have occasionally seen this kind of indirect schema definition work in transactional systems—when the systems had been designed and were maintained by really smart people. More often, the systems collapse in a burning heap the minute the requirements change or the original designer leaves the project.

It's unlikely an indirect schema like this would last even that long in an analytical system. Remember that one of the primary goals of the star schema is that it be comprehensible to the end user. An indirect schema will never meet that goal.

Summary

In this chapter we've looked at the structure of fact tables in a dimensional database. We saw that a fact table consists of two distinct types of attributes: dimensional keys and facts. Dimensional keys are similar in structure and function to the foreign keys of the relational model in that they link rows in the fact table to rows in the dimensional tables.

The facts in a fact table represent the values to be measured for a specific combination of dimension values. The ideal fact has two characteristics: it is numeric and fully additive. Non-numeric facts are not necessarily incorrect, but when presented with one, you should double-check that it's not actually a dimension in disguise.

Non-numeric facts are, by definition, non-additive. They can be counted or listed, but not summarized in any other manner. Fully additive facts can be counted and listed, and also summarized over any dimension. Semi-additive facts are numeric, but can only be added across some, not all, dimensions.

The grain of a fact table is the level of detail at which facts are captured. You should always use the finest possible grain because the more detail, the more ways the data can be analyzed. You should, however, expect that not all of the source data will be available at the same grain and that determining the formula for allocating these high-level facts to the lower levels can be a contentious process.

There are three primary types of fact tables. The most common is the transaction table, which models individual transactions such as a line item on a sales order. Transaction tables are often combined with snapshot tables, which measure values at specific points in time. The final type of fact table is the coverage table, which may not have any fact attributes at all. Coverage tables most often record that an event occurred.

Finally, we examined handling heterogeneous facts. In a process similar to sub-classing entities in the relational model, heterogeneous facts are handled using multiple fact table/dimension table pairs, a single pair at the generic level and a pair for each category. Unlike sub-classing, however, heterogeneous facts duplicate the core facts in each category-specific table. This avoids the necessity for large-table joins.

Dimension Tables

In the last chapter, we examined fact tables, the relation that sits at the core of every star schema. In this chapter, we'll examine the other type of table found in dimensional databases, the dimension table from which, of course, the model takes its name.

In some respects, dimension tables are similar to the look-up tables common to normalized databases, but despite their surface resemblance, dimension tables serve an entirely different purpose. Look-up tables are intended to reduce duplicate data and ensure consistency. Dimension tables represent the characteristics that are being measured—it is at the conjunction of a set of dimension values that a measurement is taken. Although dimension tables can, as a side effect, reduce the size of the fact table and the amount of duplicate data it contains, their primary purpose is to facilitate analysis. They are the means by which analysts drill down through masses of data.

The Structure of a Dimension Table

A typical dimension table is much wider than a fact table or, indeed, a typical table in a normalized database. Whereas the majority of fact tables contain no more than three or four facts, and normalized databases with more than 20 or 30 attributes are automatically viewed with suspicion, dimension tables with 50 attributes are common, and 100 or more attributes are not unknown. In fact, this is the one situation in which it's reasonable to push the 255-field limit imposed by many relational engines.

Perhaps the best example of this is the time dimension that forms a part of almost every fact table, such as the date of a transaction or of a snapshot row. In the source (normalized) database, the date field will usually be a single SQL date. In a dimensional database, this single field will be replaced by a link to a dimension table with over a dozen attributes. Table 8–1 shows a typical example from a retail application.

Table 8–1 A Typical Time Dimension

Attribute	Example
TimeID	8302984
FullDate	14 June 2004
DayOfWeek	"Wednesday"
DayInMonth	23
DayInYear	173
CalendarYear	2004
Quarter	"Second"
FiscalYear	0304
FiscalPeriod	"2Q"
HolidayFlag	True
HolidayName	"Flag Day"
WeekdayFlag	True
WeekendFlag	False
BeginningOfMonth	False
MidMonth	True
LastDayInMonth	False
Season	"Spring"
EventFlag	False
EventName	""

There are several things to notice here. First, if you take a moment to review the attributes, you'll see that they attempt to provide direct support for every type of question an analyst might pose. Do we sell more potato chips on Mondays or Wednesdays? Do football games affect the sales of coffee? What are the products whose sales peak at the beginning and end of the month (standard pay dates)?

Second, the actual SQL date has been replaced by the surrogate key TimeID. This is probably less critical in time dimensions than in product lists, for example, but it is always good practice to replace whatever keys you extract from the source data with meaningless surrogate keys.

The primary reason for assigning surrogate keys is to insulate the dimensional database from changes to the key values in the source system. It really doesn't matter how vehemently the administrator of the source system insists that keys are not allowed to change. They will. Given enough time, the source system will change the method of establishing keys, perhaps because the transaction system is being replaced or because the organization has merged with another, or just because the administrator was bored. (Don't laugh. I've seen it happen.)

Or, worse, the source system will re-use old keys. This is a perfectly legitimate thing to do in a transactional system that typically isn't interested in the history of the organization. But re-using the keys would be devastating for a dimensional database that *does* track historical data. Does policy PL-3957 refer to the current homeowner's policy held by Peter Levinson, or to the Public Liability policy held by Acme Corp in 1957? The question would never arise in a transactional system, but it might in a dimensional database.

A secondary benefit of using a surrogate key defined by the dimensional database is that you can use a small, neat autonumber rather than whatever data type you receive from the source system. This isn't often an issue, but it can provide you with some extra ammunition if you're engaged in an argument with someone who doesn't understand how dimensional databases work. (This happens a lot.)

By the way, notice that the original SQL date is stored in the dimension table in the FullDate attribute. Obviously you should always keep the original value. You might also want to store the name of the transactional system that originally assigned the value as a primary key. This is useful if the systems change or if the keys are re-used. (We'll discuss the issue of changing dimensional values in detail later in this chapter.)

In examining Table 8–1, another thing to notice is that many of the attributes are (or at least could be) calculated based on one or more other attributes. Month, DayInWeek and DayInMonth, for example, are easily calculated from the full date. This would, of course, be a violation of normal form were this a normalized database. But it's not, so the rule doesn't apply.

Remember that the attributes of a dimension table are used to restrict queries. In practical terms, that often means that the available values will be displayed to users in a ComboBox. Now, if we take the Month attribute as an example, populating that ComboBox is the difference between

```
SELECT DISTINCT Month FROM Time;
```

with the "de-normalized" dimensional schema and

```
SELECT DISTINCT MonthName
FROM CalendarNames
INNER JOIN NormalizedDimension
ON CalendarNames.MonthNumber = Month(SQLDate);
```

in a normalized database schema. Even without doing formal performance testing, I'm prepared to bet that the first version of this statement is going to be a whole lot faster than the second. This performance benefit is even more evident when you're working with multiple dimensions, as you would be in a typical analysis. Remember: Storage space is cheap, time is expensive.

A similar principle explains the existence of the mutually exclusive WeekdayFlag and WeekendFlag attribute pair. Yes, selecting on

```
WeekdayFlag <> False
```

will return the same set of rows as

```
WeekendFlag = True
```

but the latter is easier for the user to understand and work with.

The next thing to notice about the attributes in Table 8–1 is that there are no abbreviations. I recently placed an Internet order and received an email confirming that I'd ordered 1 FB11 T WHi. Since the confirmation came almost immediately and I'd only ordered a single item, I was pretty sure that FB11 T WHi stood for a white, twin-size, feather bed. But ask me in a month and I won't have a clue.

The point here is not that this company sends slightly questionable confirming emails (although they do), or even that my day bed is more comfortable these days (although it is). The point is that FB11 T WHi is clearly the contents of the "description" field in the company's product master file (the product number is even worse: FB11-378095X). It probably makes perfect sense to the people who spend their working days ordering, boxing, and shipping feather beds, but as a product description in a dimensional database, it's hopeless.

To start with, you can't expect anyone who is more than a step or two away from the warehouse to remember that "WHi" stands for "White", particularly since it probably stands for "whip-stitched" somewhere else in the table. Whether it's "Wednesday" rather than "Weds", as in our table, or "White" rather than "WHi", spell the entire word out rather than asking the user to guess.

In addition to this problem, notice that there are several bits of information combined in "FB11 T WHi". It tells us that the product is a feather bed, that it's style 11 (presumably—it could be the 11th featherbed entered into the system; there's no way to know from inspection), that it's twin-sized, and that it's white. Now, there's nothing particularly wrong with embedding all this information into a single description field, provided it's also available in separate fields that can be used as selection criteria. Regardless of what the schema of the product master might be, the dimension needs to look something like Table 8–2.

Unfortunately, getting to this beautiful, neat, easily understood dimension from whatever the product master might look like, a process called **scrubbing**, is unlikely to be a simple process. It will almost certainly require human intervention, and can bring on as many political battles as the allocation of costs that we looked at in the last chapter.

The biggest problem you're likely to face is determining who "owns" the product master—or whatever dimension you're examining—in the first place. In the case of a product list, there are probably several groups who claim ownership: Manufacturing, Sales, Marketing, even Shipping and you'll either have to get them all on board with the scrubbing process or resort to a higher authority to resolve the politics.

Alternatively, you might be dealing with a Cinderella dimension that is doing everyone's work but is claimed by no one. It's not at all unusual for questions about a product master in particular to be met with a vague smile and a discussion of several systems that use product lists. This latter situation is actually a good thing for the dimensional database project. It means that the dimensional database can take ownership of the product master (or other dimension), scrub it once, and then keep other systems from mucking about with it. At least, that's the theory.

Table 8–2 A Product Dimension Derived from a Sample Product Description

Attribute	Example
ProductID	10293810
ProductMasterID	"FB11-378095X"
Category	"Bedding"
Product	"Featherbed"
StyleNumber	11
Size	"Twin"
Color	"White"
Description	"Twin White Style 11 Featherbed"

Snowflaking

There's one final thing to notice about the structure of the dimensions shown in Tables 8–1 and 8–2: They aren't normalized. The one-to-many relationships in the dimension are not extracted into separate tables as they would be in a normalized database.

For example, in the dimension represented by Table 8–2 and Figure 8–1, there are almost certainly multiple Products in the Category "Bedding"; there is a one-to-many relationship between these two attributes. There is another one-to-many between Product and Style, and two more between Style and Size and between Style and Color.

A normalized database would require that each of these one-to-many relationships be modeled as a separate table, as shown in Figure 8–2. This schema makes more efficient use of space, and reduces the likelihood of data entry errors.

But as I've said repeatedly, neither of those concerns applies to dimensional databases. (I do realize that I'm nagging, but the urge to normalize really is a difficult habit to break.) The goal of a dimensional database schema is to make it easy for the analyst to understand and browse. Normalizing a dimension, called **snowflaking** in dimensional design, fails to achieve either of these goals.

There is one situation in which snowflaking is appropriate: when there is a many-to-many relationship between the dimension and the fact table. This situation is fairly rare in dimensional databases. The majority of many-to-many relationships are between dimensions, and of course in that situation the fact table is the junction table that resolves them.

But many-to-many relationships between dimensions and facts do occasionally occur, and like any many-to-many relationship in a relational database, they must be resolved using a junction table. The classic example

Products
ProductID
ProductMasterID
Category
Product
StyleNumber
Size
Color
Description

Figure 8–1 A Product Dimension

Figure 8–2 A Normalized Version of the Product Dimension Shown in Figure 8–1

of this situation is between a fact table that models a visit to a doctor's office, and the dimension that models diagnoses. Obviously, a doctor might diagnose multiple problems in a single visit, so the many-to-many relationship between the dimension and the fact table must be modeled as shown in Figure 8–3.

This solution is very similar to the schema in a normalized database, but notice that the junction table contains an attribute called "Weight", which typically isn't present in a normalized database. The Weight attribute is a numeric value used to allocate the numeric facts when the Diagnoses dimension is used to restrict a query.

The sum of the Weight values for each visit must equal 100. So, for example, if Ms. Bloggs visited Dr. Jones because she has a head cold, but while she was there the doctor also adjusted her blood pressure medication, there would be two records added to the VisitDiagnoses table with, say, 80 percent of the weight given to the cold, and 20 percent to the hypertension.

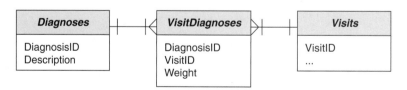

Figure 8–3 The Many-to-Many Relationship between the Diagnosis Dimension and a Visits Fact Table

If, then, an analyst asks for the total charges of all visits with a diagnosis of hypertension (e.g., the Diagnoses dimension is used to restrict the query), 20 percent of the cost of Ms. Bloggs' visit would be included in the result. If, on the other hand, the total charges of some group to which Ms. Bloggs belongs—females under 20, say—were requested, then 100 percent of the cost would be included.

Now the problem with this approach is probably clear: It's unlikely in the extreme that the required weight allocation is going to be available in the source system. If it isn't, you must either derive an artificial weighting (most often assigning each item an equal weight) or you must alter the source system. In our example, that would mean asking physicians to add the allocation to their charts. Yeah, right.

What might not be so obvious is that the many-to-many relationship between dimensions and fact tables can sometimes be eliminated by adjusting the grain of the fact table. In our example, if we changed the grain from office visit to diagnosis, the many-to-many relationship would go away.

Unfortunately, this doesn't eliminate the problem of allocation, it just moves it. Instead of assigning weights to dimension groups, you'd allocate costs to a fact table, with all the inherent problems we discussed in the last chapter.

It doesn't follow, however, that changing the fact table grain to eliminate a many-to-many relationship isn't worth considering. Occasionally thinking about the problem in a different way really can make it go away, or at least can be the prompt needed to solve the most intractable of allocation problems. Only occasionally, I'm afraid, but it's still worth a try.

When designing the schema of a traditional normalized database, the design process is most often a relatively simple matter of determining what the data means and then applying logically straight-forward rules to structure it. But the design of a dimensional database, despite its simple, predictable physical structure, is often a complex process of balancing fact table grain against the grain of the available data and the development of viable and politically acceptable allocation formulas. I'm tempted to say something about the equality of net complexity, but perhaps such discussions are a wee bit too metaphysical to be germane.

Changing Dimensions

So far in our discussion of dimension tables we've treated them as though they were largely static. We did discuss the use of surrogate keys to insulate the data from changes, but we haven't yet explored how to handle the changes when they occur. And they will occur, of course.

You have three basic choices when the values of attributes in a dimension row change:

- You can overwrite the old values with new ones (losing history),
- You can add a new row (maintaining all historical information, but complicating the design), or
- You can maintain both the original and the current values (losing interim values)

Overwriting the old values is the simplest technique for handling dimension changes. This is the technique most often used in transactional databases that typically only care about the current state of entities. But dimensional databases are interested in historical trends, and of course simply overwriting old values causes problems in that context.

Say, for example, that I am added to a Customer dimension in March 2000 as a female living in Amsterdam, The Netherlands (as I was at that time), and $1,175.32 worth of sales transactions are added to the fact table, assigned to my CustomerID. In April of 2002, my address changes to Santa Fe, New Mexico (as it did), and an additional $1,053.97 worth of sales are assigned to me.

Now, the order entry system doesn't care that I used to live in Amsterdam. It just wants to know where to send my bill. But if the values in the dimension database were overwritten, and an analyst in 2004 asked for the sum of the last five years' orders placed by residents of New Mexico, the system would erroneously include the $1,175.32 I spent while living in Amsterdam. Oops.

So the dimension database does care about historical values, and you can't blithely discard or overwrite them. The only time this technique is used is when the original values were in error—if I had never lived in Amsterdam in the first place. The problem, of course, is in knowing whether a change uploaded from the source system is an error correction or an actual change, since most transactional systems don't track this information.

I'm afraid that tackling this problem is, once again, a matter of policy. It might be possible to alter the source system, although this is, frankly, unlikely. Occasionally management is prepared to live with educated guesses—any change made within a certain time period, seven days for example, is considered a correction. After that, the system treats it as an actual change. Most often, the status of the change will have to be determined manually as part of the scrubbing process.

Assuming that you've determined that the change is, in fact, a change and not a correction, then you must choose one of the other two ways of handling it. Your choice will depend (as it so often does) on what the data means and how it is used. The choices, by the way, are not mutually exclusive. You may decide to create a new record when some fields change, but use an original/current pair for others in the same dimension.

Creating a new row when a change occurs is the most powerful solution, but it requires that the dimension identifier be expanded somewhat to include both a general identifier and a sequence number. So, for example, to maintain the fact that the Rebecca M. Riordan who currently lives in New Mexico is the same Rebecca M. Riordan who used to live in Amsterdam, the dimension would assign a general CustomerID of, for example, 35972, and a sequence number of 1 to the Amsterdam address and 2 to the New Mexico address. At any given time, my full dimensional identifier would be 35972-x, where x is the current sequence number.

In order to make it easier to pull out the most recent value, some analysts use an arbitrary number, typically 999, to indicate the current sequence. In this case, the system would have initially assigned 999 to the Amsterdam address, and then when I moved, assigned 1 to Amsterdam and 999 to New Mexico. Provided you can ensure that this policy is not overridden, this approach does, indeed, make "current value" analysis far simpler.

In addition to tracking changes, you sometimes need to know when a change occurs. There are two methods for doing this. You can store the effective date in the dimension table, which is useful for tracking the history of a particular dimensional entity or performing queries against the dimension table itself. Or you can store both the general identifier of the entity and the current sequence number in the fact table, which correctly and easily partitions the facts chronologically.

Most authors recommend the latter approach, but in reality they're not mutually exclusive, and I think it safest to combine them, storing an effective date in the dimension and the sequence number in the fact table. Remember, space is cheap...

The final approach to handling changing values is used when you don't need to track historical data so much as you need to track only the current and original (or previous) values simultaneously. This structure would, for example, make it easy to answer questions such as "How many of our New Mexico customers moved here from Amsterdam?" Now, this is a decidedly pathological example in a Sales environment, but it might make sense for a system that is interested in demographic trends—disease control systems, for example, ask questions like this.

In a sales environment, the technique is used for so-called "soft" changes, when the effective date is somewhat fuzzy and for some period of time it's legitimate and reasonable to pretend that the change hasn't occurred. The classic example of this is product formulations. Manufacturing may begin production of YaYa Gel using formula B on the first of July, but there will probably still be a supply of YaYa Gel made using formula A in the warehouse, in transit, and in stores. In most organizations, there will be an unpredictable period of time during which the YaYa Gel sold could be made by either formula.

The next time you're in the grocery store, check the number of products whose ingredient list contains the warning that it "may contain peanuts or peanut by-products." The formulation of these products changes slightly with each batch, vegetable oil or peanut oil being chosen based on commodity pricing. These are the types of situations in which you might use the Current/Original or Current/Previous attribute pair to track changes.

These situations are rare, however. In reality, you will more often be faced with "do I care or not" questions than "in what way do I care" decisions, and when you are faced with one of the latter, it's been my experience that the choice between the new row and current/previous pair techniques is, in practice, obvious.

Summary

In this chapter we've examined dimension tables. We examined their basic structure, and saw that best practice to add an artificial key to all dimensions in order to insulate the dimensional database from changes in the schema of the source data.

We also examined the snowflake dimensional schema, and saw that it is useful in precisely the same situations in which you might sub-class a relation in a normalized database.

Finally, we examined the issue of changing dimensions, and saw two techniques for handling them: either by adding a new row, or by using a pair of facts representing the current and previous value.

And this concludes our examination of dimensional database theory. Not nearly as difficult as you expected, was it? In Part III, we'll turn to the process of designing database systems.

Designing Database Systems

The Design Process

In Parts 1 and 2, we looked at the principles of relational and dimensional database design. But the structure of the data is only one component of a database system—a critical component, obviously, but still only a single component. Beginning with this part, we'll look at some of the remaining aspects of designing database systems.

In this part, we'll discuss most of the activities involved in the analysis and design of database systems, including the definition of system parameters and work processes, the conceptual database model, and the database schema. The design of the user interface, because it is such a complex topic, will be discussed in Part IV.

I'll be examining only the analysis and design of database systems here; implementation lies outside the scope of this book. But analysis and design can't exist in isolation from the rest of the process, so we'll begin with a brief discussion of project life cycles.

Life Cycle Models

Once upon a time, systems analysts used a paradigm for the development process known as the **waterfall model**. There are several versions of this model. A reasonably simple one is shown in Figure 9–1.

The process begins with systems analysis, sometimes called requirements analysis, since it focuses on what the organization and the users require the system to do. Once the systems analysis has been completed and approved, the entire system is designed in detail. This phase is followed by planning and budgeting, and then the entire system is built, tested, and released. At least it is in theory.

The waterfall model is aesthetically pleasing. Each activity is completed and approved before the next one is begun, and the model allows a fine degree of control over budgets, staffing, and time. Deliver a waterfall project on time and on budget, and your clients will probably love you.

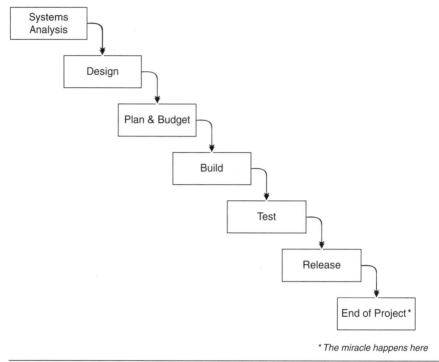

Figure 9–1 The Waterfall Model

The problem, of course, is that reality is hardly ever this neat. The model assumes that all the information required to complete a task is available during the performance of that task, and makes no allowance for new information coming to light later in the process. With the possible exception of very small systems (the sort of thing you can design and build for yourself over the course of a long weekend), this situation is unlikely in the extreme.

The waterfall model also doesn't allow for changes in business requirements during the course of the project. To assume that a system that met the business needs at the beginning of a project will still meet them at the end of a two- or three-year development process is foolhardy. Your clients will not love you for delivering a useless system, even if it *is* on time and on budget.

Understand, however, that the activities identified in the waterfall model are perfectly sound. In fact, omitting any of them from a development project is a recipe for disaster. The problem with the model is its linearity, its assumption that each phase need never be re-examined once it has been completed.

Several alternative life cycle models have been proposed to deal with the problems in the waterfall model. The **spiral model** assumes multiple iterations of the waterfall, each one expanding the scope of the previous iteration, as shown in Figure 9–2.

The problem with the spiral model is that, when strictly applied, the entire scope of the project is not considered until very late in the development project, and there is a (not insignificant) chance that later iterations will invalidate earlier work. This has always seemed to me a recipe for blown budgets and frustrated developers. The situation is particularly dangerous for database projects, where expansions in scope can change the semantics of the data, which requires a change to the database schema, and a change in the database schema can require unexpected—and unpredictable—changes throughout the system.

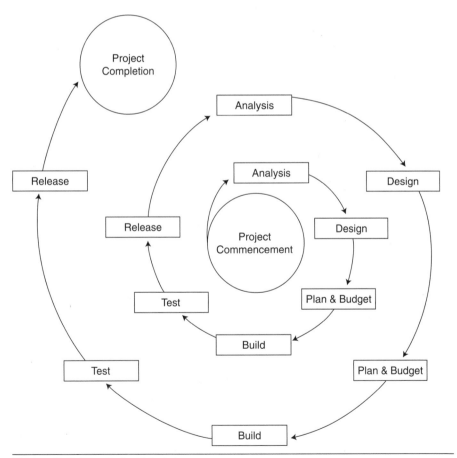

Figure 9–2 The Spiral Model

The model that I prefer for large systems, and use in my own work, is variously described as **incremental development** or **evolutionary development**, and is shown in Figure 9–3.

In this model, which is in many ways simply a variation on the spiral model, the preliminary analysis is performed for the entire system, not just a portion of it. This is followed by an architectural design, again of the whole system. The goal of the architectural design is to define individual components that can be implemented more or less independently, and to describe the interactions and interdependencies between these components. The detailed design and implementation of each component is then performed using whichever model seems most appropriate. I use the spiral model for this phase, as shown in Figure 9–3, because it allows greater flexibility in design and implementation.

Note that the spiral here includes an additional task: integration. Component integration is implicit in the spiral model as well, of course, but it's been my experience that the task is rather more complex using the incremental development approach. This is also one of the reasons I prefer to

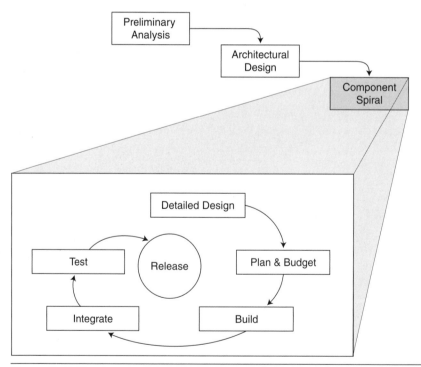

Figure 9–3 The Incremental Development Model

use the spiral model during component development. Deferring the detailed design of a component until just before it is to be developed allows you to accommodate any insights gained during the integration of previous components, and, with a bit of luck, avoid any of the problems you might have encountered during the integration.

The problem with the incremental development model is that it assumes that any large system can be decomposed into distinct components, and this is not necessarily the case for all systems. It can also result in a lot of "scaffolding" code. For example, say that a data entry screen is supposed to make a call to a COM component that will perform a lookup on a customer code and take some action if a match is found, but that the component hasn't yet been built. The development team will have to build a dummy component that allows the call to be made without error. Complex systems can include a substantial amount of scaffolding like this.

Additionally, there's always a chance that the external component will never be implemented; perhaps the budget doesn't stretch that far, or you later determine that it wasn't such a good idea after all. If you don't plan for this possibility, you could be distributing components whose only function is to keep *other* components from failing. Not an elegant situation, and certainly not one you'd like to explain to a maintenance programmer.

Because the analysis and architectural design are performed at the beginning of the project, there is the risk of them becoming obsolete, which as you will recall is one of the main disadvantages of the waterfall model. For this reason, it's important to review these two steps—particularly the requirements analysis, since it's more likely to change—before commencing the detailed design of each component. It's often a pleasant surprise how changes in requirements can be accommodated by changes to as-yet-undeveloped components, or even by changing the order in which new components are developed, without invalidating previous development work.

And despite the risks, the incremental development model does have several advantages. Because a "big picture" of the system is defined at the outset, the chances of wasted development work are minimized. Because large projects are decomposed into smaller components, the individual component projects become easier to manage. And, by breaking the system into individual components, you have a good chance of being able to deliver some core functionality to your users early in the project. This allows the system to start paying for itself and also provides a mechanism for soliciting user input to be fed into subsequent development efforts.

The Database Design Process

Whatever overall development model you choose, you must perform certain analysis and design activities. Whether you perform them sequentially or iteratively, whether the scope of your inquiry is the entire system or only a single component, whether your techniques are formal or informal, every project should include each of these steps at least once.

Defining the System Parameters

Ideally, every project should begin with a clear definition of what you're trying to achieve, why you're trying to achieve it, and how your success will be judged. Most projects won't have this definition prior to commencement, so this is what the first phase of the design process is about. The project's goal defines the "why" of the project. Based on this, you can define the "what," the project's scope. Once you understand the goal and scope, you can begin to determine realistic design criteria, the "how." Each of these is discussed in detail in Chapter 11.

Defining the Work Processes

Although ostensibly involved in the storage and retrieval of data, the majority of database systems support one or more work processes. Your users aren't just storing data for the sake of storing data; they want to *use* it in some way. Understanding the work processes the data needs to support is crucial to understanding the semantics of the data model. Work processes are discussed in Chapter 12.

Building the Conceptual Data Model

More than simply a set of table structures, the conceptual data model defines the data usage for the entire system. This includes not only the logical data model, but also a description of how the work processes interact with the data. The conceptual data model is discussed in Chapter 13.

Preparing the Database Schema

The database schema translates the conceptual data model into physical terms. It includes a description of the tables that will be implemented in the system and also the physical architecture of the data. Physical architectures and the database schema are discussed in detail in Chapter 14.

Designing the User Interface

No matter how impressive the technical performance of your system, if the user interface is clumsy, confusing, or patronizing, the project is unlikely to be successful. To most users, after all, the interface *is* the system. User interface design is discussed in Part IV.

A Note on Design Methodologies and Standards

I'm not a great fan of checklists and step-by-step procedures for the design of computer systems. It's been my experience that they can actually get in the way of good design, as the analyst can easily become more involved in ticking the boxes than in understanding the user's requirements.

In large systems, however, with multiple analysts and several teams of programmers, it's obviously necessary to establish some common procedures for managing the process. Several methodologies are around, and most have automated tools to support them. I'm not going to make any recommendations. In the first place, this tends to be a religious issue; in the second, as with variable naming, the *existence* of a methodology is usually more important than the methodology chosen.

I do understand, however, that preparing design documents can be daunting, at least the first few times you do it. Chapter 14 contains a general discussion of the process.

Defining the System Parameters

"A system is designed to do *something*, not *everything*."
— Robert Hall, Research Engineer, North American Aviation

The story goes that Bob Hall made this remark to a vice president who was trying to expand the scope of his project for the umpteenth time, and it almost cost Mr. Hall his job. (In system design, as in all else, it pays to know your audience.) Nevertheless, it remains one of the truest remarks I've ever heard about the system design process. If the project is going to be successful, you must be able to describe what you're trying to accomplish and draw reasonable boundaries around the project. If you can't say with reasonable certainty, "We're going to do this; we're *not* going to do that," I can promise you that what you *are* going to do is experience big trouble.

There are three steps to this process of definition:

1. Determining the goal, not just of the system, but of the project as a whole.
2. Establishing the system's design criteria, which will be used to judge any trade-offs during design and implementation, and also to evaluate the system's success or failure.
3. Defining the system scope—what you will and will not attempt to do.

Determining the System Goals

Defining (or discovering) the goal and scope of a system ought to be a simple process. Sometimes, if you're *really* lucky, it is. Sometimes a workable definition of the project's goal and scope are part of your initial brief. More often, defining them is a complicated process combining formal analysis techniques, design trade-offs, and more than a little diplomacy.

The goal of a development project is usually the most important factor in determining both the system's scope and the design criteria by which it will be evaluated. The goal is, after all, the reason the system is being implemented at all. Obviously, you won't be able to make informed decisions regarding any other aspect of the project until you have a clear understanding of what you're setting out to achieve.

Do not confuse "goal" and "brief." Most projects start with a description of the system to be developed and a budget. Your brief is to "automate the current order-taking system," and you have one year and half a million dollars to do it. But "automating the current order-taking system" is a brief, not a goal. The **goal** is the reason, or more likely the set of reasons, the project is being undertaken.

In fact, to talk about determining the system's "goal" at all is somewhat misleading. The vast majority of systems have many goals, both tangible and intangible, and discovering them might require some detective work. Why is the order-taking system being automated? Is it to speed up the process? Improve accuracy? Reduce costs? Position the company in the minds of the users? Make the manager look good? The system goals probably include all these reasons and half a dozen others.

Now, I'm not suggesting that you start invading people's privacy or requesting confidential company information, and some of these goals come under the general heading of "none of your business." You don't need to know that the department head is jumping on the Internet bandwagon out of fear. You do need to know that in order to pay for itself the system needs to reduce the average time to process an order from 10 minutes to 2 minutes.

You might also need to understand those vague phrases sales and marketing people use, like "product positioning" and "managing user expectations." Fortunately, this doesn't require going back to school; you can simply ask your client. Everybody means something a little different by these expressions, so you'll have to ask anyway.

The problem with intangible goals like these is that they're often difficult to translate into measurable design criteria. Sometimes a little judicious digging can turn an intangible goal into a tangible one. For example, the goal "assist in managing user expectations" usually indicates a customer service problem, which will either translate easily into measurable criteria— "we need to tell the customer how long it will take to fill the order"—or needs to be discarded.

If your client has a problem meeting delivery schedules *and* is reasonably confident that this is due to salespeople agreeing to impossible delivery dates in order to make a sale, then the order-taking system has a direct bearing on the goal of managing user expectations. You could, for example, impose a constraint on the minimum time between the date the order is taken and the date delivery is promised. If, however, the problems are due to quality control in the manufacturing process, an order-taking system can do nothing to help and it's incumbent on you to point this out to your client. That doesn't mean the project isn't worth undertaking; however, everyone involved needs to understand that the order-taking system can't *directly* impact the stated goal.

Not all intangible goals succumb so easily to translation, of course. "Positioning" is one of those. You might be asked to establish a Web site to "position the company on the cutting edge of technology." Most of these types of goals either don't actually mean anything or the fact of a system's existence will prove sufficient to meet them. It's easy enough to determine if this is the case; just ask the client how you'll know whether you've achieved the goal. Chances are good that if the other goals regarding performance and functionality are met, the intangible goal will be met as well. (Chances are also good that you'll get to watch a marketing person shuck and jive. I just love that, don't you?)

Another kind of statement that needs to be examined carefully is a goal that is stated in general terms like "improve" and "reduce." "Increase efficiency" and "improve productivity" are very common, and very vague, goals. How are you going to know if you've achieved them? A client of mine once shared a wonderful (and almost certainly apocryphal) story about the importance of measurability in job requirements. (Design criteria and job requirements are, after all, similar in purpose.) The story goes that, as a young salesman, he was told that part of his job was to "promote our goods and services." So he opened the office door and yelled, "Everybody should buy our stuff because it's really neat." This is not, I'm sure, what his manager had in mind.

During the initial analysis, unless you value your sense of humor over your bank balance, you'll have to determine the degree to which some general improvement is required. Increase efficiency *by how much*? Improve productivity *from what to what*? But there's another trap to look out for here. It's all very well to say that goals should be directly measurable, and "reduce the time required to process an invoice from 10 minutes to 2 minutes" is clearly preferable to "increase efficiency." But the first statement assumes that you know how long an invoice currently takes to process, and finding that out can be an expensive exercise.

The cost of research can often exceed the risk of making a mistake. In our invoicing example, it probably isn't necessary to send in a team of analysts with stopwatches to determine precisely how long it takes to process an invoice, although I've seen it done. Some years ago, I was involved in a project where a government department spent upwards of $50,000 determining whether it could justify the purchase of a single copy of off-the-shelf graphing software with a recommended retail price of $2,500. (And I confess, I pointed out the situation precisely once, and then I was snide all the way to the bank. I consider being paid to do something stupid by a government agency to be a unique form of tax refund.)

The solution to translating these general requirements into tangible design criteria lies in a sense of scale and the concept of "good enough." If you're betting the company or someone's career on the implementation of a new computer system, you'd better be very, very sure of what you're doing. If you're building a little system that's not going to have a major effect on the company's bottom line, you can afford to be more casual. To return to our example, it's probably "good enough" to know that the average person can currently process about 25 invoices a day. There's no need to perform a detailed study because the department manager can almost certainly tell you this; it's why you were called in. I'm sure that over-extensive research is how the Department of Defense winds up ordering $400 screwdrivers. (And before you start sending me hate mail, I had absolutely nothing to do with that one.)

Why a certain improvement needs to be made is always worth asking as well. There might be, for example, a processing backlog, and the manager is faced with either speeding up the process or hiring additional staff. If you know about the backlog and the projected increases in sales (as in our invoicing example), you can determine how much of an improvement is actually required.

The figure you arrive at might be different from the one your client initially gives you. Obviously, if your client wants to reduce the processing time by half, you should do everything you can to achieve that. But if you know the system actually only *needs* to achieve a 25-percent reduction, you have room to negotiate if you need to make trade-offs between the flat rate of processing and ease of use or system reliability.

You often overhear computer people remark that their lives would be easier if their clients knew what they wanted. Your clients *do* know what they want; they just don't know how to translate that need into a computer system. That's your job. Your clients are not going to knowingly make unreasonable demands, mislead you, or blame you for things that aren't your fault. But part of your job is to help your clients decide what the proposed database system can and cannot do to assist them. It's unreasonable to expect them to know the capabilities and limitations of the technology up front.

A variation on this theme is the client who presents you with a stack of screen layouts and sample reports that might or might not be possible to implement. This is a case of being told the solution rather than the problem. It takes a certain amount of tact to examine the reasoning behind the "system design" without implying that the individual who created it is stupid, incompetent, or simply in the wrong line of work.

All I can suggest for these situations is that you test the waters. If the client seems resistant to your questions, try saying something along the lines of "I'll be better able to help you if I understand your business environment." If this approach isn't getting you anywhere, you're going to have to either implement the system as presented or walk away from the project (which I realize is not always possible). The best you can hope for is to review the design with which you have been presented, and if you find any fundamental flaws, discuss them in terms of "I can't do this, but I could do that or that. Which would best meet your needs?"

The process of eliciting goals described earlier is not specific to database systems. The primary way in which database systems differ from other computer systems is that they have, almost as a by-product, a body of data about the organization. This body of data, whether it's a list of subscribers or a set of invoices, might have intrinsic value to the organization above and beyond the work processes that it directly supports.

Of course, I'm *not* suggesting that every project be looked at as an opportunity to create an enterprise-wide data repository. I'm suggesting that the data that forms a part of the system be examined for its value to other areas of the organization or other processes within the same area. It might be the case that the data your system will accumulate could be easily made available to some other area, although frankly, these opportunities occur far less often than some might think.

For example, if the invoicing system maintains a list of customers and the Sales department needs a mailing list for sending out newsletters, it might be appropriate to make the list available to them. If nothing else, sharing the list would save some poor clerical worker from the task of typing all those names and addresses again. But please note that "making the data available" is absolutely *not* the same as incorporating the mailing list functionality into the invoicing system—there be dragons.

The only reason I suggest considering the issue at all, given that it is fraught with the dangers of megalomania, is that it might be appropriate to make *minor* changes to the data structure to accommodate other uses. We'll look at this possibility in detail in Chapter 12, but let me give you a simple example here.

Remember that when I talked about atomic values I said that an address could be, within the semantics of a given system, simply a blob that gets printed on a mailing label. I recommended that in this case you consider treating the address as a single attribute. If, however, the data might be useful to another area, but only if the attributes are separated, then it is reasonable to add that small extra overhead to the current system in order to avoid duplicating the data entry elsewhere.

Be careful, however, that the extra overhead really is small and that sharing the data really is feasible. I have seen (and to my shame, even implemented) systems that require entire categories of information to be entered that have no direct bearing on the process at hand, simply because they might be useful to someone at some point in time. This is amazingly easy to do by accident, so be sure that when you talk about "planning for future growth" you don't actually mean "adding unnecessary overhead."

Once you've established your initial set of goals, you can move to the next activities in the analysis process: establishing design criteria and project scope. Do not make the mistake, however, of assuming that goals are stable. You must always be prepared to reevaluate the system goals during later stages of the project.

For any project that lasts more than a few weeks, the business requirements are subject to change. Sales can vary wildly from projections; company mergers can mean a surplus of staff rather than a shortage; any number of external events can require reevaluation of the project's goals. Check in with the client now and again during a long project to ensure that nothing has radically changed.

Even with projects of relatively short duration, you might discover during later stages of the project that some of the goals were either inappropriate or unattainable. One of the major problems with the classical waterfall model, you'll remember, is that it assumes that you can know everything you need to know when you need to know it. In reality, you'll be expanding your understanding of what the system needs to do throughout the project. New understanding will often require a reevaluation of the system goals, even if that means only reviewing them and saying, "Yep, these are all still valid."

Developing the Design Criteria

After you've gained a reasonable understanding of the tangible and intangible goals of the project, you can begin developing the design criteria. Of course, things are never quite that neatly sequential, and in practice you will have been accumulating criteria during the process of goal definition. But for the sake of discussion, let's assume that you've got a list of project goals and now you need to prepare a list of criteria by which the success or failure of the system will be judged.

Design criteria are closely related to project goals. If the project goals tell you where you're going, the design criteria tell whether you've arrived. All of the design criteria for a system should directly support one or more of the system's goals. If you find yourself with important criteria that don't seem to match up with a goal, it's almost certainly an indication that your list of goals is incomplete.

Matching up each criterion to the goal it supports is not strictly necessary, but it's a useful exercise, even for experienced analysts. One of the greatest dangers with any project is that you don't know what you don't know. This particularly the case if you're an outside consultant who might not have much (or any) experience with the activities of the organization. Mismatched goals and criteria are a good indication that you haven't yet understood everything you need to understand.

Design criteria generally take one of three forms:

- Directly measurable requirements, such as "Print an aging report in less than two hours."
- Environmental criteria, such as "Operate over the existing LAN."
- General design strategies, such as "Provide context-sensitive user assistance."

The specific categories aren't dreadfully important, but the ones I've listed are a useful indication of how well you understand the system. Most criteria should fall into the first or second category. If you only have a list of design strategies, I'd be willing to bet that you don't have a clear enough understanding of the problem you're setting out to solve.

NOTE: Whatever forms the criteria take, when you have met them, stop. Your project is finished. Go have a party. This injunction isn't quite as trivial as it might sound. Let me give you a common example. You're optimizing a particular piece of code. To meet the design criterion, the function must calculate a certain value in less than 10 seconds. You've got it down to 9, but you're *sure* that if you try this other approach you just thought of you'll cut that time in half. Don't. Or if you must, do it on your own time. You must not continue working after all the project criteria have been met, or the project will never be finished.

The only possible exception to this rule is with research and development (R&D) projects, but then R&D projects have different goals and hence different criteria. Rather than "complete the calculation in less than 10 seconds," the design criterion for an R&D project is more likely to be "determine the optimum method for calculating whatever." Since you can never be certain that any given solution is optimum, you can never meet the criterion; so you can explore forever or until you run out of money, whichever comes first.

It's important not to accidentally commit yourself to particular designs or architectures when you're developing design criteria. You might be certain that you're going to use Microsoft Transaction Server to support system scalability, but that's an architectural decision, not a design criterion. The design criterion is that the system must be scalable to support x users.

When in doubt, remember that a design criterion is used to determine whether a project has been successfully completed. In this case, ask yourself, "If we're using Microsoft Transaction Server, is our system finished?" Maybe, but the fact that you're using Microsoft Transaction Server isn't going to tell you that. However, the answer to "If we're scalable to x users, are we done?" is yes, provided, of course, that you've met the other design criteria as well.

Directly Measurable Criteria

I've already discussed the importance of identifying objectively measurable goals. If you've been successful in this, many of your design criteria will follow as a matter of course. If the goal is to reduce processing time by 50 percent and the current processing time is 10 minutes, then the design criteria is, obviously, "Enable processing to be completed in 5 minutes or less."

It can sometimes be difficult to distinguish measurable goals from directly measurable criteria. I don't know that the issue is terribly important. The specification police will not arrest you for listing something as both a goal and a criterion. They might give you a warning, however, if you fail to support a measurable goal with one or more design criteria.

Be careful not to micromanage your design criteria. It might be the case that for a specific process to be completed in 1 minute, a given query must execute in less than 10 seconds. But that's really an implementation issue, and you don't yet know enough about the project to make implementation decisions.

Environmental Criteria

The majority of environmental constraints represent the existing operating environment and any legacy systems with which you must interact. It's relatively rare to have a clean slate on which to specify a system. In most cases, your clients will have a hardware and software environment in which the new system will be expected to operate.

The other main source of environmental criteria is specific to database systems: the volume of data to be handled. One of my early disgraces as an independent consultant was preparing a quote for a sales-tracking system for a regional branch of a computer hardware wholesaler. After discussing their requirements, I presented them with a quote for a little system to be written in Microsoft Access 2.0, only to be told that they wanted to track sales for the entire company, with some 500 regional branches and tens of millions of dollars in sales—obviously far beyond the capabilities of Access. I had assumed they only needed to track that branch's sales. Oops. (Needless to say, I didn't get the job.)

In looking at data volume, you need to examine two issues. One is the sheer volume of data, and the other is its growth pattern. A library might have millions of volumes but add only a few records a day. An ordering system might add hundreds of records daily but archive the records after the sales are complete, so the absolute number of records is never more than a few thousand. Obviously, these two patterns require different design strategies.

Supporting data volume is one situation for which you're justified in over-designing the system. As a general rule, I'd say plan for at *least* 10 percent more capacity than the largest figure provided by your client, and round up. For smaller systems, I'd increase that to between 20 percent and 25 percent extra capacity.

Data volume is less an issue with larger volumes of data. A well-designed client/server system can support 100,000 records as easily as it can support 10,000. But a LAN-based Access system originally designed to support a few thousand records using Jet will probably not scale well to a few million, no matter how well it is designed.

The other primary source of environmental criteria is the number of users the system needs to support. Most systems have more than one category of user, and you'll need to define the requirements for each. For example, the order-processing system will have users entering orders, obviously. It will probably have a second group of users inquiring about the status of orders and perhaps updating the data, and a third group producing reports from the entire database. Each of these groups needs different support from the system, so each should be specified in separate design criteria.

You must also distinguish between users who are connected to the system and those who are actually using the system. The Jet database engine, for example, has a limit of 255 users connected to the database at any one time. This means that 255 people can have the database open simultaneously. It *doesn't* mean that 255 people can update the database simultaneously.

General Design Strategies

Some project goals don't translate easily to simple numeric measurements. A goal such as "improve data entry accuracy," for example, is extremely difficult to quantify, since this is a situation in which the cost of determining how many errors are made will probably exceed the benefit of having a number by which to measure your success.

You shouldn't ignore these kinds of goals; you can state them in terms of design strategies rather than measurable criteria. In this case, the design criterion might be "improve data entry accuracy by allowing users to select from lists wherever feasible" or "reduce the incidence of credit exceptions by implementing appropriate credit checks prior to accepting the invoice."

Just as with the measurable design criteria, you should not be too specific here and accidentally make implementation decisions. You're not designing the system; you're only establishing criteria by which its success will be judged. The previous examples talk about doing things "wherever feasible" and performing "appropriate checks"; the specifics are deferred to later stages in design when the system requirements are better understood.

But you should also avoid "motherhood" statements. "The system must be user friendly" sounds admirable—after all, nobody wants to work with a user-*antagonistic* system. But it's not a useful criterion. Determining whether a system conforms to the criterion "The system will comply with the *Windows Interface Guidelines for Software Design*" is possible. Whether a system is user friendly, however, is too often a matter of debate. You want your design criteria to reduce contention, not increase it.

Determining the System Scope

Once you know why you are implementing a system, you have a basis for deciding what functionality reasonably falls within the scope of the system (and what doesn't). As with design criteria, the functions within a system's scope should directly support a specified goal.

Say, for example, that improving the efficiency of the sales order process is a project goal. The printing of invoices directly supports that goal and clearly falls within the scope of the proposed system. The production of a product catalog, on the other hand, does not, and therefore lies outside the scope of the system. This remains the case even when the catalog is produced by the same people and shares a certain amount of data with the order-taking system.

Sometimes, when there's a lot of overlap in data or functionality between core and "extraneous" goals, it makes sense to redefine the goals of the system. In the preceding example, the system might become a "Sales Support" system rather than an "Order Taking" system, and "Produce Product Catalogs" would become one of the project's goals.

But this can also be a dangerous process. You don't want to be using the desired scope of the system to define the goals. That's very much a case of putting the cart before the horse. I know from experience how tempting it can be to expand a system's scope to include easy or interesting functions. I also know from experience how embarrassing it is when you don't have a good answer for a user who asks, "Why would I want to do that?"

Old versions of the Norton Utilities—an indispensable piece of software in the days of MS-DOS—provided a great example of this. The program used to report, on exit, how long it had been running. Having spent years considering the matter, the only explanation I've found for *why* it did this is "because they could."

Not good enough, I'm afraid. The rule is that if a function doesn't directly support a goal, then it's outside the scope of the system. Like most rules, this one can be broken, but you should do so only after careful consideration, if you're *sure* that there's a legitimate use for the function. Timing how long a piece of software is loaded may be cool, but it's hardly useful.

There are situations in which the function has clear value to the users and that value clearly outweighs the cost of implementation. The product catalog goal described previously might be a good example of this.

But even in fairly clear-cut situations like this, where you might expand the goals of the system, it's probably safer to include these extra functions under the general scope category "Added Value Functionality." This makes it clear that the functionality is not strictly necessary and it can easily be dropped from the system at a later date if you discover that its implementation is going to cost more than expected, or if you simply run out of time and money.

The second situation in which you might need to include functionality that doesn't directly support a system goal is when the client insists on including it. It might seem perfectly obvious to you that producing an employee phone list has nothing whatsoever to do with processing orders, but if the client wants it, they want it. You can point out that the functionality doesn't support any of the specified goals, but your job is to satisfy your client's requirements, not define them.

Cost-Benefit Analysis

As a final step in this phase of the design process, you might find it worthwhile to perform a cost-benefit analysis on the scoped functionality. This is particularly true if the proposed system has several components. The relative cost-benefit ratios of the various components will help you determine the order in which the components should be implemented. And if you're considering expanding the scope to include "Added Value" functionality, a cost-benefit analysis can serve as a reality check on the system.

All else being equal, components with the highest benefit per cost should be implemented first. This strategy provides the best "bang for the buck" and allows the system to start paying for itself as early as possible. This is particularly true for projects that will take considerable time to complete. If you can deliver the core functionality quickly, you have a sound basis for evaluating future development, and you reduce the risk of changes in the business environment making the system unusable later.

If the system can start paying for itself relatively early in the development process, you might also find it possible to fund some of those "fun and interesting but not strictly necessary" functions that you had to weed out while defining the system's scope. Of course, the reverse occasionally happens as well. Clients might find that the initial functionality adequately meets their goals and delay the development of future components indefinitely.

Performing a formal cost-benefit analysis is, of course, subject to the rule about the cost of making a mistake outweighing the cost of researching the answer. Cost-benefit analyses aren't difficult, but they can be time-consuming, and it's obviously not sensible to spend two days analyzing a system that will take one day to write. In many situations, an informal analysis (otherwise known as gut feel) is more than sufficient.

There are many ways of performing cost-benefit analyses, although the principle is simple. The estimated benefit of a function divided by the estimated cost of the function will give you a numeric value. The higher this value, the higher the relative value of the component when compared to other components.

NOTE: At this stage of the project, we're talking about *estimated* costs and *estimated* benefits. The only time you'll know for certain how much a function costs is after it's been implemented, and you won't know for certain how much benefit has been gained until after the system has been in use for some time. Post-mortem analyses are useful for improving future estimates, but they're a completely different activity.

Where cost-benefit analysis gets tricky is in determining common units of measurement. All costs must be measured in the same units, and all benefits must be measured in the same units, although the two units need not be the same. You can, for example, compare costs in time against value in dollars. The resulting ratio is used for comparison with other values calculated using the same units, so the result is perfectly valid.

Estimated cost can usually be measured in either hours or dollars, and it's normally straightforward to convert between these two in a business environment. Because both of these terms are somewhat loaded, however, it might be better to express costs in some derived value, like "units of work." This avoids the possibility of confusing a cost-benefit analysis with either a price quotation or an implementation schedule.

Assigning common units of measurement to benefits can be more problematic. You might estimate, for example, that automating a given work process will increase efficiency by 20 percent and reduce errors by 50 percent. The 20-percent improvement in efficiency can be translated into hours saved, and from there, if necessary, into dollars. But it might not be so easy to assign a value to the improved accuracy. It might be possible to estimate the cost (in either time or dollars) of finding and fixing mistakes, but that doesn't allow for other intangible, but very real, benefits, such as the good will gained by getting a customer's order correct.

In these situations, you can use multiple benefit estimates. For example, you might estimate benefits in terms of "Dollars Saved," "Dollars Earned," and "Intangible Benefits." You then calculate three ratios, one for each value. This can make comparison a little complex—you and your client might find it difficult to determine whether a function with the values 3/6/2 should have higher priority than one with values of 6/2/3. In this case, you can normalize the values in some way to derive a single cost-benefit estimate.

You might decide to add the values for each benefit category together if they're all of relatively equal importance. Admittedly, you're adding apples and oranges, but at this point it's acceptable to think of them simply as fruit. Sometimes an average value seems more appropriate.

If, as is most often the case, the categories are not of equal importance to the organization, you can assign a relative value to each category, and multiply each category by that importance factor. For example, given the benefit categories cited earlier, you might decide that "Dollars Saved" is not terribly important but "Intangible Benefits" is and that "Dollars Earned" is twice as important as "Intangible Benefits." So you would assign a modifier of 1 to "Dollars Saved," 2 to "Intangible Benefits," and 4 to "Dollars Earned." The resulting figures are shown in Table 10–1.

Table 10–1 A Sample Weighted Benefit Analysis

	Dollars Earned (mod: 4)	Dollars Saved (mod: 1)	Intangible Benefits (mod: 2)	Total	Weighted Total	Average	Weighted Average
Function 1	3	6	2	11	22	3.6	7.3
Function 2	6	2	3	11	32	3.6	10.6

It's often easier to assign benefit estimates in relative, rather than absolute, terms. For example, it's often difficult to assign Function X intangible benefits of 3. But it's usually possible to say that Function X is likely to have twice the intangible benefits of Function Y and that Function Y and Function Z are likely to have the same intangible benefits.

Cost-benefit analyses can be useful tools for capturing the proposed benefits of a system. They provide a simple way to compare the relative values of various components, which can be useful in scoping and scheduling projects. But they are only tools, based on best-guess estimates, and you must not mistake them for absolute values. Even though Function X has a benefit ratio of 12 and Function Y has a ratio of 2, it might still be appropriate (or technically necessary) to implement Function Y first.

The results of a cost-benefit analysis have to be reviewed in conjunction with other factors, such as system dependencies. They must also be reviewed as your understanding of the system improves. Re-evaluate your estimates prior to commencing work on each component. You might find that your experience with the actual costs and benefits of the previous components will alter your estimates for future components.

Summary

In this chapter, we've looked at the activities involved in gaining an understanding of a system at the beginning of a project. You must first determine the system's goals and then translate those goals into tangible design criteria that can be used to determine the success or failure of the project. You must also determine the system's scope—the boundaries of what will and will not be undertaken as part of the project.

These activities are a kind of step zero; they're the things you must do *before* you begin designing the system in earnest. In the next chapter, we'll examine the first step of the design process proper: the definition of the work processes the system will support.

Defining the Work Processes

Although many database systems are designed simply to store and retrieve some set of data, the majority are intended to assist in performing one or more activities. These activities are the **work processes** that the system will support. A work process is simply a set of one or more discrete tasks that together represent some activity meaningful to the organization. "Process an order" and "Find a customer's phone number" are both examples of work processes, although they are of very different complexity.

A **task** is a discrete action, a step in the performance of a work process. The sales order process, for example, might consist of the tasks "Record sales order," "Check customer credit," "Check stock availability," and "Ship order." The process of finding a customer's phone number, however, probably consists of only the single task "Find customer record," or, if you prefer more explicit detail, "Find customer record" and "Display customer record."

Distinguishing between a task and a process can sometimes be difficult; the distinction is fairly arbitrary. It's rather like determining what represents a scalar value in a data model—a single attribute in one model might be decomposed into multiple attributes in another. An activity that is treated as a task in one system might be treated as a process in another and then decomposed into separate tasks at a lower level of detail. As it is with the data modeling process, the decision must be based on the semantics of the problem space.

Some systems don't lend themselves to work process analysis. Ad hoc reporting tools, for example, don't support a specific process as much as they support certain *kinds* of activities. In these instances, it's more appropriate to build user scenarios. These are discussed at the end of this chapter.

Determining Current Work Processes

Defining the system scope is actually the first step in analyzing business processes, since the definition will tell you the processes you need to analyze. The order in which you examine the various processes within the system's scope is usually unimportant. Even if you're planning on implementing some system components prior to others (incremental development), you should perform at least a cursory analysis of all the work processes the system is going to support before you begin implementation. Doing this allows you to find any dependencies between processes that might affect the order in which components must be implemented.

Speaking to Users

Having identified the work processes that are within the scope of the system, your next task is to capture everything that is currently done in order to carry them out. You needn't worry overmuch at this point about what represents a task and what is, perhaps, a separate work process that requires further analysis. Just find someone who can tell you, "Well, we get this document from the salesperson, and first we just look through it to see if they've completed it correctly; if they have, well, then we pull the customer file, and…." Ask lots of questions, and write it all down. You should also get copies of any forms or reports that are either used as input during the process or produced during it. Your goal is to understand what happens; you're not yet analyzing the process.

By the way, many people refer to this phase of the analysis as "user interviews." I prefer "process analysis" or some other neutral term. It's easy to underestimate how intimidating computers can be, even to people who currently use them. Lots of people still worry that they're going to be replaced by a computer, and "user interview" can easily be mistaken to mean, "We're going to decide who gets the sack." This is particularly true in large organizations in which it's not usually possible to speak to everyone, and many people might be unsure exactly who you are or what you're supposed to be doing.

Whenever possible (and it isn't always), you should try to speak to the individuals who actually perform the process rather than to a manager or supervisor. My experience has been that managers tend to have a rather ideal view of the work processes under their jurisdiction. The people who perform an activity on a daily basis are in the best position to tell you the problems and interruptions they face. Of course, you should speak to supervisors as well, since they often have the best understanding of *why* specific tasks are performed and the ramifications of not performing them or performing them incorrectly.

During your discussions, be sure to look for any possible exceptions to the process. If the user says, "We check the order for completeness," for example, be sure that you know what happens if it *isn't* complete. Chances are that they just bounce it, but you need to know whether they try to find the information themselves; perhaps your system can make the process easier. In fact, for every activity that a user performs, you should ask what can go wrong and what happens when it does.

Since we're specifically interested in database systems here, you should also pay particular attention to how data is getting used during the process. What bits of information are being used? Where do they come from? What form do they take? What happens if they're not present or not in the correct form? The answers will form raw material for the conceptual data model we'll discuss in the next chapter.

Many work processes consist of tasks that are performed by different individuals. Obviously, you should speak to all the people involved whenever that's possible. This recommendation also applies to people whose tasks are ostensibly outside the scope of the system. Take, for example, the sales order process described earlier. The "Ship order" task might in fact be "Send order to the Shipping department," and what happens to it in the Shipping department might be outside the scope of your system. It's still a good idea to talk to people from Shipping to confirm that they're getting all the information they need and getting it in a form that's useful to them.

Similarly, if a report gets printed at any point in the process, you should find the person who receives the report and learn what he or she does with it. You'll be amazed at how many pieces of paper get passed around an organization for no apparent reason. (Then again, maybe you won't.) Or, as is more often the case, there *is* a reason for the report but it contains the wrong information, or it contains the right information but in the wrong format, so it's being neatly filed somewhere and is not being put to the use for which it was designed.

Identifying Tasks

After you've talked to the people who are currently performing the work your system is going to support, you should have a reasonable understanding of the activities involved. Your next step is to organize this information into a set of tasks. The key is identifying the business rules that apply to the process.

At the beginning of the chapter, I defined the term "task" as a discrete action. It's now possible to define more precisely what "discrete" means in this context. It means two things: that the action has an identifiable beginning and ending, and that all the pertinent business rules are valid before the task has begun and after it is completed. The rules might be temporarily broken, however, during the execution of the task.

A **business rule** is nothing more than a constraint that originates in the problem domain, as opposed to constraints that derive from, for example, a data type. Thus "No orders can have a ship date of April 36" is not a business rule, since it's dependent on the domain of dates. (And it's a pretty silly rule, anyway.) But "No orders can have a ship date prior to the order date" is dependent on the problem domain; it is a function of the way the organization does business. Thus it is, or at least could be, a valid business rule. The term "business rule" is used, by the way, even when the organization isn't technically a business. The database you're building to track your collection of antique thimbles is still subject to business rules.

The vast majority of business rules relate to the way data is handled. "Customer zip code cannot be empty" and "Invoice date must be on or after ship date" are examples of data-related business rules. Other rules, such as "Sales manager authorization is required when orders will cause customers to exceed their credit limit," do not directly constrain a data value, although they might be triggered by a data value, as this one is.

Don't worry; finding the business rules that pertain to a work process isn't as difficult as it might sound. This is what all those "How can this go wrong and what do you do if it does?" questions were about. You don't need to worry too much at this point about what the details of the rules are. The details are part of building the conceptual data model, which you'll do later. All you need to do here is group the various activities you've identified in such a way that you're reasonably confident the business rules will be valid on either side of the action.

Let's look at an example. Say your list of actions for processing a sales order includes the following tasks:

1. Check sales order for completeness.
2. Retrieve customer file if existing customer.
3. Record shipping information.
4. Enter order details.
5. Assign customer number for new customer.
6. Check item availability.
7. Check customer credit limit.
8. Pick order.

9. Pack items.
10. Prepare shipping documents.

The first thing to notice about the list is that things seem to be done in a somewhat random order. That's OK. You're only trying to understand how things are currently done. Cleaning up the process happens later. Some of the items also seem to contain a different level of detail. We'll look at that in a minute. For now, let's just identify the tasks.

Item 1, "Check sales order for completeness," has a discrete beginning and ending. The action takes place when a new order is received, and it is completed when the entire document has been checked. We can assume that all the business rules are valid at the beginning of a process, so there's no problem there. If the initial sales order document doesn't comply with the business rules, it will be rejected. So we know that if the process continues to the next step, the rules will be valid. So item 1 qualifies as a task.

The only business rule that pertains to item 2, "Retrieve customer file," is that the individual retrieving the file must have access to it. We'll assume that anyone performing this process has access to the files, so that task criterion doesn't apply. The action begins when the sales order has been checked, but since the file is used during later actions, it doesn't have a discrete end point. So it's not a task; it's one of the steps within a task.

In fact, the customer file is used in item 3 ("Record shipping information") and item 5 ("Assign customer number"), which is the first clue that these items belong to the same task. Indeed, it's clear that items 2 through 5 can be grouped together into a single task, called perhaps "Record order." In this case, item 4, "Enter order details," is clearly a part of recording the order. Don't be surprised, however, to find that some tasks are performed simultaneously. In a manual system, it's easy for someone to be filling out two forms at the same time. The fact that the forms logically belong to separate tasks doesn't matter.

We now have a new task consisting of four discrete steps. It begins when the original document has been checked for completeness, and it ends when the entire order has been recorded. But there's a problem. Your client doesn't allow customers to place orders that exceed their credit limit, but the credit limit isn't checked until item 7, "Check customer credit limit," *after* the user has checked that the ordered items are available. Until the order is confirmed to be within the customer's credit limit, however, you can't be certain that the business rules are valid on either side of the task. So item 7 is part of the "Record order" task.

Item 6, "Check item availability," isn't logically part of recording the order, however. In fact, item 6 represents a discrete task that begins once the "Record order" task has been completed and ends upon confirmation that there is sufficient stock to ship. So item 6 is a task on its own. Don't say I didn't warn you.

In situations like this, be sure to find out *why* the tasks appear to be done out of order. It's most often simply a matter of convenience, but occasionally these inconsistencies result from some operational constraints that can have an impact on your system processes.

In this instance, if the item availability is checked first simply because that's logistically an easier check to make, you can rearrange the activities. But you might discover some interaction between the order entry process and the production process that requires stock levels to be checked immediately, and this interaction would have to be accommodated in your system.

If we were to discover later that an order shouldn't be accepted unless there is sufficient stock to fill it, the "Check item availability" task would become a step in the "Record order" task. As we'll see in the next section, moving activities around between tasks and between logical levels is a fairly simple process. The crucial issue here is to identify the activities.

Analyzing the next three items on the list—8, 9, and 10—depends on the scope of the system. If shipping of products is part of the system to be developed, these items need to be looked at carefully. If, as is more likely the case, the scope of the system ends when the completed order is passed to the Shipping department, these items can simply be lumped under a single task, "Submit order."

We happen to know, of course, that several things will occur after this point, and there's no reason to throw that information away. From inspection, it's clear that all of these remaining items are tasks. In fact, the final item on the list, "Prepare shipping documents," might even be an entire work process. But all of those tasks lie outside the scope of the project, so we'll list them as steps to preserve what we know but we won't otherwise concern ourselves with them. Our revised task list is shown here:

> Task 1: Check sales order for completeness
> > Exception: Reject order if incomplete
> Task 2: Record order
> > Step 1: Retrieve customer file
> > > Exception: Hold order if file unavailable
> > Step 2: Record shipping information
> > Step 3: Enter order details
> > Step 4: Assign customer number
> > Step 5: Check customer credit limit
> > > Exception: Refer to sales manager

Task 3: Check item availability
   Exception: Refer to sales manager
Task 4: Submit order to Shipping department
   Step 1: Pick order
   Step 2: Pack items
   Step 3: Prepare shipping documents

During the process of organizing activities into tasks and processes, you will almost certainly discover things that you don't understand as well as you thought, in which case you should go back to the users for clarification. In any case, you should review the processes with the users. Often, seeing the process written down will prompt them to provide additional information—steps they've missed or exceptions that you forgot to ask about.

Analyzing Work Processes

Now that you have a clear idea of how things are currently done, it's appropriate to examine the work processes for possible improvements. As I said earlier, most organizations have a great deal of inertia. This applies equally well to processes as to working with documents. The deployment of a new computer system provides an excellent opportunity to clean up some of the dead wood.

There's an old efficiency rule that says you should never handle a piece of paper more than once. Like many rules, this one isn't always practical, but it's not unusual to discover that a work process can be simplified by reordering the tasks so that bits of work aren't traded back and forth between individuals or processes. For some reason, this sort of "I do A and give it to you, then you do B and give it back to me, then I do C" process is difficult to see when you're involved in the actual work but is immediately apparent when the activities are written down.

To do this kind of analysis, you must be very clear about the task dependencies. Within any given process, some tasks are dependent on others and must be completed in a specific order. You couldn't, for example, transmit the order to Shipping before you record it. The order of other tasks can be reasonably independent. It doesn't matter greatly, for example, if you assign the customer number before or after recording the shipping details.

It's particularly important to look at data dependencies. Some tasks are responsible for creating information, such as customer numbers, that is used by other tasks. One client of mine, for example, used a sales order process similar to the one outlined in the previous section, except that the Accounting department established the customer number and initial credit limit rather than the Sales department, which was responsible for order processing.

The client's initial work process looked like this:

Task 1: Check sales order for completeness
Task 2: Record order
      Step 1: Retrieve customer file
      Step 2: Record shipping information
      Step 3: Enter order details
Task 3: Perform customer credit check
      Step 1: Check customer references
      Step 2: Check customer credit limit
      Step 3: Assign customer number
Task 4: Complete order
      Step 1: Check item availability
      Step 2: Submit order to Shipping department

Task 3 was performed by the Accounting department, which returned the order to the Sales department only if the results of the credit check were acceptable. The problem with this, of course, was that the initial data entry had already been performed. Not only did this mean the work was wasted if the customer wasn't approved, it also meant extra work, since the dead orders had to be periodically removed. It also involved the data entry personnel in arguments between the Accounting department and the salespeople, who wanted their orders filled (and their commissions paid). Changing the order of the tasks so that the credit check was performed *before* the order was given to the data entry people eliminated the inefficiency and hassle.

In addition to confirming the dependencies between tasks, you should check for tasks that no longer need to be performed. These are rarely obvious, but sometimes if you trace the data through the process you find items that are being created for use in another task or process that no longer needs them. It is less likely that whole tasks, or even steps within tasks, are unnecessary. Most people are pretty smart about avoiding busy work, but the situation can be masked by the interaction between processes. The production of unnecessary reports is the most common example of this.

This is not, of course, a justification for making wholesale changes to your client's business practices. Nor would I recommend telling your great aunt Gertrude that she should change the way she organizes the knitting patterns she's asked you to computerize. And, in fact, it is rare to find major inefficiencies in work processes. But your job is to help your clients do their job better where you can, and reviewing the work processes is a part of that.

Documenting Work Processes

As with all other areas of the design process, the amount of time you spend analyzing the work processes and the formality of your documentation should be in proportion to the complexity of the system. A simple system for tracking names and phone numbers might require nothing more than an hour's conversation and some quick notes for your own use.

Unless you're the client as well as the designer, however, I'd recommend at least two meetings for even the simplest projects. The purpose of the second meeting is to review your understanding of the client's needs and confirm that what you've understood and plan to do is, in fact, correct.

More complex projects might require weeks of discussion with dozens of people and correspondingly complex and formal documentation. A structured list of tasks and steps like those used in this chapter might still be sufficient to document simple processes. For more complex processes, I prefer to use a picture.

Although the Entity Relationship (E/R) diagrams used to document data relationships are reasonably standardized across the industry, there is less consistency in work process diagrams. The diagramming methodologies in use tend to be closely related to specific analysis techniques and subject to fashions.

If you know one of these methodologies and are comfortable with it, there's no reason to change. The purpose here is to understand and convey information. UML, data flow diagrams and process quality diagrams are all useful tools. Specific diagramming techniques have always seemed to me a rather silly thing to get religious about, although people certainly do often enough.

In the absence of a formal technique, you can easily derive your own. You need five symbols, representing the task, the document, the data item, the decision point, and events such as the start point and end point of a task. The symbols I use in my own work are shown in Figure 11–1.

If there are relatively few steps required to complete a task, I list them within the Task box. If there are too many steps for this to be convenient, I expand each task as a separate diagram and use the Task box to represent each step. Sometimes, for clarity, I will use shading or a bold outline to indicate that a task is done by an external group, such as when the Accounting department performs the credit check for new customers.

The data item symbol can represent either a single attribute, such as a customer number, or an entire entity, such as the customer as a whole. When the item is actually created by the task, you can use either shading or

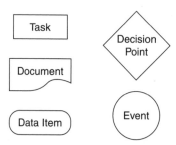

Figure 11–1 The Work Process Symbols

a bold outline to indicate this. Some analysts also like to indicate when a data item is "consumed" by a task; that is, when the item is used by the task but never shared with any other tasks later in the process. Frankly, I have rarely found this to be useful information and prefer to keep my diagrams uncluttered.

Having determined the symbols you will use (and I strongly suggest you choose symbols that are easy to draw freehand rather than those that have any intrinsic meaning), you then need a way of organizing them. I use an arrow to indicate dependency and a branching line to indicate that tasks can be performed in any order. An open circle on a line indicates that the task is optional, just as it does in an E/R diagram. These connections are shown in Figure 11–2.

If you find that your work processes are too complex to capture using this simple technique, I suggest you look into one of the more developed methodologies described in any good textbook on systems design and analysis. Several are listed in the Bibliography.

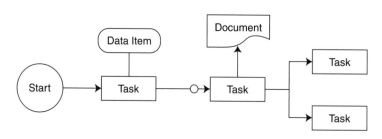

Figure 11–2 The Work Process Connections

User Scenarios

An alternative to formal work process analysis is the identification of **user scenarios**. A user scenario consists of two components: a set of one or more **user profiles**, which identify the various types of users of the proposed system, and **usage scenarios** for each user profile, which are narrative descriptions of the way the user is expected to interact with the proposed system—the activities he or she is expected to perform.

Although user scenarios can be used to capture the same information as a work process analysis, user scenarios tend to focus more on the ways users interact with the proposed system rather than on the specific steps of a transaction. Because of this focus on user interaction, it can sometimes be difficult to prepare a user scenario that doesn't anticipate the user interface of the system.

The intention, however, is to focus on users' goals and expectations, and as such, the user scenario is particularly useful for systems that must support a variety of ad hoc activities. It allows the analyst to focus on the *kinds* of tasks users need to perform without getting bogged down in the mechanics of processes that have not yet been defined.

For example, even the rather simple scenario "Sales representatives will use the system to track the status of their customers' orders through each of the phases of the process, from initial entry through shipping, invoicing, and eventual payment" adequately explains how this user group will interact with the system. But it does so without forcing any decisions to be made regarding the detailed functionality of the user interface.

The development of user scenarios and work process analyses are not, of course, mutually exclusive. Work process analyses are a useful tool for thinking about the processes themselves, while user scenarios allow the designer to focus on how each type of user will interact with the system. For most systems, these are equally important issues. When the project is large enough to warrant the effort, it is certainly worthwhile to perform both types of analysis, particularly since user scenarios can generally be based on the information gained during the work process analysis without additional interviewing or analysis.

Summary

In this chapter, we've looked at how to gain an understanding of the activities a proposed system is intended to support. This can be done by performing work process analysis of various degrees of formality, by the creation of user scenarios, or by a combination of techniques. In Chapter 12, we'll look at the design of the conceptual data model: the logical description of how data will be created, structured, and used by the system.

The Conceptual Data Model

At this point in the design process, you should have a clear understanding of what you're setting out to achieve. You've defined the scope of the project, compiled a set of design criteria, and analyzed the work processes. Now it's time to start building the data model.

Remember that a conceptual data model contains a description of the entities, their attributes, and the relationships between them. It isn't a database schema, which describes the physical layout of the tables. You don't yet know enough to create this. You need to understand the user interface and the architecture that you'll use to implement the system before you can create the schema.

Identifying the Data Objects

In the earlier phases of the analysis, you will have gathered or created a set of source documents. These include both the documents provided by the client—sample input forms, reports, and so forth—and the work process documentation you prepared. The first step in creating the data model is to review these sources and make a list of all the bits of data the system needs to deal with.

Start with a work process. It doesn't really matter which one, but I usually choose one of the central ones for the project, since the core processes usually involve the majority of the entities. Most work processes are triggered by some piece of paper, like when a salesperson hands the order entry clerk a sales order. Sometimes they're triggered by some other kind of an event, in which case one of the first tasks is usually filling out a form. Continuing our order-processing example from Chapter 11, a sample Sales Order form might look like the one shown in Figure 12–1.

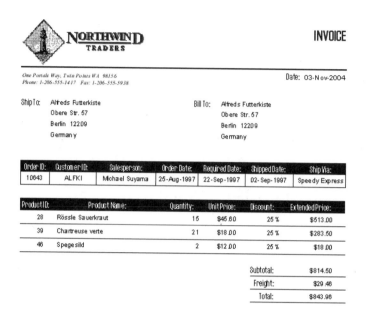

Order ID:	Customer ID:	Salesperson:	Order Date:	Required Date:	Shipped Date:	Ship Via:
10643	ALFKI	Michael Suyama	25-Aug-1997	22-Sep-1997	02-Sep-1997	Speedy Express

Product ID:	Product Name:	Quantity:	Unit Price:	Discount:	Extended Price:
28	Rössle Sauerkraut	15	$45.60	25 %	$513.00
39	Chartreuse verte	21	$18.00	25 %	$283.50
46	Spegesild	2	$12.00	25 %	$18.00

Subtotal:	$814.50
Freight:	$29.46
Total:	$843.96

Figure 12–1 Most Work Processes Are Triggered by a Piece of Paper Such as This Sales Order

Find a sample of this first chunk of data, and write down all the bits of information it contains. Don't worry about classifying these bits as entities or attributes yet, just write them down. Do make a note of any repeating groups, and you'll also want to include any data items that your work process analysis has identified as missing. Your initial list of data items might look like the one in Figure 12–2.

Sales Order
Bill To Address
Ship To Address
Salesperson
Ship Via
Order Date
Date Required
Product
Unit Price
Quantity
Discount

Figure 12–2 This Initial List of the Sales Order Form's Data Items

Now that you've compiled the list, you can start to extract the entities, attributes, and relationships. For each item on the list, you identify whether the item is an object or some fact about an object. Objects become entities, and the facts become attributes of the entity. The results of this analysis will probably look something like Figure 12–3.

As you can see, the Bill To and Ship To items have been identified as facts belonging to the added Customer entity. It's not, however, immediately apparent whether the two addresses belong only in the Customer entity, only in the Sales Order entity, or in both. The principle at work is the same as that for including the Unit Price in an Order Detail item. Just as the current selling price for a product is logically different from the price at which a specific product was sold, the current billing and shipping addresses for a client are logically different from the addresses to which *this* invoice and order were sent.

Whether the shipping and billing addresses are also attributes of the Customer entity is something of a judgment call, based on the nature of the system and its users. Including these attributes in the Customer entity allows defaults to be set during the order entry process, which reduces the

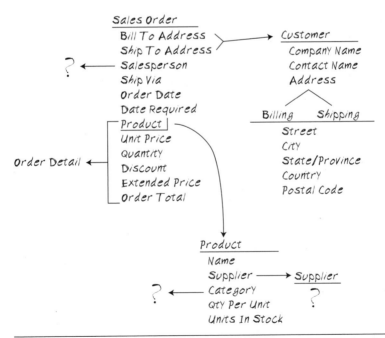

Figure 12–3 The Initial Definition of the Entities and Attributes in the Sales Order Form

time required to enter the order and the opportunities for making data entry mistakes. It does, however, add the overhead of maintaining these values in the Customer entity. If the organization's customers typically have many shipping addresses (retail chains, for example), this overhead might be onerous, and a better solution is simply to enter the shipping address as part of the order entry process.

Sometimes it makes sense to walk a middle ground. You can add multiple shipping address attributes to the Customer entity, for example, but not require that users fill them out. If there is a single address, the system can use that as a default. If there are multiple addresses, the system could present users with a list and allow them to choose. Or you might implement some conditional processing that uses the most recent address entered as a default but allows users to choose another from the list as required.

You might also consider having the Customer entity updated by the order entry process. If there is no address, or if a user enters a new address, the system could ask whether it should be added to the customer record. These are user interface issues, not really data model issues, but the two are sometimes so closely tied that it's impossible to separate them entirely.

The Salesperson data item also seems to indicate that an Employee entity exists somewhere, but we don't yet know what that needs to look like, hence the question mark. Chances are that other documents or processes will use this entity. If so, we can add the required attributes. If not, you might decide to leave Salesperson as an attribute of a Sales Order entity. Remember, these decisions must always be based on the semantics of the system. There's absolutely no value to be gained from creating an Employee input screen with managers, departments, and phone extensions if the data is only going to be used to list a name on a Sales Order.

The Product item has been identified as an entity, and the group of items identified as repeating in the first diagram (Product, Unit Price, Quantity, and Discount) is identified as an Order Details entity. An initial set of attributes has been identified for the Product entity, presumably from another source document, and from this list the Supplier and (Product) Category entities have been identified, although again no details are yet available.

Because we're defining the entities on a conceptual level, we don't care at this point whether attributes such as the Extended Price of an Order Detail entity or the Units In Stock of a Product entity are stored as values or calculated when required. We don't yet know whether they can in fact be calculated. That will come later.

One interesting bit of data is the Ship Via attribute. Many order forms have a couple of check boxes for the shipping method, listing the values "Parcel Post", "FedEx", and "2nd Day Air", perhaps. Are these entities or attributes? It depends. (You guessed, didn't you?) How many options are there? If there are more than two, you won't be able to conveniently model this as a single attribute. How stable are the options? The chances are that you're dealing with external service providers here. Is the organization likely to change providers or add additional ones? How responsive does the organization need to be to special delivery methods? Will they turn down a sale that requires sending the goods by Sherpa to the top of Mount Everest? If not, your model needs to be able to account for all these options.

Modeling the shipping method as a separate entity allows the items to be changed or added at any time, but at the cost of more complexity in both the data model and the user interface. The difference might be only a matter of a few keystrokes, selecting an item from a ComboBox rather than clicking in a check box with the mouse. But those extra keystrokes can, if you're not careful, add up to a clunky, slow interface.

If the company must allow for special delivery methods, you'll need to consider carefully how to account for this. You must walk a fine line between allowing sufficient flexibility to handle all reasonable cases and imposing unnecessary overhead on users. In this example, the best solution would probably be the addition of an optional Special Instructions attribute, but this must also be accounted for in the data model and in any system processes.

These decisions can affect the system constraints in unexpected ways. In this instance, although the organization clearly needs to know how to send the goods to the customer, it's no longer simply a question of requiring that a shipping method be specified. The system must specify that the Shipping Method and Special Instructions attributes cannot *both* be empty, a slightly more complex rule that must be implemented at a different level in the model.

If the actual shipping of goods is within the scope of the system, treating the Shipping Method as a distinct entity might be a good idea and might in fact be required, but allowing for exceptional methods can add significant overhead to the system. How does one capture the shipping details for a shipping method one can't know about in advance? You can either create a generic shipping entity containing the attributes most methods provide, such as a docket number and pickup time, or you can specify the known methods and leave special handling as just that—an exceptional case to be dealt with outside the system.

The danger here is in overcomplicating the system and placing unnecessary overhead on users. It's far too easy to get excited about the functionality the system is capable of providing and lose track of the overhead involved. Yes, providing default values is a good thing, *provided* they can be easily maintained and the maintenance is done regularly (preferably as a by-product of some other task). Making it possible for the receptionist to handle delivery inquiries is good, but is it worth the effort to enter shipping details for a thousand orders just so that they're available for the five customers who inquire?

These decisions only require thinking through the implications of the design decisions you make. But this is easy to overlook when you're in the first flush of thinking, "Isn't this cool? It will save us *so* much time." When you capture a piece of data anywhere in the system, consider whether it can be used elsewhere in the system, either to provide a default or as a constraint. If you're entering the shipping details *anyway,* why not make them available to the receptionist?

Conversely, whenever you use a piece of data, consider where it will be created and how it will be maintained. As a general rule, it's better to present users with a list of choices than with a text box. But there's a cost in creating and maintaining the list, and in building the maintenance interface. All of these things must be balanced when you're making decisions about the structure of your data model.

Certainly, your goal is never to require that a piece of data be entered twice. But by the same token, you don't want to force users to go somewhere out of their way to enter a piece of data just so that it can be used for the task they want to do. We'll talk about this issue a great deal in Part IV, but identifying where bits of data are created and where they're used is the crucial first step in the process.

Defining Relationships

After you've been through all your source documents, you'll have a draft description of the entities and attributes in the problem space. Two tasks remain: establishing the relationships between these entities, and reviewing each entity's attributes and constraints.

Although theoretically you could review the attributes first, I find it easiest to start with the relationships, because some of these will become additional entities and some will require that attributes be added to entities you've already identified.

If you're like me, what you have after your first pass through the source documents is a bunch of handwritten notes with arrows and scribbles and "see page 12"s that nobody else could possibly decipher. So the first step in defining relationships is to get these organized neatly. You can start by building the first draft of the Entity Relationship (E/R) diagram of your data model. (If your notes are really messy and you're worried that even *you* might not be able to read them in three weeks, you might also list the attributes you've identified for each entity.)

Figure 12–4 The First Draft of the Order Processing E/R Diagram

Start by choosing an entity, usually one of the core entities in the system, and then add the entities that have some relationship with it. You can define the nature of the relationships (one-to-one, one-to-many, many-to-many) as you go, or you can simply draw a straight line to remind yourself that there *is* a relationship, and then come back and analyze it later. I usually analyze as I go, but you might find it easier to get all the entities down first and then review them.

The first draft of the E/R diagram for the order-processing example is shown in Figure 12–4. This is a simple example, and the diagram is quite easy to read. (Assume we've decided that Salesperson is an attribute only of the Sales Order entity and not an entity in its own right.) If you're working on a complex example, you might want to create multiple diagrams, each one describing only a subset of the data. In this case, it's a good idea to use some sort of automated support for the diagrams. Otherwise, making sure they're synchronized can get tedious.

Once you have your draft E/R diagram prepared, you can begin to analyze the relationships in more detail. For each relationship, you want to determine the following:

- The cardinality of the relationship
- The optionality of each participant
- Any attributes of the relationship
- Any constraints on the relationship

Figure 12–5 shows the Order Processing E/R diagram after review.

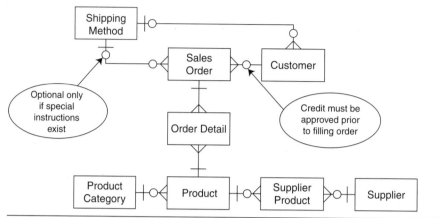

Figure 12–5 The Order Processing E/R Diagram after Reviewing the Relationships

The Cardinality of the Relationship

You might already have indicated the relationships between entities in your first draft, as I did in Figure 12–4. If not, now is the time to do so. Even if you did, it's a good idea to review your decisions now that you have a more complete picture of the whole model.

Where you discover a many-to-many relationship, you should add the junction entity to the model, with a one-to-many relationship on each side. The relationship between Supplier and Product in our model is many-to-many, and so we need to add the entity Product Supplier to resolve it. Note that the relationship between Sales Order and Product is also many-to-many, but in this case the Order Detail entity functions as the junction.

The Optionality of the Relationship

Having established the kind of the relationship between any two entities, you should now consider whether the relationship is optional for either or both participants. In our example, the relationship between Customer and Shipping Method is optional in both directions—that is, customers are not required to have a default shipping method, and shipping methods can exist without being used by a customer.

The relationship between Product Category and Product, on the other hand, is only optional in one direction. A Product Category need not have products assigned to it, but all products must be assigned to a Product Category.

The relationship between Sales Order and Shipping Method is even more complex. A shipping method can exist independently of a sales order, so the Sales Order side of the relationship is optional. The Shipping Method side of the relationship, however, is optional only if the sales order has special instructions. This is an important constraint and should be noted on the diagram.

The Attributes of the Relationship

In most situations, all that you need to record about the relationship between two entities is the fact of its existence. We need to know, for example, that a specific Customer placed a given Sales Order, and that's *all* we need to know. Sometimes, however, we need to know additional facts about the relationship—when it began or how long it lasted, for example. These facts are attributes of the relationship itself, not of either of the participants.

Where the relationship itself has attributes, it must be modeled as an entity. In the order-processing example, we might decide to designate one Supplier as having "Preferred Supplier" status. Since we already have a junction entity between Product and Supplier, the Preferred Supplier attribute can simply be added to that entity. If that were not the case, we would have needed to add an entity to represent the attributes of the relationship.

Additional Constraints on the Relationship

Finally, we want to consider whether any additional constraints pertain to the relationship. What are the minimum and maximum number of records that can exist on the many side of a one-to-many relationship? Are there any conditions that must be met before the relationship is allowed to exist? Are there any conditions under which the relationship *must* exist?

In our example, the requirement that the relationship between a Sales Order and a Shipping Method is optional only if Special Instructions have been indicated is one such constraint. The rule that customers cannot place an order until after their credit has been approved is another. Again, this rule has been indicated by an annotation on the diagram. If there are many constraints or the constraints are too complex for a simple annotation, you might need to document them elsewhere. You should, however, at least indicate on the diagram that such constraints exist.

Reviewing Entities

Now that you've begun to get a picture of the entities in the system and how they're related, it's time to start analyzing each entity in detail. For each entity, you'll want to identify the following information:

- The relationship between the entity and the problem space
- The work processes that create, modify, use, and delete the entity
- Any other entities it might interact with or depend on
- The business rules and constraints pertaining to the entity
- The attributes of the entity

The Relationship between the Entity and the Problem Space

Identifying the relationship between the entity and the problem space is usually straightforward. "The Customer entity models the individuals and organizations who buy our products." The biggest problem here, I've found, is thinking up a sentence that isn't hopelessly tautological. "The Employees entity models the organization's employees" seems hardly worth saying.

If a relationship is modeled as an entity, things can be trickier since the entity won't map directly to the problem space. "A supplier can provide multiple products, and any given product might be provided by any number of suppliers. The Product Supplier entity models this relationship, as well as the Preferred Supplier status of any given Supplier for a specific Product."

Some things in the problem space—a Sales Order is probably the best example—are modeled using one or more logical entities in the data model. I refer to these as **composite entities**. The sales order document is represented by *both* the Sales Order and Order Detail entities.

I have generally found it cleaner to handle composite entities as a single object for documentation purposes. For example, "The Sales Order and Order Detail entities represent a single order placed by a Customer. The Sales Order entity models the order itself, while the Order Detail items represent each product being ordered."

Work Processes that Affect the Entity

Although you might have already identified where data items are used during the work process analysis you performed earlier, it's useful to include that information in the entity documentation as well. That way, if it's necessary at some point to make a change to the structure of the entity, such as adding an attribute, there's a single place to identify all the processes that can be affected.

Identifying the processes that operate directly on an entity is also usually a straightforward process. Identifying those that indirectly interact with the entity might require more work. It might not be immediately obvious, for example, that the order entry process can modify a customer's default shipping method, or that a "Special Bonus" identified for a product category can affect the discount and thus the total value of a sales order. And yet these are exactly the kinds of interactions that are a maintenance programmer's nightmare if they're not carefully documented.

Most analysts document these interactions in the work processes analysis, which is obviously useful if your changes are to the processes themselves. Sometimes, however, the changes are to the model itself, either directly because of a change in the business environment or indirectly because a change to an existing process requires alterations in the model. In this case, it's far easier to scan the entity documentation for the specific entity you're changing than to sift through all the work processes to determine which might be affected by the change.

Think of including work process information in your entity documentation as cross-referencing, which it is. Like all cross-referencing, it can be tedious to implement and maintain, but it will make your life a lot easier in the long run.

Interactions between Entities

E/R diagrams are wonderful tools, but they're capable of showing only so much information. If the entities in your system have complex interactions that can't easily be represented on the diagram, it's important to document them in the entity descriptions. Even if you've added annotations to the diagram, you should expand on any interactions that aren't immediately apparent in the notation.

If the model is complex enough to warrant multiple entity diagrams and a given entity appears in multiple diagrams, it might be useful to list all of the entities to which it is related in the entity description. This tends to be the case with entities that provide look-up values in multiple places. A Courtesy Title entity, for example, that contains entries such as "Mr.", "Mrs.", "Dr.", and "Ms." might be referenced in a dozen places. If you need to make changes to the entity, it's useful to be able to find all the referencing entities in a single spot.

As a general rule, however, the E/R diagram provides adequate documentation for the interaction between entities. Only exceptional cases like those cited previously warrant additional information.

Business Rules and Constraints

The next bit of documentation required for an entity is to note any entity-level constraints that pertain to it. Any constraints that reference multiple attributes, such as the "Shipping Method and Special Instructions attributes cannot both be empty" rule in our example, should also be documented, and this is the time to do so.

Attributes

The final bit of documentation required for the entities is a list of attributes and their domains. In compiling the list, you'll want to start with the list of attributes you identified when going through the source documents, and then be sure to add any foreign keys that are required for referential integrity.

You'll also want to check that each entity has at least one candidate key that can be used to uniquely identify each instance. This will become the primary key for the table in the database schema. Remember that primary keys cannot contain Null values. Because of this, it might not always be possible to use an existing attribute or combination of attributes as a key. If this is the case, you'll need to add an arbitrary, system-generated identifier.

In our example, the Customer entity probably needs an artificial identifier like this. If we assume that a customer might be either a company or an individual, you might have an initial attribute list like that shown in Figure 12–6.

Even if we set aside for the moment the issue that names are not unique, we still have a problem. If the customer is an individual, the Company Name will be null. If the customer is a company, the Individual Name

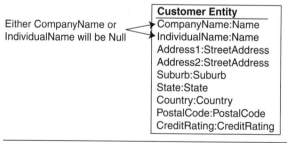

Figure 12–6 The Customer Entity Attribute List

will be null. Something is *always* going to be null. So these fields cannot be used as the candidate key even if we could assume that they uniquely identify the record, which we can't.

This leads me to the next problem with the Customer entity. Names are not unique. In our example, the entire list of attributes doesn't even guarantee uniqueness, since it's possible for two individuals with the same name to live at the same address. John Smith is not guaranteed to tell you that he's actually John Smith Jr. and not to be confused with his papa, who lives in the same house.

There is certainly no question that John Smith Sr. and John Smith Jr. are different people and should be represented by different records. However, the attributes that uniquely identify them are none of our business. Can you imagine being asked about your living arrangements when you place an order for groceries? "Pardon me, sir, but do you happen to have a relative of the same name residing with you? Just checking for our computer system." Not in the best tradition of customer service, really.

Fortunately, there's a simple answer: the Customer Number. And if the organization doesn't already have a method of assigning these numbers, both Microsoft Jet and Microsoft SQL Server provide a mechanism for assigning them automatically (the AutoNumber and Identity data types, respectively).

If you do use an arbitrary identifier, though, be sure to provide an alternate form of identification. You don't want to put a user in the situation of having to refuse an order because the customer has forgotten his or her customer number. Asking a customer, "Are you the John Smith who lives in Oakridge or the one who lives in Cincinnati?" is one thing, asking him to call back after he's found an old invoice is quite another.

The Customer entity is also an example of the second reason to use an arbitrary system identifier. Even if we could assume that the combination of name and address were sufficiently unique for our purposes, that still leaves way too many fields to copy everywhere. Remember that the primary key of an entity will be used as a foreign key in any entities that reference it. It's obviously much more efficient to duplicate a single attribute than five or six.

Domain Analysis

In Figure 12–6, the attribute listing takes the form Name:Domain. Many analysts ignore the existence of domains and specify the attributes directly in terms of their data types and constraints. So if you ignore this step of the process, you'll be in good company. You won't be *correct,* but it's unlikely that anyone will fault you for it.

The reason I perform domain analysis in my own work, and recommend that you do so as well, is that it saves work and provides additional information. As far as I'm concerned, anything that's easier and better is a good idea. And this task has the added advantage of being technically correct, as well.

Let's take just one example: The CompanyName and IndividualName attributes in Figure 12–6 all specify that they derive their values from the domain of Name.

We can now define the Name domain as follows:

"A string of one or more words in proper case, with a maximum length of 75 characters. Only characters and the punctuation marks period (.) and comma (,) are allowed."

We have to define the domain only once, and we can reference it any number of times throughout the system. We could have defined these constraints for each applicable attribute, but why bother? Furthermore, because these attributes are defined on the same domain, we know that they can be logically compared. This wouldn't necessarily be clear if we had defined the attributes directly.

Finding the customer with the same value in the CompanyName field as in the IndividualName field might not be the most useful thing to do, but it is at least a possible thing. The same could not be said of comparing company names to customer numbers that might, coincidentally, have the same structure and constraints.

The technical definition of a domain is "the set of values from which an attribute can draw its values." This is conceptually straightforward, but how does one define a domain? Essentially, you need to identify three things:

1. The data type of the domain
2. Any restrictions to the range of values accepted by the data type
3. Optionally, any formatting that pertains to the domain

Choosing a Data Type

The first step in defining a domain is to choose the core data type that will be used in the database schema to represent it. This is one instance where it's practical to break the rule about separating the database schema from the conceptual data model.

The data type serves as a shorthand description of a range of values. While "Integer" is not a domain unless you're modeling mathematics, values of the domain "Quantity" are almost certainly integers. I wouldn't recommend getting too involved with the specifics of database engine types, however. At this point, the choice of database engine is still subject to change.

The "data type" of a domain can also be another domain. You might have already defined a generic Date domain, which specifies, for example, that all dates in the system must be on or after 1 January 1900 and formatted using a four-digit year. It's perfectly acceptable to define the Event Date as "A Date after 23 October 1982 (the date on which trading commenced)".

Restricting the Range of Values

Having identified the base data type for your domain, the next step is to specify the values within that data type's range that are valid for the domain. Sometimes the easiest way to do this is by specifying a rule: "Quantities must be positive whole numbers."

Sometimes it's simpler to list the valid values for a domain. "Region must be one of these: Northwest, Northeast, Central, Southern." In this instance, you will almost certainly want to include the domain as an entity in the data model. This is far easier than typing the values everywhere they're referenced, and also allows them to be easily changed after the system has been implemented.

The only possible exception to this rule is when the domain values are few in number and cannot possibly change. Say, for example, that you're modeling a questionnaire and an exam, and you have an Answer domain that consists of the values ""True" and "False". There is no point in modeling these two options as an entity. There are no other possible values, and referencing a table during implementation will almost certainly be more trouble than typing in the rule directly.

You will also use an entity to model domains that must be defined using more than one attribute. The best example of this is the domain of State. If you must account for multiple countries, you cannot determine whether a given state value is valid without reference to the country specified.

If a customer is located in Australia, for example, "New South Wales" is a valid state, but "Alabama" is not. In this case, the domain look-up entity would consist of both the Country and State attributes. This example is not strictly a domain definition, and it's modeled using required relationships in the E/R model. It is, however, easy to think of this sort of situation as a kind of composite domain, and treat it as such.

After all, the point here is to simplify the task of identifying the constraints that pertain to the system, and bending the domain definition for domains that appear repeatedly in the data model saves time and reduces the chance of error.

Your domain specification must also indicate whether nulls or zero-length strings, or both, are acceptable values for attributes defined on the domain. It's useful to explicitly declare this in your definition even if you're modeling the range using a system entity, in which case the nullability can be determined by the relationship between the two entities.

Performing the domain analysis and identifying the list of attributes for any given entity are closely related, iterative processes. In actual practice, you'll probably find it most effective to define the domains at the same time that you're listing the attributes. If the domain of an attribute is already defined, you can simply list it. If not, you can define the domain while you have an example in front of you.

During this process, you might find that certain attributes have restrictions in addition to those defined for the domain. This is perfectly proper and not at all unusual. You might have defined an Event Date domain, for example, that represents the date on which any event can occur. This date is restricted to dates after the company began trading. In the Sales Order example, both the Order Date and the Shipping Date would be defined on the Event Date domain. The Shipping Date attribute, however, must also be after the Order Date. This is an entity-level constraint and should be listed as such in the entity description.

In defining domain constraints (and additional attribute constraints, for that matter), you should try to be as specific as possible *without compromising usability*. We'll discuss this in greater detail in Part IV, but at this point you should be aware that the more precisely you define a domain, the more assistance you can provide users. If you accidentally eliminate values, however, you will get in the users' way and can ultimately make the system unusable.

Defining the Format

It's not strictly necessary, but it's often a good idea to specify the appropriate format for a domain. If you specify once that all dates must be displayed as DD-MMM-YYYY, you need never do it again.

Normalization

It might have come as a surprise that nowhere in this discussion of data modeling have I discussed normalizing the data model. It's been my experience that if you start with the data bits and then organize them into entities, reconciling repeating groups and many-to-many relationships as you go, you're likely to have a data model that is in third-normal form.

But it certainly does no harm, particularly when all of this is fairly new to you, to review the model for compliancy. Remember, every entity in the model should be dependent on "the key, the whole key, and nothing but the key."

Summary

In this chapter, we've looked at building the conceptual data model of the system. The process begins with a review of all source materials to identify the data items used by the system, which are then organized into a set of entities. The relationships between the entities are reviewed, and then each individual entity and its attributes are analyzed.

In the next chapter, we'll look at translating the conceptual model into the physical database schema that will be implemented against the chosen database engine.

The Database Schema

In the last chapter, we examined the conceptual data model, which defines the logical structure of the data. In this chapter, we turn to the database schema, which describes the physical structure of the data. Remember that the database schema is still a logical construct. In building it, you will describe the physical structure of the data in fairly abstract terms, albeit ones that correspond to the physical representation of the data. The actual physical representation is the responsibility of the database engine and need not concern you.

Systems Architectures

Before describing the database schema, you must make some decisions about the architecture your system requires. Unfortunately, the literature uses the term "architecture" to describe two distinct (although interrelated) models. To clarify things, I'll call one of these models the **code architecture** and the other the **data architecture**. But be aware that these are my names; you're unlikely to find them elsewhere.

Code Architectures

What I call the code architecture is variously called the "application model," the "layered paradigm," and the "services model" in the literature. The code architecture describes the way code is logically structured. Code structure is largely an implementation issue, and as such it lies outside the scope of this book. However, the code architecture can affect whether data integrity constraints are implemented in the database schema, and so we will discuss it here, although somewhat superficially.

In the bad old days, system architectures were monolithic: huge blobs of code with minimal structure. Anyone who's had the misfortune of trying to modify (or even understand) a monolithic system of any complexity will never look at a plate of spaghetti in the same way again. To impose some order on this mess, programmers began to structure their code into discrete components in various ways: subroutines, modules, or objects, depending on language capabilities. The problem with this approach is that instead of creating spaghetti, you can easily create tortellini—independent chunks of code that interact in *some* way, but it's anybody's guess how.

To manage this modern pasta, many developers are organizing components into services, sometimes called "layers," which perform tasks at a discrete logical level. There are innumerable ways of organizing the layers. We'll look at two of the most common types: the three-tiered and four-layer models. (Please don't ask me why when you have three of them, they're "tiers," and when you have four, they're "layers." Just to confuse us, I suspect.)

Three-Tiered Model

The three-tiered model organizes components into User Services, Business Services, and Data Services. Code components that present information to users and respond to user actions are assigned to the User Services tier. The entire user interface is encapsulated within this tier. The Business Services tier is responsible for enforcing business rules and validating user input. Business Services components interact with both the User Services and Data Services tiers. Code components in the Data Services tier, which interact only with the Business Services tier, are responsible for maintaining data.

The three-tiered model is clean, but I've found its use in actual development problematic. There always seem to be certain types of functionality that don't clearly belong to any specific tier. For example, say a given piece of data needs to be formatted before it's displayed to users. A social security number might be stored as a string of nine digits but displayed as 999-99-9999. Does the formatting belong to the User Services or the Data Services tier? You could make a case for putting it in either tier. Similarly, is transaction management part of Business Services or Data Services? When you begin to design complex systems using hierarchical data and data shaping, these types of decisions can get hairy.

Provided that you're consistent, I suppose it doesn't really matter where you put these types of functions, but this is precisely where the model fails. If you must refer to a set of external conventions—such as "formatting belongs to the User Services tier, and building hierarchical data sets is a part of the Business Services tier"—then the overhead of the model begins to outweigh its benefits.

Four-Layer Model

Dividing the code architecture into four layers instead of three eliminates many of the problems associated with the three-tiered model. The four-layered model, often called the "layered paradigm," organizes code components into a User Interface layer, a Data Interface layer, a Transaction Interface layer, and an External Access Interface layer, as shown in Figure 13–1.

The User Interface layer corresponds to the User Services tier of the three-tiered model. The User Interface layer is responsible for user interaction, including presenting information to users by means of window objects; responding to changes in the state of window objects, such as a form resize; and initiating user requests.

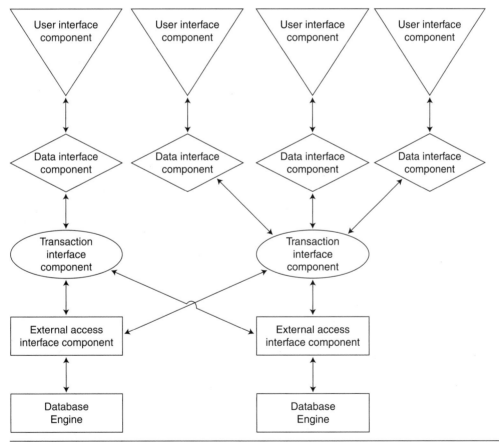

Figure 13–1 The Four-Layer Model

The Data Interface layer is responsible for maintaining data in memory (as opposed to maintaining it permanently, which is handled by the External Access Interface layer and the database engine, as we'll see). It explicitly includes most of the functionality that can be contentious in the three-tiered model, such as being able to format data and create virtual record-sets. (A *virtual recordset* exists only in memory; it's not permanently stored anywhere.)

In most cases, a component in the Data Interface layer is tightly coupled with a specific component in the User Interface layer. Theoretically, however, a Data Interface component can support multiple User Interface components, as Figure 13–1 shows. A system might include, for example, a Customer Maintenance form showing information for a single customer and a Customer Summary form showing information for multiple customers. Since both of these forms represent a Customer entity, they might share the code for formatting and validating the CustomerNumber, which is a function of the Data Interface layer.

In physical terms, a User Interface component usually corresponds to a form in Microsoft Visual Basic or Microsoft Access, and the associated Data Interface component is typically implemented in the form's class module. Certain procedures might be shared by multiple forms, however, in which case the procedures would be implemented in a shared module.

The Data Interface layer is responsible for validating data but is not responsible for business processes. The code that ensures that the Customer-Number value specified in an order is known to the system, for example, is part of the Data Interface layer. The code that enforces a specific sequence of events, such as preventing an order from being shipped until the customer's credit is approved, belongs to the Transaction Interface layer.

The Transaction Interface layer coordinates the use of data by the application. Components at this level are responsible for building and initiating queries, receiving information from the External Access Interface layer, enforcing business processes, and handling errors and violations reported by the External Access Interface layer.

The components in the Transaction Interface layer are more likely to be reused than Data Interface components. Transaction Interface layer components are good candidates for implementation as objects in both Visual Basic and C#. A Customer object, for example, might expose an *Update* method that is called by multiple components in the Data Interface layer. Note that because the Data Interface layer should (at least ideally) be independent from components at the User Interface layer, the values to be updated must be listed explicitly. In other words, the call would take the following form:

```
MyCustomer.Update CustomerNumber, CustomerName …
```

The Update method would then create the UPDATE query statement, hand it to the External Access Interface layer for execution, and handle any error conditions that might result, either by resolving them directly or by handing them back up the chain for display by the User Interface layer.

The External Access Interface layer is responsible for communication between the application and external data sources. In database systems, the code components at this level handle the communication with the database engine. They execute queries and hand the results (including any error messages) back up the component chain.

Ideally, you should design the procedures at this level to isolate the transaction from the specifics of the database engine you choose. Theoretically, it should be possible to upsize an application originally designed to use the Microsoft Jet database engine to SQL Server simply by replacing the External Access Interface layer. In reality, this can be a little difficult to pull off.

Remember that the Transaction Interface layer is responsible for building queries; the External Access Interface layer only executes them. Given the syntactic differences between various implementations of the SQL language, implementation is rarely so straightforward. A recordset created by a single TRANSFORM query against a Microsoft Jet database requires multiple statements to be created using SQL Server.

If you can predict all the queries executed by the application in advance, you can avoid syntax problems by including the queries in the database schema. Parameter queries can be enormously helpful here. You don't need to create the SQL statement to select the customer named Jones on the fly—you can pass "Jones" in as a parameter to a pre-existing query, thereby simplifying your code architecture and probably improving performance.

Unfortunately, it isn't always possible to predict all the necessary queries in advance, particularly if you're providing an ad hoc query capability to users. In this case it's almost impossible to insulate the Transaction Interface layer entirely. (At any rate, I've never found a complete solution to the problem; if you figure it out, I'll be grateful if you'd share it with me.) In the meantime, you might have to write some conditional code in the Data Interface layer components.

If your application is intended to support a single database engine, it's tempting to roll the Transaction Interface layer and the External Access Interface layer together. I don't recommend it. Although it does take a certain amount of time to design the External Access Interface layer, the process isn't difficult, and once written it will save you hundreds of lines of code elsewhere in the system. Furthermore, once you've written a component that communicates to, say, SQL Server 2000 using ADO.NET, you need never write it again. You can use it in any other systems you write, without modification. The only time you need a new External Access Interface layer component is when either the underlying database engine or the object model changes.

Code Architectures and the Database Schema

The code architecture you choose impacts the database schema in two areas: insulation of the External Access Interface layer (or the Data Services layer, if you're using the three-tiered model) and data validation. We've already talked about insulating the External Access Interface layer from a change in database engines by predicting necessary queries and including them in the database schema. This approach has the added advantage of improving performance, sometimes significantly. Data validation is a somewhat trickier issue. We'll look at the "what" and "how" of data validation in detail in Chapter 19. What we'll consider here is the "when" and "where."

Some designers advocate embedding all data validation functionality in the database engine itself. This approach isn't without merit: All of the data integrity constraints and business rules are implemented in a single place, where they can be easily updated. Unfortunately, the approach is not without problems, either.

In the first place, certain rules *can't* be implemented at the database-engine level. For example, without triggers in the Jet database engine, it's impossible to enforce a rule that prevents a primary key value from being changed once the record is created. Even in SQL Server, which is generally more powerful in this area, you can't implement every rule directly in the database engine.

YUKON NOTE: SQL Server Yukon allows triggers, code and stored procedures to be implemented in any procedural language, which will remove any effective limits on implementing constraints at the server level.

Secondly, waiting until the data has been submitted to the database engine before validating it can reduce the usability of the system. As a general rule, you should validate data as soon as it's entered. In some cases, this means validating the data as soon as a key is pressed, such as when you prevent the entry of alphabetical characters in a numeric field. In other cases, you should validate the data when a field is exited or when the last of a sequence of fields is entered, such as when you're enforcing the rule that the DesiredDeliveryDate value must be equal to or later than the Order-Date value.

Even in a standalone application running on a single machine, submitting a data set to the database engine after each keystroke, or even after each field is exited, results in deplorable performance. If you're making a round-trip across a network or, heaven forbid, across a wide area network or the Internet to a database engine at a remote site, performance will be so poor your users will be better off using index cards (and they might).

The only solution, if all validation is handled by the server, is to submit the data to the database engine for validation after the entire record has been completed. But by this point, a user's attention will have turned to the next task. To report a problem that resulted from an entry made 10 minutes ago is disruptive and confusing.

To make the system as responsive and usable as possible, then, you must implement data validation in the application. If the database is used by only a single application and the validation requirements are relatively stable, you might decide to implement data validation *only* at the application level and entirely forego any validation by the database engine. This eliminates duplicate effort, but it's a fairly dangerous approach.

If another application is implemented against the same database in the future, nothing but good intentions prevent the new application from inadvertently undermining the integrity of the database, and we all know which road is paved with good intentions. Even if the database is never shared with another application, it's vulnerable to users using ad hoc tools such as Access or the SQL Server Enterprise Manager to manipulate the data. A strict security model that prohibits data changes except by the application itself can help prevent this, but at a cost of restricted access to the data, which may be inappropriate.

For these reasons, I believe that best practice is to implement data validation in both the application and the database schema. Access implements this automatically. When you define a validation rule for a field at the table level and then drag that field onto a bound form, the form inherits the validation rule.

In versions of Access prior to 2000, this feature is unfortunately also a good example of the problem with duplicate validation. If, after including the field on a bound form, you then change the validation rule at the table level, the changes are not reflected in the form. Microsoft Access 2000 does update the rule, but the problem remains in Visual Basic. If you reference the field on multiple forms (in the same or multiple applications), you must manually change the validation rules in each of the forms (or rather, in the Data Interface layer components supporting each of the forms).

To overcome this problem, you can query the database engine for validation rules at runtime. This technique has a certain amount of overhead, but if your validation rules change frequently, the overhead might be offset by the ease of updating the rules in a single place.

Retrieving the validation rules from the database engine can be done when the application first starts, when a form is loaded, or before each record is updated. I recommend doing it when the form is loaded. If you do it on application startup, you might download unnecessary information pertaining to forms a user never loads. If you do it before each record is updated, you can be absolutely sure that the rules you're working with are as current as possible, but it means re-querying the schema for each record and, realistically, how many systems are *that* volatile?

In the extremely unlikely event that a rule changes while a user has a form open *and* the user enters data that complied with the old rule but violates the new rule, the problem will be caught by the database engine anyway, so no major harm will be done. Besides, the very thought of tinkering with the database schema while the system is being *used* is enough to give me nightmares.

Data Architectures

In addition to making decisions about how the code for your system should be structured, you must also decide on a data architecture. You will recall from Chapter 1 that a database system consists of a number of discrete components: the application itself, the database engine, and the database. (See Figure 1–1.) Based on the four-layer code model, we can now refine this structure somewhat, as shown in Figure 13–2.

In determining the data architecture for the application, you decide where each of the layers will live. Theoretically, each layer (or even each individual component) can exist on a different computer, communicating across a network of some kind. At the other end of the scale, all the components can exist on a single, standalone computer. In reality, a few more-or-less standard configurations have been shown to be effective in various situations, and we'll examine each of these in turn.

Single-Tier Architectures

Each logical grouping of components in the data architecture is referred to as a **tier**. The simplest architecture, of course, is a single-tier system, in which all the components exist in a single logical tier, and the simplest version of a single-tier data architecture is a standalone system.

Figure 13–2 A Database System Consists of Six Discrete Layers

In a standalone system, all the components exist on a single machine and are available only to the user physically working at that machine. Although the machine might incidentally be connected to a network or the Internet, the database system is not available to other users. Because all processing occurs on the local machine and the data is stored locally, the only performance constraints are the capabilities of the machine—its processor speed and memory. Standalone systems tend to be very memory-hungry; that's one of the reasons other configurations are sought.

The majority of standalone systems use the Jet database engine, although Microsoft is encouraging developers to use the Microsoft Data Engine (MSDE), a standalone version of SQL Server distributed as part of the Microsoft Data Access Components (MDAC). It's certainly possible to implement a SQL Server system on a single machine, but for reasons that will become clear later, it's debatable whether such a system qualifies as single-tier.

A common variation in the single-tier architecture is the networked database. In this model, you physically locate the database (or at least parts of it) on a computer across a network, but all processing is performed locally.

NOTE: Don't be tempted to put the application itself on the network drive. This is theoretically possible—but definitely *not* recommended—because of the load it puts on the network. Instead, you should put the application on the local computer and use linked tables to access the networked data.

A networked database—which is possible only using the Jet database engine, not SQL Server—allows multiple users to access the data simultaneously. The maximum number of simultaneous users of a Jet database is theoretically 255. In reality, the practical maximum depends on what they're doing and, ultimately, on how efficient the system design is. Clearly, 20 people entering data as fast as their sweet fingers can type are going to put more strain on a system than 50 people reviewing sales and pondering product strategy.

Reducing the network load has the most direct effect on the database schema. Remember that all processing occurs on the local machine; in a sense, you treat the computer on which the database resides as nothing more than a remote hard disk. But response time across a network is typically much slower than accessing a local hard drive. Furthermore, the network has a limited capacity, and all users on the system must compete for it. So you want to reduce the amount of information you're shuffling back and forth. Again, this is largely an implementation issue; if you're directly involved with implementation, I suggest you consult the sources listed in the Bibliography that accompanies this book for more information.

However, two aspects of the database schema can directly impact network performance: the location of database objects and the appropriate use of indices. I've already mentioned the importance of having the user interface objects stored locally. In addition, you might want to consider placing copies of data that doesn't change very often on users' machines.

For example, product lists tend to be fairly stable, and they're typically referenced frequently. Provided the Products table isn't too big (a few megabytes is fine; a gigabyte is pushing it), you might want to consider storing a copy of it on each user's machine. In most situations, this will reduce network traffic and improve performance. Of course, you'll need to provide some mechanism for updating the data when necessary, but this doesn't present too much of a problem. If the system is implemented using Microsoft Access, replication will do the job beautifully.

Lists of postal codes, states, countries, and an organization's regions or branches are also good candidates for local storage, since these lists tend to be small and stable. They also tend to be referenced frequently. (There's no point in storing a copy of a table that's used only by the system administrator once a year on every user's workstation.) Sales orders or lists of customers or students, on the other hand, are typically not appropriate for local storage. The data in these tables changes frequently, and sharing the most current version is the whole point of a networked database.

The second way the database schema can affect network performance is in the use of appropriate indices. You can think of an index as a sort of mini-table that is maintained in a specific order. It contains only the fields required to order the records and a "pointer" to the record in the real table, as shown in Figure 13–3.

Note that I'm using the word "pointer" rather loosely here. This pointer isn't the same as a "memory pointer" or an "object pointer" as those terms are used in programming. In fact, the physical implementation of indices doesn't match the model presented here very closely at all, but the model will work. If you *really* want to know the ugly details, the *Microsoft Jet Database Engine Programmer's Guide* is a good place to start.

Instead of physically rearranging the records in the base table, a task that would be prohibitively time-consuming in most situations, Microsoft Jet sorts only the index file. This is (usually) substantially faster and also allows the base table to be quickly and easily accessed in multiple orders, since more than one index can be maintained for any given table.

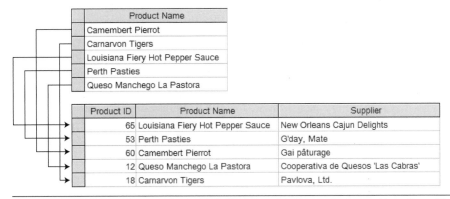

Figure 13–3 An Index Is a Kind of Mini-Table, with Records Stored in a Specific Order

SQL Server provides a special kind of index, called a **clustered index**, that does control the physical ordering of data. There can be only one clustered index per table.

The importance of indices from a performance point of view is that in many cases the database engine can perform an operation using only an index, without reading the base table itself. This often provides a noticeable performance improvement even for standalone systems (even reading data from a local drive takes time), and in networked situations the improvement can be critical.

To take just one example, say you have a Customers table containing 100,000 records, each 1500 bytes long. The application needs to find a specific record, say the one for Jones Construction, whose CustomerID is JONSCON. You execute a statement like the following:

```
SELECT * FROM Customers WHERE CustomerID = "JONSCON"
```

Without an index or a primary key declared for the table, the Jet database engine must read each of those 100,000 records to determine which ones match the specified condition. That's at least 150 megabytes of data being sent across the network. If the CustomerID is indexed, either explicitly or by declaring it a primary key, the Jet database engine needs to read only the index, which is probably just a few kilobytes, and can then quickly locate the correct record in the base table.

The performance improvement from using indices can be amazing, but of course you don't get it for free. There's a certain amount of overhead involved in using indices: Every time you add or update a record, the database engine must update the indices on the table. Usually this overhead is negligible, but if you are using too many indices on any one table, it can start to impact performance. Taken to extremes, the time required to maintain the indices will exceed the time saved by using them.

Two-Tiered Architectures

In a two-tiered architecture, the database and the database engine are both located on a remote computer. They can be on the same computer or on different ones. In fact, the database can be spread across several physical computers; logically, the system will still be two-tiered. This architecture is possible only using SQL Server or another database server such as Oracle; it is not possible with Microsoft Jet.

At first glance, the difference between a networked database and a two-tiered system might not seem great. Use Microsoft Jet or SQL Server on a remote computer—what's the big deal? The big deal is that in a networked database all the processing is performed on the local workstation, but in a two-tiered system the processing is spread across two processors. The workstation is responsible for handling user interaction, and the remote computer handles the data access. SQL Server performs all the data manipulation, including query execution, and "serves" the results to the client workstation. For this reason, two-tiered database systems are better known as **client/server** systems.

To make the difference between a networked database and a two-tiered system clearer, take the following SQL statement, which we used when we talked about the importance of indices:

```
SELECT * FROM Customers WHERE CustomerID = "JONSCON"
```

In a networked database, the Jet database engine will read the index (assuming one is present), determine the correct record, and then fetch the record. The index and the record are both transported across the network. In a client/server system, the application will submit the statement to SQL Server and get the correct record in return. Only the record is transported across the network. (Of course, what actually happens in each situation is rather more complicated, but this simple model will serve.)

With a request like this, the performance of either architecture will be good enough that you might not see much difference between a networked database and a client/server database. But with complex queries and scores of users, using a client/server system significantly improves performance and responsiveness.

In addition to reducing network traffic, system responsiveness can also improve in a client/server system because while the server is busy calculating the results of a command, the workstation can be doing something else, like responding to additional user requests. The reverse is also true. While the workstation is busy responding to a user (or waiting around for the user to do something), the database server is free to process other requests. SQL Server is more sophisticated than Microsoft Jet in many ways, but this system responsiveness is essentially why client/server systems can support more users than a networked database. This is yet another case of the whole being greater than the sum of its parts.

To make a client/server system work, you must push as much data processing onto the server as possible. Whereas in a networked database it often makes sense to store queries locally, in a two-tiered client/server system they should remain on the server.

If you're linking to SQL Server through Access, you need to be careful about issuing commands that will execute locally. For example, a SELECT statement that contains a user-defined function will be executed by Access rather than being passed to SQL Server, because SQL Server doesn't support Access functions in SELECT statements (neither does Microsoft Jet, which is why a query containing a user-defined function can't be executed from Visual Basic, even if the query is stored in an .mdb file). If you force local evaluation, you'll lose all the benefits of having the database engine perform the data manipulation.

From an implementation standpoint, there are many more issues to consider in building client/server databases. Again, I refer you to one of the many excellent books available on the subject, some of which are listed in the Bibliography.

N-Tiered Architectures

Spreading the processing load between two systems in a two-tiered system can, if implemented correctly, significantly improve application performance and responsiveness. Spreading the load across additional systems can provide similar benefits. Referring back to the four-layer code architecture shown in Figure 13–1, it's usually the Transaction Interface layer and External Access Interface layer components that are distributed to additional intermediate systems.

Unfortunately, the implementation complexity seems to increase exponentially, as well. Connectivity, security, process management—all these issues become infinitely more complex when you move to three or more logical tiers. Since the complexity of these systems often requires additional servers of various descriptions, such as the Microsoft Transaction Server, these systems are usually referred to as "n-tiered." (Apparently, with physical tiers, as with ex-husbands, one stops counting after the third.)

Fortunately, this implementation complexity is just that—an implementation issue. Your development team might decide to explore a new career in basket weaving, but an n-tiered architecture doesn't affect the *design* of the database very much. You must be especially rigorous in keeping the logical levels of the code architecture distinct, but a database schema that performs correctly in a two-tiered environment should scale to n-tiers without alteration.

Detached Architectures

Deploying a database across the Internet or an intranet is essentially a special form of n-tiered architecture. The specifics of the technologies are different—you'll use HTTP as a transfer protocol, and the user interface is more likely to be Internet Explorer than Access—but logically the architectures are very similar.

The most important difference between a database system deployed on the Internet and one deployed in a more traditional environment is that the Internet is stateless. Unlike an Internet application, in a typical client/server environment the application will request a username and password when it first starts up and then use this information to connect to SQL Server. Once the connection is established (assuming the username and password are accepted), the server usually maintains the connection for the duration of the session. As long as the connection is maintained, the server knows who the client is, and when the client makes a request, it can respond appropriately. All this "I know who you are" business is called a **state** and is maintained by the database server.

When the database system is deployed across the Internet, however, the database server will no longer maintain state information. Each time the application makes a request from the database server, it must reestablish the connection and re-identify itself. Once the database server has complied with the request, it forgets all about the application that made it.

Detached architectures used to be restricted to the Internet and intranets, but this is the architecture enforced by ADO.Net, no matter what the physical architecture, so they're becoming difficult to avoid.

Under most circumstances, the slight overhead involved in making a new connection for each request has very little impact on the database system, and it certainly doesn't affect the database schema. But the stateless nature of the Internet has another implication that *does* affect the application and might also require changes to the database schema.

Most Internet applications aim for a **thin client**. This means that applications do as little processing as possible on the client, usually just the user interface. But consider the case of a query that returns a lot of records, more than can be reasonably displayed on a single screen. In a traditional application, the result set is cached, either on the client or the server.

But in an Internet application, the results can't be cached on the server side because the server wouldn't know where to send the next batch. If they're cached on the client side, the data-handling components (the Transaction Interface and External Access Interface layers) must reside on the client as well, and these components are certainly not "thin." They're decidedly pudgy, in fact.

ActiveX Data Objects (ADO) and the Net Framework both provide a mechanism called **paging** for handling these situations. Paging allows you to return a specified number of records in the resultset. It's rather like the

TOP N clause of a standard SQL SELECT statement, except that you have a "middle N" capability as well.

On the server side, paging results in the re-execution of the query each time a user requests a new page. For queries having a reasonably fast response time this represents no problem. For complex queries that are relatively slow to calculate, you've got big problems. An application that makes a single user wait a couple of minutes for a response is marginally acceptable. An application that makes several thousand users wait minutes every time they want to see the next five records is going to be pitched in the rubbish bin where it belongs.

If you're faced with a complex query in a detached application, you have a couple of options. The first, and in most cases preferable, option is to optimize the query to within an inch of its life. Create temporary tables, de-normalize the data, do whatever you need to get the response time down to an acceptable level.

If this isn't possible, you might have no choice but to create a fat client by moving the data-handling components out to the client side. This architecture allows you to cache the query results on the client side, effectively reproducing an environment similar to a networked database (with a few complications, just to keep you on your toes).

However, as a general rule, fat clients are more appropriate on an intranet than the Internet, Microsoft's Web Services Architecture notwithstanding. Many people have a perfectly reasonable aversion to downloading code components, but this situation is less likely to arise in an application that's publicly available. If it does arise, you can only hope that your content is sufficiently valuable to overcome their resistance.

Database Schema Components

Once you've completed the conceptual data model and decided on the system architecture, you have most of the information you need to build the database schema. The database schema is a description of the data objects you will include in the database. If you've chosen anything other than a standalone data architecture, the database schema will also define where each object is to be deployed.

If you're implementing your system in Access, your database schema will include the definition of each table, query, and relationship. It will not include a description of the system's forms, reports, and code components, even though these are also stored in an .mdb file. If you're implementing the system in SQL Server, your database schema will include the definition of each table, view, stored procedure, and trigger in the database.

Defining Tables and Relationships

The definition of the physical tables in the database schema is derived directly from the conceptual data model. Entities become tables, and the table's fields are the entity's attributes. For the most part, this is a simple process of direct translation. The only areas that require special attention are constraints, relationships, and indices.

Constraints

As part of defining the conceptual data model, you defined constraints for entities, attributes and domains. Whether or not you implement these constraints in the database schema depends, as we've seen, on the choices you made about the system architecture. As I've said, some designers prefer to implement all constraints only at the Data Interface and Transaction Interface layers of the four-layer model, or the Business Services layer of the three-tiered model.

In most circumstances, I recommend that you implement constraints at both levels. Assuming that you agree with me and have decided to include constraints in the database itself, you will define them as part of the database schema. We discussed implementing data integrity in detail in Chapter 4, but it's worthwhile to review it here.

Most domain and attribute constraints will become field-level constraints in the database schema, usually as validation rules in Access. Access also supports the CHECK constraint clause used by SQL Server if you chose to create the database using SQL statements rather than DAO or the Access user interface.

Entity-level constraints usually become table constraints, again, either as validation rules or through the SQL CHECK constraint. You implement the entity integrity constraint, which specifies that each instance of an entity be uniquely identifiable, by defining a primary key for each table.

Whether you're implementing the database using SQL Server or the Jet database engine, you might find that some of the constraints defined in the conceptual data model can't be implemented as part of the table definition. In SQL Server, you might be able to enforce the constraint using a trigger. Since the Jet database engine doesn't support triggers, you'll need to implement these constraints as part of the application.

Relationships

We discussed the ways relationships between entities are modeled in a relational database in Chapter 3 and again in Chapter 13. The first step is always to include a unique identifier from the primary relation in the foreign relation. At the level of the database schema, this means that the primary key fields from the primary table will be included in the foreign table.

Some designers stop there, preferring to handle referential integrity only in the application rather than allow the database engine to do so. As with all database validation, in my own work I do both: I validate referential integrity in the application for usability and in the database engine for safety. I suppose if I were a man, I'd wear both a belt and suspenders.

We discussed previously the importance of indices for system performance. Every table should have at least one index, which the database engine will create automatically when you declare the primary key. In addition, you should create an index on any field or combination of fields that you will use to join tables. This usually isn't a problem for the table that represents the primary relation since the fields used for the join are the primary key. However, you might need to declare additional indices in the table representing the foreign relation if the field or fields used for the join don't make up the entire primary key in the foreign relation.

If the foreign key field or fields participate in the primary key but aren't the *whole* key, I define a separate index on the foreign key. For example, an OrderItems table usually has a primary key of {OrderID, ItemID}. Even though the primary key index could be used to join the table with the master Orders table in most circumstances (well, every circumstance I can think of), I would probably still create a separate index on OrderID just to be certain.

Any fields that will be used to sort the data should also be indexed. For example, customer lists are usually sorted by customer name and orders by date, even though neither of these fields usually participates in the primary key or forms part of a join. Indexing the fields will make the sorting process easier and more efficient.

It's possible to go overboard in creating indices, so be careful here. Remember that a small, but cumulative, amount of overhead is involved in maintaining each index. Any field that will be used for sorting the table frequently should be indexed, but you can always use the SQL ORDER BY clause to sort records without using an index.

The practical maximum number of indices per table really depends on how often the table is updated. (The overhead is incurred only when a record is added or the indexed field is updated.) For a table such as Orders that the system will update more or less constantly, I'd be careful about maintaining more than 10 or 15 indices, including those used to support joins and the primary key. You might be justified in using more indices on a Products table, on the other hand, which is typically updated infrequently but used in many ways throughout a system. As always, you must base the decision on how the data is to be used.

Views and Queries

Both Access and SQL Server provide a mechanism for storing SQL SELECT statements. These stored statements are called **views** in SQL Server and **queries** in Access. (I'll call them queries here, as that's the more common term.) In most cases, using a stored query will be faster than executing a SELECT statement on the fly; this isn't always the case, but the situations in which it isn't are so quirky that you can take this as a general rule.

You can begin deciding which queries to include in the database schema by examining the conceptual data model for complex entities. Remember that a complex entity is a single logical entity that is modeled by two or more tables for efficiency. You should include a query that de-normalizes any complex entities in your model. Most of these will be tables in a one-to-many relationship such as Orders and OrderItems, but you might also have complex entities that have been sub-classed with one-to-one relationships, and you should include queries to support them as well.

Users will frequently need to find particular records in the primary entities in the system—a specific customer or order, for example—and this is the second place to look for queries to be included in the database schema. All these common searches should be supported by a parameter query allowing users to specify the particular record to be found at runtime.

Sometimes you'll need to provide more than one "find" query for an entity. A user might need to find an Order by looking up the OrderDate, CustomerID, or OrderID, for example. Each of these should be supported by a separate parameter query.

On the other hand, users won't search through all tables. You might have a table in the database schema that contains a list of U.S. states. These lookup tables are extremely useful, but it's extremely unlikely that users will ever need to search for a specific state record.

You should also look for queries in the forms and reports implemented by the application. You'll need queries to link the fields and also to support lookups such as those used for combo boxes. If the system has form dependencies, you'll need a parameter query to support them as well. An example of this might be a dialog box that's called from an order entry form to display Customer details.

Based on the system's work processes, you will also want to include in your database schema queries (and perhaps stored procedures in SQL Server) that perform actions. If you know that the system will regularly archive orders or update product prices, it will be more efficient to support these activities with queries or stored procedures than to issue the commands on the fly.

Additional action queries will probably be added to the database schema during implementation. Unlike indices, essentially no overhead is involved in queries and stored procedures once they're implemented, so you need not hesitate about adding them to the database schema.

Remember that systems development is not a strictly linear process. While changes to the tables themselves during implementation can cause problems (and the further in the development process, the greater the problems), adding queries to the schema is trivial and to be expected.

Security

After you understand the system work processes and build the conceptual data model, you must consider the administrative requirements for the system. Administrative requirements don't necessarily impact the database schema directly, but they are nonetheless business rules that must be accommodated in the release system.

Administrative requirements are, in a sense, "meta-requirements," in that they concern the system *itself* rather than the problem space the system is modeling. They fall into two categories: security requirements, which determine who can access the system; and availability requirements, which determine such things as how often the system must be online (24 hours a day seven days a week, or normal working hours, for example) and how users will back up data. Since availability is almost exclusively an implementation issue, we'll discuss only security here.

The implementation of a security scheme can be a complex business. Fortunately, the processes are well documented for Access and the Jet database engine and for SQL Server. Even more fortunately, database design is distinct from implementation, so you need only consider the logical security arrangements during this phase of the process, and at a logical level the principles are simple.

Security Levels

You must first decide the level of security required. Note that we're talking about securing the *data* here, not the system code, which is an implementation issue. At the lowest level of security is a completely unsecured system that allows everyone access to the database at any time. This is obviously easy to implement and administer, as you don't need to do anything in particular.

If your data has any value, however, implementing a completely unsecured system is reckless. It might make sense, however, if the client has implemented a network security scheme by which access can be restricted. There's no need to duplicate security precautions.

The next level is **share-level security**. At this level, you assign the whole database a password, and anyone knowing the password has full access to the system. This is also easy to implement and administer, requiring only that the password be changed periodically. Share-level security is adequate in many situations.

User-level security, although it requires more effort to implement and administer, provides the most discrete control over the database. User-level security allows the system administrator to assign specific privileges for each object to individual users: "Joe can add and edit information in the Customers entity but can only view Orders. Mary can add and edit information in the Customers and Orders entities. Neither Joe nor Mary can delete records of either type."

Actually, to call this "user-level" security is somewhat misleading. Security privileges *can* be assigned to individual users, but they can also be assigned to generic user roles to which individuals are assigned. This is a more effective mechanism for implementing security, as it requires far less administration.

Using this model, you first identify the types of users—system administrators, order-entry clerks, salespeople, and so forth—and then determine the security privileges each role has for each object in the system. It's not necessary to assign privileges for the data objects; in fact, it's not a good idea to do so. You might decide that salespeople need to be able to add, edit, and delete records in the Customers table, but you don't want them messing about with the table itself. You can make a Customer maintenance form available to them, but not the table. This ensures that they can't inadvertently bypass the special processing provided by the maintenance form.

Often you need to allow people to view only a portion of the data. For example, you might allow everyone to view the Name and Extension fields of the Employee table but allow only managers to view the Salary field. Or you might allow salespeople to see the Orders placed by their own clients but not anyone else's. To accommodate both these situations, you can assign privileges to queries and deny access to the underlying tables.

Auditing

In addition to controlling who has access to the data, perhaps you also need to know what users have done. These requirements can vary widely. Some organizations want to track who logged on to the system and when. Others require a detailed audit trail of who made what changes. Others require something in between.

How you model your auditing requirements depends on the exact requirements. If you simply need to track who used the system, a single entity with the attributes UserName, LogOn, and LogOff will probably suffice. Simply create a record when a user logs on, and update it when he or she logs off.

Sometimes you also need to know who added a record. This can be accommodated in the primary entity with one or two additional attributes: CreatedBy and perhaps CreatedOn.

Tracking deletions can be more complex. In a relational database, you have a couple of options. You can prevent users from actually deleting records at all and set a Deleted flag instead, perhaps adding DeletedBy and DeletedOn attributes as well. This is a useful technique if you want to copy the records to an archive file before removing them from the database.

Alternatively, you can allow the deletions but write the necessary information to a log file, in the same way that you would if you needed to track the users who logged on. Of course, you'll probably have to create additional attributes. There's not much point, after all, in knowing that someone deleted a record unless you have some way of reconstructing what the record *was*.

If you need to know in detail which changes were made, you'll need to use one of the techniques we discussed in Chapter 8 for tracking changes to dimensional records.

If you're going to implement any of these auditing features using a Jet database, you'll have to prohibit users from direct access to the tables, since that would allow them to bypass your security measures. SQL Server doesn't require this, since it supports database triggers, which cannot be overridden.

However you model the auditing requirements, you must also consider how this information will be used, by whom, and under what circumstances. Obviously, you need to restrict access to the audit tables. You might also need to add work processes to your system design to accommodate the auditing. Do the system administrators need to be able to reverse changes made? Are usage reports necessary?

In my experience, most auditing requirements are simply a form of insurance, and the information is intended to be used only in exceptional circumstances. If this is the case, you might not need to expand the work processes at all. The system administrators can easily use Access interactively or use the SQL Server Enterprise Manager to manually interrogate the data and perform any actions required.

Summary

In this chapter, we've looked at translating the conceptual data model into a physical database schema. We began by examining two architectures for structuring the code in your system—the three-tiered model and the four-layer model—primarily from the perspective of how the choice of code architecture can impact the database schema.

We've also examined several possible data architectures. A single-tier system locates both the application and the data on the same logical machine. A single-tier application can run as a standalone application, or the data can reside on a network but be accessible only to a single user. Networked applications implemented using the Jet database engine are also logically single-tier, but the data may be accessed by multiple concurrent users.

You can implement two-tiered, or client/server, applications using SQL Server. In this logical architecture, the server machine performs the data manipulation, while the client is responsible for responding to the user. The basic principles of two-tier applications can be elaborated to three or more machines in what is known as an n-tiered application.

We then turned to the translation of the conceptual data model into a database schema. This is usually a straightforward process, as the only new information is the definition of indices and queries to be implemented in the database. Finally, we looked at the impact that security requirements can have on the database schema, and we briefly reviewed the design of a security scheme at the logical level.

In the next chapter, we'll take a quick look at some of the issues involved in communicating your system design to the client and the development team.

Communicating the Design

Unless you're building a database system for your own use, you need to be able to communicate the results to other people. Please note that I just said "communicate." I didn't say "document." Yes, you'll be creating at least one document as part of communicating the design, but I've seen far too many analysts produce "system design documents" that consist of data dictionaries, screen shots and report layouts, with nothing to explain how these bits fit together.

All the documentation in the world isn't going to accomplish anything if it's obscure and unreadable. You can't learn a language by reading a dictionary, and you can't understand a project by reading tables of data.

Now, a word from my soapbox: Basic written communication skills are critical to this task, so if you have any doubts about your abilities, get a good book (some of my favorites are listed in the Bibliography) or sign up for a course at a local community college. I *promise* it will be time well spent. If your grasp of English grammar is faulty, your clients are bound to wonder what else you haven't understood quite as well as you should have. (And here endeth the sermon.)

Audience and Purpose

Understanding your audience is important in any writing, but particularly so in communicating a system design, since you're likely to have several types of readers with different requirements.

You need to consider what you and your readers are trying to achieve. Your clients primarily need to confirm that you've understood their requirements and secondarily want to gain some assurance that the system will achieve their goals. Your clients don't need (or want) to understand the details of how the system is to be implemented. But if the document is going to be used as the basis for development, the development team needs to see exactly those gory details that will make the client's eyes cross.

Sometimes the best solution is to prepare several documents: one for the client and a different one for the development team. This is a particularly good approach if you're using an iterative development model, since it closely matches the model. In these situations, I usually write multiple documents:

- A Requirements Specification, aimed primarily at the client, that documents my understanding of the system in (relatively) non-technical terms.
- An Architectural Specification, read by both the client and the development team but aimed primarily at the latter, that details the interactions and dependencies between components.
- A separate Technical Specification for each component, for use by the development team.

For simpler systems, a single document will usually suffice. Just be sure that you've considered the needs of each of your audiences and provided the information required by each in a format that they can easily understand.

Document Structure

Unless you're working in an organization that has specific documentation standards with which you must comply, the ultimate structure of your document depends on its scope and your own taste. It can be as simple or as complex as you think is appropriate; there is no standard format. I'll give you some guidelines in this chapter, but I'm doing so on the assumption that you'll adapt them to your specific needs.

If you've followed the recommendations I've made regarding the system analysis, you'll find that the document easily falls into several well-defined sections that (not entirely accidentally) coincide with the previous chapters in Part III. You'll probably also want to include an Introduction or Executive Summary aimed at management.

Executive Summary

In large organizations, a steering committee often oversees development projects. Even with small projects, usually someone in a management position who isn't directly involved in the implementation of the project has oversight or budget responsibilities. If someone is overseeing your project, it's a good idea to include an Executive Summary aimed directly at that person.

These individuals are generally not terribly interested in the details of the system. They have a few specific questions they want answered, and the more efficiently you answer them, the better. Management is usually looking for answers to questions like the following:

- What problems does the proposed system address?
- Is this the best and most cost-effective solution?
- What other solutions have been considered?
- How long will it take to implement the system?
- How much will it cost?
- What are the risks?

Answering the first question should be simple if you've defined the system's goals and scope. You only need to re-state them here. I like to be as explicit as possible about listing anything that might have been considered for inclusion in the system but was rejected. I find that it's good insurance against finger-pointing later.

If you're an outside consultant, you might not be able to address the second and third questions regarding other solutions. If you do have access to this information, however, it's useful to include a brief description of other solutions that might have been considered and the reasons for their rejection. Management finds it reassuring to think that due consideration has been given to alternatives.

But do keep your answers to the second and third questions brief. If you've done an extensive evaluation of off-the-shelf applications and rejected them in favor of a custom solution, you'll probably have detailed information comparing cost, functionality, support, and so on. This isn't the place for it; put it in an appendix. As a matter of fact, the entire Executive Summary shouldn't be more than a few pages long.

Answering questions about time and cost can be tricky, and it's almost always scary. But answering these questions becomes more manageable if you consider what you're asking management to buy into. If you're developing a simple system, you probably have a good idea of the answers, based on the defined scope. With large, complex systems, you won't yet know how long or how much, but that's OK. You'll know what the next step is, and that's all you need approval for at this point.

If you can realistically say something like, "It is not yet possible to estimate the actual time or cost for full implementation, but we expect it to be in the range of x to y. The next phase, however, will require only z to complete, and will result in…", then you should be fine. Just be sure that whatever follows the "result in…" is tangible and intrinsically valuable to the organization. In my experience, people are very hesitant to commit funds to "additional research."

I've also found that adequately addressing the final question, regarding risks, is one of the most effective ways of establishing your credibility. Spend time thinking about what could go wrong. Are there technical issues that haven't been resolved? Are things likely to take longer than expected? Where? Why? Be paranoid.

Now go back and be realistic. How likely are these things to happen? Yes, it's *possible* that your entire development team will be incapacitated by an outbreak of the Bubonic plague, or that the office will be destroyed by a sudden flood. But it's not very likely. What *is* likely is that sometime during the project *something* will go wrong, and management will want to know that you've thought about likely issues and have contingency plans. You needn't list everything, perhaps only the top two or three concerns in a few paragraphs, but it is important that the risk issues be addressed.

If you're an outside consultant, I recommend that you not skirt the issue of your competence. Obviously, the first question anybody considering hiring you will ask is whether you can do the job. The Executive Summary probably isn't the best place to talk about your credentials, but you should address the risk of non-performance. The details of risk negotiation are up to you; I won't presume to make recommendations. It's just been my experience that directly addressing the issue helps establish your credibility as a businessperson.

System Overview

Whether you have included a formal Executive Summary or a less structured Introduction, the first section of the document proper is the System Overview. This is one section of the document where the needs of all sections of your audience are similar. Both the development team and the client need to understand the overall scope of the project. The difference is only one of detail.

If you haven't prepared a formal Executive Summary, some of the information that might otherwise have been in that section should be included in the System Overview. Even if you have prepared an Executive Summary, you might want to discuss some of the issues in greater detail. Alternatively, some issues—such as the comparison of alternative solutions or risk management—can be extensive enough to warrant separate sections.

Whether you include these topics or not, your main goal in this section is to establish the "big picture" of the system, which you should be able to accomplish by explaining the system parameters: the system's goal and scope, the design criteria, and perhaps an overview of the work processes.

There isn't a great deal to say about communicating the system goal and scope. If you've understood them, you simply write them up in terms your audience can understand. If you haven't understood them, you better go back and find out now.

Again, I recommend being as explicit as possible about areas that are *excluded* from the scope of the system, including those that might be implemented later. Anything considered for inclusion in the system should be listed here, even if you've decided to exclude the area from the system's scope. Spend some time identifying areas that you think *might* have been considered for inclusion but were never explicitly discussed. This is the time and place to make sure you and your client are operating under the same assumptions.

If you have prepared a cost-benefit analysis for the system, it should be included in this document but not necessarily in this section. It's a question of style, but I prefer not to embed pages and pages of tables in the main document. It makes for a much more readable document if you include only summary information—perhaps one or two tables—in the main document and put the rest in an appendix.

The same holds true for documenting goals and scope. You might have prepared a detailed analysis of functionality, cross-referenced by the goal it supports, and normalized by the importance of the goals. This is a wonderful tool and will be useful throughout the project. But if the table is more than one page long, it belongs in an appendix rather than in the main text. Just include a summary table with a textual description and refer the reader to the appropriate appendix for more details.

Work Processes

The best way to communicate system work processes depends on how you've captured them. If you've used an outline format, you can include that in the text. If you've prepared work process diagrams, you'll want to include them in the document as well. Just be sure to include an explanation of the symbols you're using. In either case, be sure to explain what you mean by the terms "process," "task," and "activity" (or whatever terms you're using).

No matter what form your work process description takes, include a narrative description of the work process. In the first place, preparing a narrative is a good double-check on the formal description. It's amazing how often you'll find minor errors this way.

In the second place, it's critical that people evaluate the work processes, and in my experience, outlines and diagrams tend to be glanced at rather than understood. By providing a graphic and a narrative version, you're encouraging people to understand, and the two forms of information will help clarify each other.

If you're proposing changes to the work processes, include both the current and the new versions and highlight any changes in the narrative. Obviously, you'll want to explain why the proposed changes will improve workflow or resolve problems. You'll often find that the client will point out something that was overlooked in your initial analysis if you include an explicit discussion of the changes you're proposing.

Documentation of work processes is one area in which the needs of your various audiences can conflict. The development team will be expecting a discussion couched in technical terms: transactions being committed and data items being updated. Clients, on the other hand, need the process to be described using whatever terms they use. These can, coincidentally, be the same as computer terms, but they probably won't be.

When in doubt, err on the side of the client. On practical grounds, it's likely to be far less a stretch for the development team to understand the client's terms than the other way around. If you must use technical terms, make sure that you've adequately defined them in the document.

Unfortunately, this is much easier to say than to do. When you work full-time with computers, it's easy to forget that some of these terms aren't really in common usage. I keep a checklist of words like "transaction" and even "file" and do a final review before submitting a document to a client. It's not difficult to do using the Find functionality of your word processor. Confused clients are rarely happy clients.

Conceptual Data Model

After completing the initial analysis of the system, you'll probably have a set of Entity Relationship (E/R) diagrams, a listing of domains used in the system, and some notes regarding data constraints. It's simple to get these organized into a presentable format. The entity analysis, perhaps illustrated by an appropriate E/R diagram for complex entities, is adequate documentation of the model. I usually treat the domain analysis as a kind of glossary in a separate section, referenced within the model proper.

This is one place where page after page of tables is probably inevitable. And there is no avoiding the fact that this is a fairly technical discussion, but it's one your clients can't avoid. All you can hope to do is make the process as painless as possible.

First, use the least technical terms you can, and use no more of them than you need to. "Table," "field," and "record" are probably unavoidable, for example, but "entity," "relation," and "attribute" are best avoided. I know that less technical terms are imprecise. But they are close enough. Also make sure to define any terms you use (preferably *without* giving your users a short course in database design).

In practice, this isn't much of a problem. Once you've explained that each table represents a "thing" and that the fields are the "bits of information" about that thing, your clients are usually ready to go. You might have an occasional query about zip codes being handled as character fields or some such, but I prefer to deal with such issues informally as they arise.

If the document is doing double duty as a technical specification, you'll need to include the technical details the development team requires. I try to keep these details separate from the main tables, usually as a subheading under each entity. It doesn't take long for the clients to realize that they don't need to understand "this stuff." In these situations, I usually tell my clients that they need to review the attribute list for completeness and the domain analysis for accuracy, but they can ignore the rest.

In theory, the client should review the relationships among entities as well, but in practice I've rarely had clients catch any errors or misunderstandings in this area, and then only when I reviewed the model with them face to face. It's all just a little too foreign.

You'll have better luck asking users to review field sizes and data types. But even here, if you have serious concerns, it's safer to schedule a review meeting with the appropriate people.

I personally find this extraordinarily tedious—hours of "Now, is 25 characters long enough for a Surname, do you think?" is hardly my idea of a good time—but it's critical that these things be correct, so it might be unavoidable.

Alternatively, you might highlight the items you're concerned about. People's attention tends to wander when they're presented with 50 pages of tables to review, so if you highlight the items you need confirmed, you're likely to get better results.

Database Schema

The information in the database schema is critical to the development team, but since it contains little additional information, it's largely irrelevant to the client. If you're not preparing separate documents, consider putting the table and query specifications in an appendix. The data architecture and security specifications, however, need to be confirmed by the client.

Dimensional databases can be an exception to this "developer-only" principle, however. As we saw in Part II, the data models for dimensional databases depend on the production databases from which they derive their data. Clients may very well want to confirm the data sources, and will certainly need to see a discussion of how the data will be derived, and the impact of implementing the dimensional database on the production system(s).

Whatever type of system being implemented, I usually document the data architecture using a combination of diagrams and a narrative description. This is another case of the two forms of communication reinforcing each other. The security requirements can be documented by a simple narrative description, but sometimes an outline or graphic can be useful if the security structure is complex.

User Interface

It's a good idea to prepare a draft user interface document to discuss with the client before you go too far into the user interface designs discussed in the remainder of this book. For small systems, however, a draft might unnecessarily delay the design process.

Even when you don't intend to perform a formal user interface design, it's often useful to dummy up some sample screens marked "DRAFT" or "SAMPLE." Sample screen layouts such as these can help users visualize the proposed system. You need to be careful, though. No matter how often you indicate that screen shots are only samples and subject to change in the release system, they inevitably set user expectations. If the released system looks *too* different, all your good intentions might have only muddied the waters.

Setting user expectations is usually a problem only if the functionality for which you've provided a sample screen gets dropped from the scope of the project later. I have had users expect all the screens shown in the initial requirements, even though they'd seen and approved a later interface specification that excluded them. In these situations, I've learned to include the dropped screens in a section called "Functionality No Longer Included" or words to that effect. A brief description of the functionality being excluded and the reasoning behind the decision are extra insurance that everyone knows where they are.

Once you have defined the user interface, you need to communicate it to the users. There are two primary mechanisms for doing this: a prototype and an interface specification. I almost always prepare both, if for no other reason than building a nonfunctional prototype is the easiest way for me to prepare the illustrations around which I structure the specification.

Interface Prototyping

The best tool I've found for communicating the interface for a new system is the interface prototype. Many users, particularly those without a lot of experience with computers, have trouble making the leap from seeing a set of screens on paper to imagining what the system will look like and how it will operate. Giving them an interface prototype means they don't have to make the leap.

Prototypes come in all shapes and sizes, and they can be used for any number of purposes. One of the simplest is just dummy screens and menus tied together to model the flow of the release system. The only code in an interface prototype is that required to link the screens together. All the controls are in place, but they are not tied to data or otherwise functional. Likewise, the only menu commands that do anything are those that display a dialog box. (Well, that's not quite true. I usually give the other menus secondary windows that say, "This command will do such and so. This functionality has not been implemented in the prototype.")

The only exception to the "no-code zone" rule is when the physical display is determined by the data. For example, say you've designed a screen for entering and editing customer details, but the screen details depend on whether the customer is an individual or a company. You might decide to have the visibility of controls dependent on the choice a user makes in an option box. You'll need to implement this in the prototype.

I usually build the interface prototype using whatever front-end tool I expect to use in the final system. Because I work in several different development environments, this technique eliminates the "ah, hell, I forgot that you can't do multi-column combo boxes in VB" syndrome.

But using the development environment is dangerous. You're building a prototype here, not a system, and so it's appropriate to take all kinds of shortcuts that would never be acceptable in production code. But it's hard to resist the temptation to use the prototype as the basis for the release system.

After all, all those screens and menus are already built, and it's a waste of time not to use them, right? Wrong. Those screens and menus are *prototyped*, not built. If you use the interface prototype as the basis for the release system, you run the risk of perpetuating the shortcuts you took, and they *will* come back to haunt you.

Because of this danger, some designers recommend that your interface design be done using a drawing tool rather than using a programming tool. Visio, for example, provides some limited support for designing interfaces.

You should use whatever tool suits you best. For me, that means the programming tools I use every day. For you, it might be a drawing tool or even a presentation tool such as Microsoft PowerPoint. (I have one client who religiously takes screen shots of my prototypes and transfers them to PowerPoint for his internal presentations. He doesn't add anything to the screen, he just likes PowerPoint.) The important thing is to be clear about what you're doing—you're documenting a design, *not* building a system.

Interface Specification

Although an interface prototype is a wonderful tool for giving users a sense of how the system will operate, it has intentionally limited functionality. For this reason, it cannot replace an interface specification. (The reverse of this is not true, however. A careful interface specification *can* eliminate the need for a prototype.)

Like the documentation of the data model, the user interface specification must include technical information that can't be entirely avoided by the client. The same recommendations apply—keep the technical terminology to a minimum, and wherever possible separate any really technical stuff that can be conveniently ignored by the client from the main body of the document.

If you've built an interface prototype, preparing the interface specification is straightforward. I include a bitmap of each screen, a narrative description of its purpose and any processing it implements, and a table listing each control and the control's data source (if any). If you haven't built a prototype, you'll want to describe the layout in some other way, but the remaining information is the same.

In most systems, it's useful to include an overview of the system flow. If the system will support a number of distinct work processes, you might want to provide a model of the screen flow for each process. It's simple enough to do this by annotating the work process diagrams.

Change Management

Your design documentation will probably go through a couple of revisions before it stabilizes. Once it's reasonably stable, and certainly before you go to the next phase of the project, you'll want to place the document (or document set) under change control.

Note that "change control" is not the same as "freezing the specification," which I don't believe is realistic for even the smallest systems. If you plan for the inevitable changes, you'll make your life easier in the long run.

There are several ways to implement change control. I generally resist editing the documents; I've found it much easier to issue change sheets that function as additions to them instead. If the changes are extensive it might be easier to rewrite and replace either the whole document or sections of it, but this is an unusual occurrence.

If it's possible to establish a central location for the master specification, it might make sense to change or annotate the document. You can do this, for example, using the revision tools provided by a word processor such as Microsoft Word. The document could then be placed on a network share or perhaps published on an intranet.

The only problem I've found with putting the document in a central location is ensuring that people are working from the current version of the document and not from hard copies they've printed to scribble on. I confess, I've been guilty of this myself. Often.

Summary

In this chapter, I've given you some guidelines for communicating the system design to the client and the development team. You can consider them one designer's opinion. The strategies outlined here work for me, but more than in any other area I've discussed, you should adapt them to suit your own working methods and the needs of your clients.

Although this is the end of Part III, we have not yet finished our examination of the database design process. In Part IV, we'll turn to the most critical component of your application: the user interface.

Designing the User Interface

The Interface as Mediator

After you've completed the analysis tasks described in the previous section, you should have a good understanding of what the system you're designing needs to do. In Part IV, we'll look at some issues you need to consider when building the interface to the system.

We'll begin in this chapter by looking at general approaches to designing interfaces and the different models you'll want to think about. The amount of information I can provide here is, of necessity, limited. To refine your user interface design skills, you'll need to turn to other sources. Several excellent books are listed in the Bibliography, and a visit to your local technical bookstore will undoubtedly reveal others.

Effective Interfaces

In the minds of users, a system's user interface *is* the system; everything else is just stuff they're happy to ignore. The design of the user interface is therefore critical to the success or failure of a project. Get it right, and your users will forgive the occasional infelicity in implementation. Get it wrong, and it won't really matter how efficient your code is.

The irony here is that if you *do* get it right, hardly anyone will notice. Really elegant interfaces are invisible. Even if you get it wrong, no one may notice. The interfaces of many computer systems, particularly database systems, are so awkward that your system will be just one more of the mediocre, mildly abusive computer systems people have come to expect.

So if no one's going to notice, why bother? Well, why not? It is, after all, your job. At the risk of sounding like your mother, if you're going to design computer systems at all, doesn't it make sense to do it as well as you can?

Designing effective interfaces *does* require more work than simply slapping a front end on a database. Effective interfaces can also require more work to implement, although this isn't necessarily the case. But the payoffs can be huge, and they're not all of the "virtue is its own reward" variety.

An effective user interface minimizes the time users require to learn and implement the system. Once the system is implemented, productivity gains are higher if users don't have to struggle to bend it to their will. Chances are good that both of these issues were addressed in the project goals. They certainly impact the infamous bottom line.

Effective interfaces that closely match the users' expectations and work processes also minimize the need for external documentation, which is always expensive. And while users might not consciously notice how wonderful your user interface is, they'll certainly notice that your system seems to just work better than the one designed by UsersAreScum, Incorporated. That can affect *your* bottom line the next time a project or promotion comes up.

So, what constitutes an effective interface? To my mind, it's one that helps users accomplish their tasks and otherwise gets out of the way. An effective interface doesn't impose its requirements on users. It *never* forces users to play by its rules; it plays by the users' rules. An effective interface doesn't force users to learn a bunch of uninteresting stuff just to use it. And finally, it doesn't behave in unexpected ways.

We'll look at these three principles in this chapter, but first we'll take a brief look at a few models that are useful to consider when thinking about the design of user interfaces.

Interface Models

Alan Cooper, in his groundbreaking book *About Face: The Essentials of User Interface Design*, describes the way users think about systems (and the way systems think about users) in terms of three models: the mental model, the manifest model, and the implementation model. These three different ways of thinking about systems are useful tools for making decisions about the design of your application's user interface.

A user's **mental model** describes what the user *thinks* is happening. This doesn't often match what's really happening, but that's OK. For example, I have a vague notion that my body "burns" food to provide me energy in the same way that an automobile engine "burns" gasoline. I do know that the processes are really quite different, but I don't care. I have to put gasoline in my car to keep it running and food in my body to keep *it* running. My mental model is perfectly adequate to get on with things.

The same is true of computer systems. Whether I'm using a typewriter or a word processor, if I hit a character key, a character appears. The mental model is the same. What's actually happening, of course, is quite different. What *actually* happens is the **implementation model**. All that behind-the-scenes stuff about pulling levers or running code is part of the implementation. Users don't care, and shouldn't be forced to.

The user interface is the **manifest model** that sits between a user's mental model and the developer's implementation model. It is, if you will, the model of the process that the system reveals (manifests) to the user. Your goal in designing an interface is to hide as many details of the implementation model as possible. The ideal system interface exactly matches the users' mental model. It won't often be possible to match the mental model of the process exactly. But the closer you can get, the better.

If you're interested enough in computers to be reading this book, your mental model won't match the users' mental model. My mental model of using a word processor is that I hit a character key and a Unicode value is stored in RAM somewhere. This isn't very close to the implementation model, but it doesn't resemble what the average clerical worker thinks is happening, either.

This is the great danger of designing interfaces: Even if you aren't directly involved in the implementation, you almost certainly will know something about it. You have to either develop a knack for temporarily forgetting the implementation details or ask a user guinea pig to provide you with his mental model.

The best practice is to conduct formal usability tests using a prototype of the system. Although this is rarely possible, any kind of usability research is worthwhile. If you've built a prototype, find a few users and have them play with it. Ask them what they think is going on. You'll get some surprises. If you haven't built a prototype, you can ask about a similar system or even use a paper mock-up. I haven't had a lot of success with this last technique, however. I've found that users get confused between an interactive screen and a report when both are presented on paper.

When you've gathered as much information as you can, think about where the implementation model (what's really going on) is intruding on the users' mental model, and then resolve those areas. Are you using the wrong terminology? *Always* use the words the users use. Are you forcing users to think about "editing records" when what they want to think about is "changing addresses"? This could be a terminology problem, or it could be a problem in the system structure. (We'll look at those in the next chapter.)

User Levels

I can't imagine that anyone ever intentionally set out to build a system that wasn't "user-friendly." Perhaps usability wasn't a high priority, but no one would set out to build a system that's user-antagonistic. The problem is that "user-friendly" is one of those nice, well-intentioned expressions that doesn't mean much, so you're left scrambling around to find ad hoc definitions.

Two definitions of user-friendly that are often mooted are "easy to learn" and "easy to use." If we put aside for the moment the question of what, exactly, "easy" means, we still have to ask ourselves, "Easy for whom?" The system that's easy for a beginner to learn is not necessarily easy for an expert to use. Your best approach is to consider the needs of each level of user and accommodate each with different facets of the interface.

Beginner

Everyone is a beginner at some point. Very few people remain that way—they will either pass through the "newbie" stage to intermediacy, or they'll discard your system entirely in favor of someone else's. For this reason, you must be careful not to build in support for beginners that will get in the way of more advanced users.

Beginners need to know *what* your system does before they start to learn *how* to use it. The best way to present this information is outside the main system itself. For simple systems, an introductory dialog box that describes the system can be sufficient. (Just be sure you always include a means of dismissing the dialog box permanently.) For more complex systems, a guided tour might be more appropriate.

Online help isn't a good option for beginners. They might not know it exists or, if they do, how to use it. I have had some success using an online user's guide, however, by including a link to it from both the introductory dialog box and from the Help menu. To be successful with beginners, these guides must be task-oriented. Beginners don't want to know what "menu item" means; they want to know how to create an invoice.

Intermediate

For most systems, the majority of users fall into the intermediate category. Intermediate users know what the system does, but they often forget the details of how. This is the group you must support directly in the user interface. Fortunately, the Microsoft Windows interface standards provide a lot of tools for helping these users.

A well-designed menu system is one of the best tools for reminding intermediate users of the system capabilities. A quick scan of the available menu items will immediately remind them of the functions available and at the same time that it allows them to initiate the appropriate task.

An excellent second level of support for intermediate users is online help. Unfortunately, writing online help is outside the scope of this book. In this context, however, I will mention that most intermediate users will use the index as their primary access mechanism. The index should therefore be as complete as you can possibly make it.

Expert

Expert users know what to do and how to do it. They're primarily interested in doing things *quickly*. The more shortcuts you can build into your system, the happier you will make this group of users. In my experience, expert users tend to be keyboard-oriented, so make sure that you provide a way to move around the system using the keyboard if you're catering to this group.

Expert users also appreciate the ability to customize their working environment. Providing this functionality can be an expensive exercise, however, so you will want to carefully evaluate the benefit before including it. If you do decide to include some level of interface customization, even if it's only a matter of arranging windows on the screen, be certain to maintain the changes between sessions. Nothing is as irritating as having to rearrange everything every time you load a program.

Putting Users in Charge

Just behind "user-friendly" in the nice-but-useless terminology stakes is the expression "user-centered." What does that mean? Well, unlike "user-friendly," it does have a meaning, albeit a rather vague one. A system is user-centered if it *always* responds to the users' requests and *never* imposes a specific method of working.

This principle is perhaps easiest to understand by way of an example. An acquaintance of mine, a developer for whom I have a great deal of respect, described his method to ensure that users enter data in the order most convenient for the system. He locks all the controls on the form except for the first one; once data is entered in that control, he unlocks the second, and then the third, and so forth.

Not only is this technique as far from user-centered as one can get, it's not going to work in the long run. Actually, I'm surprised it ever worked in the short run. Users often have good reasons for not entering data in a specific order. It might be unavailable, or simply inconvenient to enter at the moment.

If you force them to enter something, they will. They'll enter any old garbage that the system will accept. So by forcing an entry, you've offended them, imposed on them, and ultimately accomplished nothing. We'll look at this issue in some detail in Chapter 19, when we discuss data integrity.

Artificially enforcing data integrity is the primary way database systems try to wrestle control from users. The second way is by being obsessively modal. A **mode** is a system condition that limits users' interactions. The classic modes in database systems are add, edit, and view. A system that requires users to return to a main menu before editing the record they've just been looking at is ridiculously inefficient. Requiring them to choose a menu item or click a button before editing is not much better.

Unfortunately, many designers implement this kind of modality as a matter of course. Perhaps in a mistaken attempt to protect users from accidental changes or because the use of Add, Edit, and View menu items was conventional 20 years ago, they perpetuate the paradigm in the Windows environment, where it is inappropriate. I *strongly* recommend that you assume the users know what they're doing. (I realize this is a shocking proposition, but trust me. More importantly, trust *them*.) If a user wants want to change a record, let her. Nobody should be forced to ask permission to do her job.

Of course, if you're going to allow users this much freedom, you must give them safety nets. Multiple levels of undo are easy to implement. You might even want to include a "Revert to Last Saved" menu option to allow a user to discard all changes to the current record.

Applying the same theory, I don't like asking users to confirm changes before saving a record, although in some situations it might be justified. The whole idea of "saving" is foreign to most users. Remember the users' mental model. They've just made a change, and now you're asking them if they want to make the change, which is very confusing.

Confirmation messages of this type are another instance of imposing on users without accomplishing much. Once they sort out what this whole "saving" thing means, most people just get in the habit of choosing "OK" every time the confirmation dialog box appears anyway, so the dialog box doesn't do much good.

In the few instances when I have implemented confirmation messages (usually at the insistence of the client), I've provided a mechanism for turning them off (generally in the Properties dialog box).

However, some extensive changes can't be undone, or at least not easily. Accidentally changing a field on a record can be easily fixed. Accidentally deleting all the records in a table can't. If you allow users to do things that you consider really dangerous, the best option is to provide a method for undoing the action. If that's not feasible, then by all means get them to confirm the action.

Just be sensible about how you define "really dangerous" and give your users useful information about the implications of their actions. The message box shown in Figure 15–1 will only scare them.

The message box shown in Figure 15–2 is much better. Not great, perhaps, but better. Not only does it explain the situation in the users' terms, it also provides them with options besides OK and Cancel (which the average user interprets as "I am an idiot" and "I am an idiot. I offer my most humble apologies," respectively.)

Figure 15–1 This Is a Spectacularly Unhelpful Message Box

Figure 15–2 This Message Box Explains the Implications of a User's Actions and Gives Her Several Options

Minimizing the Memory Load

People aren't particularly good at remembering things, which is one of the reasons we use computers in the first place. It follows that a good user interface doesn't make users remember any more than is absolutely necessary. Obviously they're going to have to learn (and remember) what your system does. And they'll need to remember some things about how to use it. But you should minimize the amount of information users need to remember wherever possible.

One approach is to comply with Windows interface standards and conventions. The *Windows Interface Guidelines for Software Design* gives one a set of conventions. You will rarely have a reason to change them and shouldn't do so arbitrarily. The Microsoft Office products—in particular, Microsoft Access—set other de facto standards. If you vary from the standards, make sure you have a good reason. Otherwise, you probably aren't doing your users any favors.

You might think that your navigation widgets are *much* cooler than the default video buttons provided in Access. But pity the poor users. They've learned to press the "Play" button to move to a new record. Now you're making them remember that in *your* program they must click on that incredibly cute photograph of your cat having kittens.

Of course, the Windows interface guidelines only go so far, and they don't cover all situations. But in most cases, you'll be able to extend the general guidelines to cover the specific situation you address. Where you do have to make decisions, stick to them. We'll talk about the importance of consistency in the next section.

It should be obvious that if you're trying to reduce the amount of information users have to remember, you should never make them enter the same information twice. We've talked about the use of default values in this situation. You'll also want to make sure that you carry forward any relevant information if users must work through a series of forms.

Furthermore, users should never be asked to enter information that could reasonably be selected from a list. Computers are notoriously picky, and users shouldn't have to worry about whether John Doe's Customer record was entered as "John Doe", "J. Doe", or "J.C. Doe". But note that I said "reasonably." Asking a user to wait while the system fills a combo box with 65,000 records is not reasonable. What is reasonable is providing them with a means of filtering the list and then picking from a manageable subset.

When you do present lists to users, include as much additional information as possible, particularly if the list items are not necessarily unique.

Users shouldn't have to remember that "John Smith" is the one who lives in Madrid, while "Johnny Smith" lives in Milan. Microsoft Access list boxes and combo boxes allow you to show multiple columns of data. In Visual Basic, you can concatenate the relevant fields.

In both environments, consider displaying subsidiary information by means of a context menu. Technically, the display should be by way of a command, such as "Details", on the context menu. (Note that there is no ellipsis following the menu item, even though it displays a dialog box. Including an ellipsis is a common error.) However, if the details are short, you might want to display them directly in the context menu. This saves users a little time.

Finally, users should never be forced to remember obscure coding schemes. You might be using a system-generated number to ensure uniqueness of a record, but in most cases users should be unaware of its existence. Unless the number has some objective use, like an invoice number, don't even display it.

Many organizations have developed lists of abbreviations representing things like product categories or sales regions. The rule I use to decide whether or not to use these abbreviations in the system is whether they're used in casual conversation. You want to avoid a situation where people *talk* about "the Southwest region" but have to enter "SWR". Only if they use "SWR" in conversation should it be used by the system. Even then, I would probably allow entry of both "SWR" and "Southwest" in the region field.

Being Consistent

Consistency in a user interface means more than just getting the File and Edit menus in the right place. The way your system interacts with users should also be consistent. When designing database systems, you need to pay attention to three areas: how users move through records in a table, how complex entities are represented, and how users initiate editing and adding records.

Most systems have a series of forms that represent each of the major entities in the system. You might, for instance, have a Customers form, a Products form, and a Sales Orders form. You must decide how users will move through the underlying recordsets. Unless you have a strong reason for using different mechanisms, you should choose one method and use it in every form.

By default, bound forms in both Access and Visual Basic display the first record in the underlying recordset and contain navigation buttons that allow users to move through the recordset. For various reasons, you might want to change this default interface. You might, for example, want to display only a single record and provide some other mechanism for choosing records to be displayed—perhaps a separate search form or a combo box control from which users can choose a record. Figure 15–3 shows an example of the latter technique, taken from the Access Developer Solutions sample database.

Changing the default navigation mechanism is fine—in fact, there are often good reasons for doing so—but having chosen one, you should use it for all the forms in your system. It's unnecessary and confusing for users to have standard navigation buttons on the Customers form, a Find Order button on the Sales Order form, and a Products form presented in datasheet view.

The exception to this rule is if you have several categories of forms. For example, you might decide to handle the forms used to maintain lookup tables differently than those used for entering primary entities. In this case, as long as the interface is consistent within the category, you're not placing an undue burden on users.

The second area where you need to be consistent is in representing complex entities. If you have entities that are modeled using more than one table in a one-to-many relationship (Sales Order entities are the classic example), you should be consistent in how you present them to users. You wouldn't want to present the line items of a sales order in a datasheet and the multiple contacts for a customer in a list box.

Figure 15–3 A Combo Box Can Sometimes Be a Useful Mechanism for Users to Choose a Client, but You Must Use It Consistently

Unfortunately, consistency in this area is more difficult to maintain, particularly if there are more than two recordsets involved. A single form that has one datasheet for customer contacts, a second for addresses, and a third for products ordered can get ugly. You need to be inventive in these situations. Perhaps you can embed each datasheet in a tab control or use pop-up forms containing the datasheets. You might have to decide on *two* display methods and keep them as consistent as possible.

The final area to watch for consistency is the mechanism for creating and editing records, which must be absolutely consistent throughout the system. If one form allows editing in place but another requires users to explicitly enter edit mode by clicking on an Edit button or choosing a menu item, you've got a real user-confuser on your hands. Of course, edit modes aren't a good idea in general, as we've seen.

Sometimes, there are good reasons for locking records—that is, for not allowing editing in place—once they're saved. For example, you might allow users to change orders only prior to their shipment, after which time they become historical records that shouldn't change. Some designers implement a mechanism to check whether the order has been shipped when a user asks to edit it. Doing this is acceptable (barely) only if *all* forms behave this way.

A better solution is to allow editing in place but to lock all the fields on the form when a shipped order is displayed. This requires more work to implement, but it's work done by the system, not by the users, so it doesn't count. And it allows editing in place to be implemented in the rest of the system, where the locking of historical records doesn't apply.

Summary

In this chapter, we've looked at some of the underlying principles in designing user interfaces. We began with a look at three interface models: the users' mental model of the system (what they *think* is going on), the system's implementation model (what's *really* going on), and the manifest model (what the system *shows* users about what's going on).

We then looked at three categories of users: beginner, intermediate, and expert. We briefly discussed the special requirements of each category and how those requirements might be best met by the system's user interface. Finally, we examined the three cardinal rules for user interface design: putting users in charge, minimizing the memory load, and being consistent.

In the next chapter, we'll turn to the overall system architecture and look at more tangible issues in user interface design.

User Interface Architectures

When you set out to design the user interface for your system, the first decision you must make is how to structure the overall system interface—the **user interface architecture**. In this chapter, we'll discuss several more-or-less standard architectures that are described in *The Windows Interface Guidelines for Software Design* and implemented in popular software.

You can invent your own user interface architecture, but as always when you're wandering away from existing standards, you should have a good reason for doing so. Remember that consistency, not just within applications but also between them, makes life easier for users.

Supporting the Work Processes

The most important principle in deciding how to structure the interface is that the choice must be based on the work processes your system supports, *not* on the structure of the data. Pay attention to what your users are trying to accomplish, and structure the system to support those activities.

It's an easy mistake to make: You look at the Entity-Relationship (E/R) diagram for the system and see an entity called "Customers," so you build a Customers form for creating and editing customer records. Then you build an Orders form that has a read-only reference to the Customers table. In an effort to make the system "user-friendly," you allow users to choose the customer name from a list, and you fill in the rest of the fields for them based on the information in the Customers table. Your form might look like the one shown in Figure 16–1, taken from the Northwind sample database.

This isn't a bad form, as forms go, but think about the users' task: they're entering a sales order. What if they open the Orders form only to discover that the customer isn't yet known to the system? They have to leave this form,

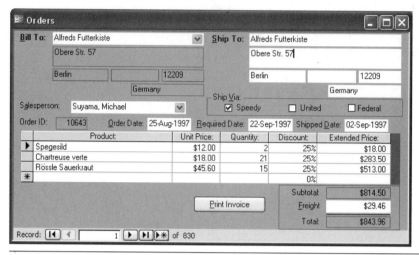

Figure 16–1 The Orders Form from the Northwind Sample Database

go someplace else in the system and enter the new customer, re-open the Orders form and then *finally* they get to enter the order. If the Orders form hasn't been closed, they'll probably need to remember to press Shift+F9 (or something equally self-evident) to refresh the Customers list. Painful.

Some designers address this problem by using the NotInList event of a ComboBox to allow users to enter a new name. When the event is triggered, these designers display a message box asking whether to add a new customer, and if a user confirms the addition, the Customers form opens.

This solution saves a few keystrokes, but it still forces users to stop what they're doing (entering a sales order) and do something else (maintain the customer list). It would be far better to allow users to complete the task at hand without interruption. If a user enters a customer name that's not in the list, the fields that would otherwise have been filled in will be blank. (This is sufficient notice that the customer is new, by the way; there's no reason to scare people by beeping at them and displaying unnecessary message boxes.) After a user has filled in the fields, the system can quietly add the new customer record in the background.

If all the fields in the customer record can be obtained from the Orders form, you're done. If additional fields exist (as is often the case), you *might* decide to ask users whether they'd like to add that information after they finish filling in the sales order. (But be sure not to ask until the order is finished—it's rude to interrupt.) You should base your decision on the circumstances under which the order is being entered—in other words, on the work processes.

If the order is being entered by a sales clerk with the new customer standing in front of her, after the order is taken is an excellent time to capture that information. "Since you're a new customer, would you mind providing some additional information...?" In the same way, if the additional customer information (or at least some of it) is on the Orders form being used for data input, allowing users to easily enter the information while it's in front of them will save them from digging the papers out later.

But if users have a stack of sales orders to enter and the additional customer information *isn't* immediately available to them, they're going to dismiss the dialog most of the time without entering the additional information. Constantly prompting users to enter information they don't have isn't helpful, it's harassment. A better approach would be to flag the incomplete records to allow users to easily find them later when the information *is* available.

You might want to ask users whether they want to go directly to Customers maintenance (or whatever it's called in your system) when they exit the Orders form. But do this *only* if finding and entering this information is a sensible next step for the individuals who enter the sales orders.

Document Architectures

User interface architectures can be divided into two groups based on whether the application displays only a single window—a **single document interface (SDI)**—or displays a primary window inside of which additional windows can be opened—a **multiple document interface (MDI)**.

Neither style of interface is intrinsically better than the other. They both have advantages and disadvantages that we'll discuss in this section. Your choice of user interface architecture should be based on the work processes the system will support.

Single Document Interfaces

The SDI, as you might expect, presents users with only a single primary window. It can display additional dialog boxes for supplementary information. The SDI approach is suited to systems that are intended to maintain a single logical entity (which might be represented by any number of physical tables in the database). For example, a simple system for maintaining employee information might best be presented using an SDI.

The SDI has much to recommend it, since a single window is so easy for users to manipulate and keep track of. It conforms to the document-centered approach to user interface design recommended by the user interface wizards at Microsoft.

SDI systems are simple to build in Microsoft Visual Basic. It isn't possible to directly implement them with Microsoft Access, since all forms are contained in the Access window. You can, however, achieve the effect of an SDI by maximizing the system's primary form on application startup and eliminating its minimize button. In Access 2000 and later, you can also specify that the form window be shown in the task bar. So with careful management, your Access system can be, for all intents and purposes, an SDI application.

Workbook Applications

A workbook interface architecture is a special kind of SDI. In a workbook, different views of data are shown on tabs of a single window rather than in separate windows. Microsoft Excel is a good example of a workbook.

This interface architecture has the advantage of providing a secure context for users without restricting them to a single form. It can, however, be mildly tricky to implement with acceptable response times. But provided performance concerns are adequately addressed during implementation, the workbook is an extremely useful paradigm for presenting different views of an object or for presenting views of a closely related set of objects when users don't need to compare them.

For example, you might want to use a workbook to display a summary report of the month's sales on one tab, a pie chart showing sales by category on another tab, and a bar chart displaying year-to-date sales on a third tab. These are related bits of information, and it's reasonable to expect that users would want to view the reports as a group. But they probably don't need to see all the reports simultaneously, since the different reports are related but not directly comparable.

The tabs in a workbook have an implicit order that can be useful. Say that you're supporting a work process that consists of a number of discrete tasks and, further, that these tasks are often, but not always, performed in a specific order. You might use a workbook tab for each task. The order of the tabs supports the order in which the tasks are performed without forcing users to comply with that order.

On the other hand, a workbook isn't generally a good method for representing separate work processes—which tend to be quite distinct activities—or for presenting information that needs to be directly compared.

Remember that only a single tab is visible at any given time, and you don't want to place an unfair burden on your users' short-term memories.

The Outlook-Style Interface

Another special kind of user interface architecture is what I think of as the "Outlook-style interface," since Microsoft Outlook is where I first saw it. This style of interface divides the application window into two panes, one containing a set of icons and the other containing documents, as shown in Figure 16–2.

I like this style of interface for applications that support multiple work processes. The icon bar on the left provides an immediate context for users, and dividing the bar into panels allows icons to be grouped into functional areas.

Unfortunately, neither Access nor Visual Basic provides intrinsic controls for implementing this style of interface, despite the fact that it's implemented in the Microsoft Access Database window, as shown in Figure 16–3. However, Outlook-style controls are available from third parties for both environments.

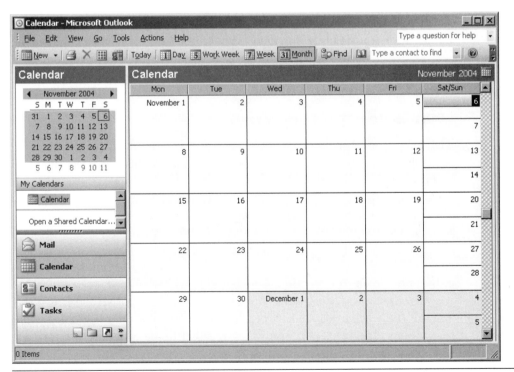

Figure 16–2 The Outlook Interface Divides the Application Window into Two Panes

Figure 16–3 The Database Window in Microsoft Access Uses an Outlook-Style Interface

If you do adopt this architecture, it's a good idea to allow users to hide the icon bar, as Outlook does. The icon bar is a good navigation mechanism, but once users have loaded the document they want to work with, they tend to stay there awhile, and the icon bar takes up scarce screen real estate.

Multiple Document Interfaces

The majority of database systems use some version of an MDI, allowing multiple child windows to be opened within the primary window. The child windows of an MDI application can contain different kinds of information, such as a form showing customers and a form showing orders. Or they can also show different views of the same information, such as a form with information about a customer and a report showing sales for that customer. Finally, they can show multiple instances of the same kind of information, such as one customer form showing details for Jones and another instance of the same form showing details for Smith.

As with SDI architectures, there are several ways of structuring MDI applications, each of which is suited to different requirements. We'll discuss the primary structures here, but be aware that these configurations are not exhaustive, nor are they necessarily mutually exclusive.

The "Classic" MDI Architecture

The classic structure for an MDI application is for a primary window to contain multiple child windows of either the same or differing types. MDI applications are useful in many situations where users need to compare several different bits of data or the same data in different formats. But MDI applications can be scary for new users: Choosing "New Whatever" from the File menu doesn't occur to a lot of people when they're presented with an apparently empty window.

The MDI versions of Microsoft Word (prior to Office 2000) allowed a command-line startup switch (/n) to automatically open a new document window on application startup, and you might consider doing something similar in your own application if you adopt this interface architecture. You might, for example, provide a switch that causes the Orders form to open for data entry.

Be sure to provide a mechanism for turning this functionality off, however, as it can be irritating to users for whom it's inappropriate. You also need to be careful during implementation that you aren't inadvertently displaying error messages to users who immediately close the window or, worse yet, adding empty records to the database.

The major problem with the MDI interface is the inconsistency in the containment model. The parent window visually contains the child windows opened within it, but the application it represents doesn't necessarily contain the objects represented in those windows. This tends to be a more acute problem in applications such as Microsoft Word, where the documents are actually distinct objects in the file system. Database applications usually do a far better job of isolating users from file system complexities. But even simple database applications are not completely effective in accomplishing this.

For example, look at Figure 16–4 from the Northwind sample database for Microsoft Access. Assume that a user has been switching back and forth between the windows and that uncommitted changes are pending in all of them.

If the user selects Save from the File menu, what's going to happen? Only the changes in the Suppliers window will be committed. *You* know that, because you know that menu options only apply to the current window. But does the user know that? Isn't it reasonable to expect that when you tell "Northwind" to save, "Northwind" will save all the changes you've made regardless of where you've made them?

Figure 16-4 The Containment Model in MDI Applications Can Confuse Users

The Windows Interface Guidelines for Software Design (woefully out of date, but still the best definition of the interface conventions) specifies that the item "Save All" can be added to the File menu to save all uncommitted changes in all open windows. This is undoubtedly a solution, but it's at best a compromise. It still requires that users understand that there's a difference between the MDI application and the objects on which it operates.

This difference is part of the implementation model, not the users' mental model, and it's a surprisingly difficult concept for users to understand. Even relatively sophisticated users can get confused about what's stored where. *I* still get confused about what formatting is stored with the document and what is stored with the style sheet in Microsoft Word, and I've been using the product extensively for many years.

All this having been said, however, classical MDI applications do have their place. They remain the best available solution for the majority of applications that require multiple windows to be open simultaneously.

Switchboard Interfaces

A switchboard application displays a central form on application startup, as shown in Figure 16–5, again from the Northwind sample database. Most of the buttons on the form are tied to either forms or reports.

The databases generated by the Microsoft Access New Database wizard use the switchboard structure, and so this structure has become quite common for database applications developed in that environment. It would be easy to implement similar behavior using Visual Basic.

I must admit to a prejudice against switchboards. Something about them feels DOS-like and clunky. I also worry that they encourage the "Find a Record/Edit a Record/Print a Record" menu structure that is so incredibly tedious for users.

Switchboard applications can be useful, however, if you have several distinct work processes that are being supported within the same application, and you either don't want to buy into the implementation complexity of the Outlook-style interface or your application requires multiple windows open simultaneously. A top-level switchboard that contains a button for each work process is an elegant mechanism for guiding users into the application.

The important thing to remember in designing switchboard applications, as with any other interface architecture, is to structure the switchboard choices around the work processes, not around the data. You should have a button for every activity users will want to perform, *not* for every form and report in the system.

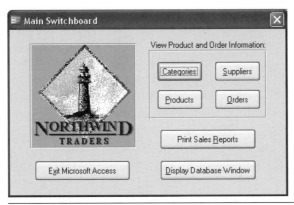

Figure 16–5 A Switchboard Is Displayed when the Application Starts

Project Interfaces

I think of a project interface as a switchboard application without a containing window. Instead, a "Project" window (which need not be called that, of course) provides a mechanism for opening windows independently on the desktop. The Visual Basic 6.0 SDI interface is a good example of a project interface, as shown in Figure 16–6.

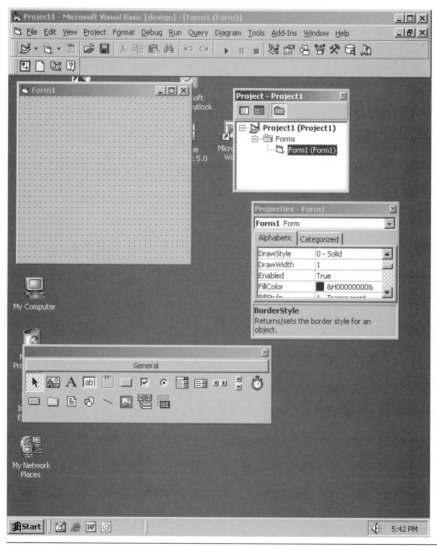

Figure 16–6 Visual Basic in SDI Mode Is a Project Interface

Once open, these independent windows are displayed in the taskbar and users can manage them independently. They are also controlled by the Project window. When the Project window is minimized or closed, the secondary windows are also affected.

The project interface, by eliminating containment, avoids the model inconsistency inherent in classic MDI applications, but it substitutes another inconsistency: the relationship between the Project window and the (apparently) independent secondary windows.

Consider this scenario: A user opens a secondary window by double-clicking in the Project window, and then to free up space on the desktop, minimizes the Project window. Poof, the window the user just opened has disappeared. Yes, it can always be restored from the taskbar, but what a user-confuser.

If you like the idea of a project window, I think that the model of the Database window in Access is preferable to a conventional project interface. The Database window provides the navigation advantages of a project window without the potentially frightening side effects, since it's part of a classic MDI application.

Wizards

The final form of interface architecture that has a role in database applications is the wizard. Wizards are made up of a series of pages displayed in a dialog box, as shown in Figure 16–7.

Wizards are most often used to support tasks that are performed infrequently, such as installation or hardware configuration. But it's certainly appropriate to use them to support infrequent work processes in database applications.

Wizards can also be useful to support complex work processes. If a work process consists of many distinct tasks that must (or at least can) be performed in a specific order, a wizard might be a good interface choice. Wizards are particularly useful if the work process has a lot of conditional tasks: "If condition a, perform task 3 and then task 4; if condition b, skip to task 6."

Using wizards for complex work processes is feasible, however, only if the individual tasks can be completed in the order in which the wizard presents them. This occurs less often than one might expect. If the tasks needn't be entered in a specific order, a wizard isn't the best interface, or at least shouldn't be the *only* interface for completing the task.

When using a wizard in a database application, you need to give careful consideration to how and when data entered by users should be stored. The usual model is that, if a user presses Cancel at any point during the process,

Figure 16–7 Microsoft Access 2000 Uses Wizards Extensively

the system is returned to the state it was in before the wizard was initiated—that is, any data the user might have entered is thrown away.

Depending on the application, you could consider either saving the data as each wizard page is completed or giving users the option of saving previously entered data when they cancel. I don't recommend either of these as a general rule, but if the wizard has a lot of data entry, it might be justified.

Alternatively, you might consider allowing users to temporarily halt a wizard and continue it later. This is a very usable solution, but it does add quite a bit of implementation complexity, since it requires a temporary data store, some mechanism for determining where a user stopped, and the ability to resume from that point.

Summary

In this chapter, we've looked at various ways you can structure the forms in your system. At the highest level, you have a choice between an SDI system that displays all its data in a single window and an MDI system that uses multiple windows.

SDI systems have two variations: workbooks and the Outlook-style interface, each of which has advantages in certain situations. More variety exists in MDI applications, from the classic MDI through the switchboard architecture supported by the Access Database Wizard applications, and including the project architecture exemplified by Visual Basic. Finally, wizards can be a useful architecture for supporting infrequent tasks and complex work processes.

In the next chapter, we'll turn from the organization of forms to the structure of the forms themselves, when we look at determining form layout based on the structure of the entities in the data model.

Representing Entities in Form Design

We've been concentrating so hard on work processes in the last few chapters that you might be wondering why you did all that data modeling. Never fear, in this chapter, we'll look at how to structure individual forms based on the way the entities displayed on them are represented in the data model. Your decisions about what data to include on any given form are based on work processes, but having made those decisions, the form layout and choice of controls will be determined by the actual data structures the forms represent.

The first decision you must make is how a form maps to the Entity Relationship (E/R) model. Does this form represent a single entity, two entities in a one-to-one relationship, two entities in a one-to-many relationship, or more than two entities? Each of these entity structures lends itself to certain kinds of form layouts, which we'll look at in this chapter. Of course, just like the architectures we explored in Chapter 16, these layouts are only general guidelines, not rules. These are the layouts that, in my experience, most naturally fit certain types of data structures.

Simple Entities

The easiest kind of entity to represent on a form is a simple entity that is represented by a single table in the database. If such an entity participates in any relationships, it is either on the many side or the table on the other side of the relationship will not be included on the form.

For example, look at the E/R diagram in Figure 17–1, representing the Customers entity and its relationships.

Somewhere in the application, you will probably have a form for maintaining customer information. This is true even if all the data is initially captured as a by-product of other activities. The Customers entity is on the

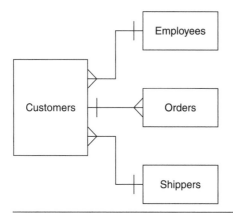

Figure 17–1 The E/R Diagram Shows the Entities that Are Related to Customers

many side of all the relationships shown in the diagram except for the relationship with the Orders entity, which you probably won't include on this Customers form anyway. Orders are logically distinct, and users would maintain them elsewhere in the system.

The Customers entity is therefore on the many side of all the entities that are included on the customer maintenance form. This means that only a single record will be included from any of the other tables, and so Customers can be treated as a simple entity.

This makes for a straightforward form layout. You don't need sub-forms or grid controls. Simply choose the control that best represents each field (we'll look at that issue in the next chapter), slap it down on the form, and you're finished.

Well, you won't *slap* it down; you'll arrange all the controls neatly, with a seven-unit margin and four units between each control, and with the most important items placed in the upper-left corner, right? But you get the idea. There's nothing tricky required unless you run out of space on the form.

But you might very well run out of space. Technically, you can add 754 controls during the lifetime of a Microsoft Access form or report (with deleted controls still counting toward the total) and have a maximum of 254 controls on a form in Microsoft Visual Basic (with control arrays counting as a single control).

Practically, you won't want users to have to deal with more than about 25 to 30 controls or control groups at one time. (Note that I said "controls or control groups"; a group box containing three or four radio buttons is perceived as a single control.) So what do you do if you have a simple entity with 75 attributes? You must show only part of the data at any one time.

The easiest way to structure a form that represents an entity with too many attributes to display comfortably is to break the fields down into groups or categories. I usually start by picking out the attributes that are used to firmly identify the entity. By this, I mean not just the candidate key attributes, but also whatever descriptive attributes users will need to be certain they're working with the correct instance.

In a Customers entity, for example, this group of identifying attributes probably includes the name and address details, and perhaps the Sales Representative attribute. For a Products entity, it might include the Product-Category, Name, and Description attributes. This group of attributes should be on the top of the form and always visible.

The remaining attributes are then divided into groups that are related and need to be viewed together. For a Customers entity, you might combine those attributes that represent sales terms—standard discount and payment terms, for example—into one group, and contact information—purchasing officer, sales manager, and so on—into another. For a Products entity, you might combine technical specifications in one group and packaging-related attributes in another.

Having organized the attributes into groups, you have a couple of options. You could use a tab control on the main form with each group on a separate tab. This is the solution I use most often. Tab controls provide the most context for users—they know immediately that additional information is available and what that information is. If you have more than five or six groups, however, a tab control is unworkable.

In this case, you might have to move some or all of the groups to subsidiary forms. Subsidiary forms are also useful if the individual groups contain more attributes than you can comfortably fit on one tab. You could allow users to open the subsidiary forms from command buttons on the main form, in a structure similar to a switchboard. With too many command buttons, however, your form will once again become unworkable. A better solution in this case would be to have the subsidiary forms available from a menu.

Be careful to maintain context for users when using subsidiary forms. Users should always be sure to which instance of the entity the displayed details pertain. The easiest way to identify the entity is by having the subsidiary form repeat details from the main screen. It's not usually necessary to repeat the entire identifying group—just enough of the group to tie the subsidiary form to the master form.

Alternatively, you could make the subsidiary forms modal. This is one of the few places where modality can be justified in a system, since it helps maintain users' context. However, modal forms always constrain users, which is something you should avoid doing wherever possible. I use this

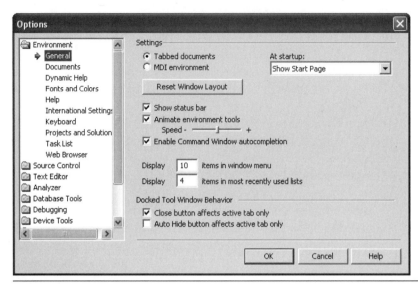

Figure 17–2 A Panel Structure from Visual Studio Provides a Good Alternative to Tabs

technique only as a last resort, when there absolutely isn't enough real estate to include the few attributes required to maintain context.

An alternative to subsidiary forms is a panel structure. It's then a fairly simple matter to provide the user with a mechanism for changing the display, either from a menu or (preferably) from a control on the main form. Figure 17–2 shows an example from Visual Studio that uses a TreeView to control the display.

One-to-One Relationships

In most cases, forms that present information from two entities that have a one-to-one relationship can be handled just like forms that represent simple entities. You create a query that combines the appropriate fields from the two tables, and then you treat it as a single simple entity. If you have more attributes than can be comfortably displayed on a single form, the same techniques as for simple entities apply.

If the primary entity participates in multiple one-to-one relationships, the nature of the relationships determines the most natural layout. If the relationships can coexist, you can treat them as one big recordset and show the information on a single form or on multiple forms, as we discussed doing for simple entities.

Many times, however, the relationships are mutually exclusive, as when any given Product can be either a Beverage or a Cheese, but not both. This is a good time to use multiple sub-forms or panels, providing you have enough real estate. You needn't worry about users understanding that more related information is available in a given context; there isn't any more information. In fact, using a tab control in this situation would be misleading.

If you have real estate problems, you'll need to use one of the techniques for grouping and displaying attributes that we talked about for simple entities. If the controls representing the attributes of the subclass are placed on a tab, it's best to try to find some generic term for the tab label. It can be confusing for users if a tab label (or command button label) changes as they move through the table.

For the same reason, if users are able to move through the primary recordset, I try to avoid having the controls displaying the attributes of the sub-classed entity on the first tab of the tab control. Since the controls for each subclass are different, the form display will jump as users step through the records. By keeping the sub-classed attributes off the first tab, you can keep the display stable and can incidentally provide some performance benefits by not recalculating the display unnecessarily.

One-to-Many Relationships

Many forms need to display entities that are linked in a one-to-many relationship. Determining the best layout for these forms is easy, as long as you remember that the form needs to display a one-to-many relationship, *not* a many-to-one relationship. When you're modeling complex relationships, it's often easier to think in terms of records rather than instances of entities. So in this case, you must be certain that the record on the one side controls the display of records on the many side, and not the other way around. Try to control the one-side record from the many-side record, and you'll tie yourself (and the system, and your users) in knots.

This sounds obvious, at least to me, but it's a fairly common mistake. I made a whole bunch of money years ago fixing all the many-to-one forms that had been designed by a woman with the title of "Senior Interface Designer" at a major Australian bank. It was the first time I gave any credence to the theory that "real programmers don't work for banks."

Having established that the record on the one side controls the form display, you need to decide how the records on the many side are to be displayed. You have two choices: You can display them all at once or one at a time.

Your choice is largely determined by the amount of detail users need to see for each many-side record. If you need to show only a few fields, you can usually display them all at once. The form shown in Figure 17–3, from the Northwind sample database, uses a sub-form to display four fields for each record on the many side.

The vertical scroll bar on the sub-form indicates that not all the records are visible at any one time. For design purposes, this still counts as "all at once." In the next chapter, we'll look at some other ways to display multiple records.

I like the "all at once" form layout because it provides the most context for users. You can always provide a mechanism for displaying additional details on a subsidiary form if you have real estate problems. But this style of layout isn't always appropriate or possible, and you might need to display the many-side records one at a time. Here, there are two issues you must address: making it clear to users that there are multiple records, and providing a mechanism for users to move between records.

The form in Figure 17–4 is identical to the one in Figure 17–3, except that the sub-form is shown in single record view rather than as a continuous form.

The "video button" record selectors at the bottom of the sub-form are the default record navigation mechanism provided by Microsoft Access. As a rule, I stick to defaults wherever possible, but look at the result here: Two record selectors are stacked on top of each other, with only their position to

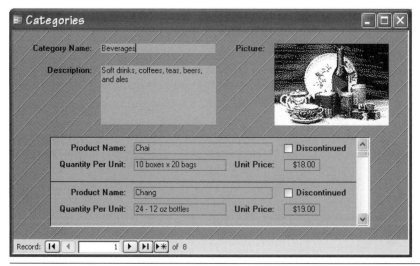

Figure 17–3 This Form Displays the Records on the Many Side of the Relationship Using a Sub-Form in Continuous View

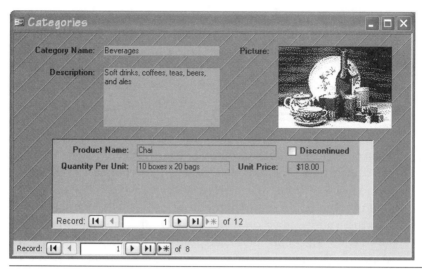

Figure 17–4 This Form Displays the Records on the Many Side of the Relationship One at a Time

indicate which record selector is for the recordset in the sub-form and which is for the primary recordset. This isn't the end of the world, but it's not an optimal solution.

You can sometimes remove the record selectors from the primary form. This could be feasible for the form in Figure 17–4 if you provided a good interface for finding product categories. Users aren't all that likely to page through a maintenance form such as this one anyway, and a good find facility would almost certainly meet their needs.

Alternatively, you could replace one of the record selectors with some other movement mechanism—command buttons or a custom scroll bar, for example. However, using a different technique for moving through records can be difficult to handle because you're introducing inconsistency into the interface. It can be done, though, if you're careful about choosing a paradigm and sticking with it.

For example, you could decide to use something like the Forward and Back toolbar buttons in Microsoft Internet Explorer to control movement between records on the one side, and use the video button record selectors for moving between records on the many side. This will work as long as you use this paradigm consistently within the application. Thus even forms that represent simple entities, and therefore don't have many-side records, should use the Forward and Back buttons.

Occasionally, a form will display a primary table that has multiple one-to-many relationships, and you will need to display more than one of the tables on the many side of the relationships.

If you take my advice, you'll avoid these situations wherever possible. Multiple many-side tables on a form can be messy to design and even messier to implement, but sometimes you have no choice. If you must display multiple one-to-many relationships on a single form, the easiest solution is to use a tab control to separate the many-side displays. This solution provides a clear context for users. It can also improve performance, since the records for the tab control only need to be loaded when the control is displayed.

What you should try most earnestly to avoid is having a whole bunch of multi-record controls simultaneously visible. They would be slow and ugly, and their appearance on a single form implies a relationship between the entities on the many side that probably doesn't exist. In Figure 17–5, for example, it's unclear whether the listed phone numbers pertain to the company or the contacts.

Figure 17–5 It's Unclear Whether Phone Numbers on This Form Are for the Company or the Contacts

Hierarchies

Any one-to-many relationship is technically a hierarchy, but the term is usually restricted to relationships consisting of three or more recordsets: a one-to-many-to-many relationship, if you will. Hierarchical relationships occur frequently in data models, but they don't often need to be represented in forms.

In Figure 17–6, for example, the Customers to Orders to Order Details relationship is a three-level hierarchy.

With this kind of structure, most applications would have a Customers form that, if it displays order information at all, shows it in a summary format. A separate Orders form would display the Orders and Order Details items. The Orders form would reference the Customers entity, of course, but would display the one-to-many relationship between Orders and Order Details only. Not many applications require a form that displays the details from all three tables.

However, it's difficult to know whether this tendency to avoid displaying hierarchical relationships is due to a lack of real need or to the difficulty of displaying them sensibly. Suppose, for example, that the client has requested the ability to review orders using the customer maintenance form. It would be easy to provide this functionality by displaying the records from the Orders table (the middle level) one at a time and the Order Details records all at once. Essentially, this would mean embedding the form shown in Figure 17–3 as a sub-form on the Customers maintenance form.

A one-at-a-time view of Orders records isn't really appropriate in these situations, however. Users are more likely to be asking, "How many orders has this customer placed?" or "What was their average order total?" than they are to be asking about specific products. Answering these common questions would be tedious if you represent the Orders records one at a time.

To avoid this problem, you might decide to display only summary order information on the Customers form and provide a mechanism for opening a subsidiary Orders form if users require more details. Unfortunately, this "summary with details" approach has some serious drawbacks as well.

Figure 17–6 This E/R Diagram Shows a Three-Level Hierarchy

If users want to review order details to determine what products the customer orders most often, they must endure the overhead of opening a second form. Since the subsidiary Orders form usually displays an order in single form view, it's also difficult to compare the products ordered on multiple occasions.

One option is to use a TreeView control. TreeView controls are wonderful tools, but they are limited in the amount of data they can show at each level of the hierarchy, since all the data must appear on a single line. This restriction would make a TreeView inappropriate for our example. Imagine trying to display all the customer details in a single line.

Microsoft Access 2000 introduced the sub-datasheet to support the presentation of hierarchical data in an outline-like format, as shown in Figure 17–7.

Sub-datasheets aren't very pretty, but they work. They can be nested up to eight levels deep, but you can nest only a single recordset at each level. You couldn't, for example, create a sub-datasheet that included both Addresses and Orders at the same level.

Visual Studio .NET supports a DataGrid control that provides similar functionality, but somewhat awkwardly—although it maintains the hierarchical

Figure 17–7 Microsoft Access 2000 Sub-Datasheets Display Hierarchical Data relationship between DataSets, it only displays one at a time. In our example, once the user displayed data from the Order table, the Customer data would disappear, and they would need to use a Back button to display it.

Many-to-Many Relationships

The final type of logical relationship that you might need to display in a form is the many-to-many relationship, which is represented by three or more tables in the database.

In the vast majority of cases, you can treat many-to-many relationships as though they were one-to-many relationships. For example, Figure 17–8 shows a many-to-many relationship between Customers and Products, with the Orders and Order Details tables acting as the junction tables.

It's reasonable to display all the products a customer has ordered (in which case, you would treat the Customers table as the one side of the relationship) or all the customers who have ordered a product (in which case, the Products table is the one side). You can use the same presentation techniques as for any other one-to-many form. You need only address where to include data from the junction tables and how to handle duplicates on the many side.

Most junction tables contain only the primary keys from each side of the many-to-many relationship. As we saw in Chapter 3 and as shown in Figure 17–8, however, the relationship itself sometimes has attributes that are modeled as part of the junction table. If you need to include these attributes in your form, they should be displayed with the many side.

In our example, if the form is to display the products for each customer (the Customers table being the one side), the order date—which is a field in

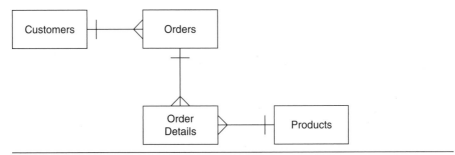

Figure 17–8 Customers and Products Have a Many-to-Many Relationship

the Orders table—is clearly part of the product information, not the customer information. "Customer X bought product Y on the 15th and product Z on the 18th..." The order date would be part of the customer information if the display were the other way around, with Products being the one side: "Product X was purchased by customer Y on the 15th and customer Z on the 18th...," as in this case the Customers table is treated as the many side.

It's quite likely that there will be duplicates, or at least partial duplicates, on the many side of the display. You must decide whether to display each item individually or to show summary information. For example, if you are listing the customers who purchased each product, you might choose to list the customer once for each product purchased; or you might just list each customer a single time, and show the total number of times the customer ordered the product and the total (and perhaps the average) quantity purchased.

You need to be careful here to avoid listing complete duplicates. It's of no use whatever to simply list a customer name 27 times if you're not providing any additional information, such as the order date. The only reason users might want to see this information is to determine the number of orders a customer placed, and the application should do this arithmetic, not the users.

Although treating a many-to-many relationship as a one-to-many relationship meets most requirements, there are times when you need to display the relationship fully. A product manager reviewing the customers who purchased a specific product might want to know what other products those customers purchased in order to develop "package deals," for example.

Fortunately, this type of analysis is most commonly performed against a dimensional database and, as we've seen, dimensional databases interface tools, such as Microsoft's Data Analyzer, are specifically designed to handle this situation. But the requirement is perfectly valid as part of an administrative function in a production database.

One relatively simple solution in this case is to treat the relationships as hierarchies and use sub-datasheets or DataGrid controls for display. The danger in this technique is that it isn't necessarily clear what the additional information represents. If you insert a sub-datasheet that lists only customer names into a product listing, for example, it might not be immediately clear whether these are the names of customers who purchased a product or suppliers who are the source of the product.

If you're concerned about the potential confusion of a hierarchical display, or if the client doesn't commonly require hierarchical information, it might be better to provide the information in a secondary window, where you can make its meaning clear. Using a secondary window also allows you to provide summary information in addition to or in place of the straight details.

A product manager looking at other products bought by a customer might prefer a list of products purchased by all customers who bought the primary product to be organized according to the percentage of overlap— for example, all the customers who bought a widget bought a gizmo, but only 10 percent of these customers bought a doohickey. You can, of course, provide some of this summary information on the main form, but since the calculation is fairly complex (and therefore time-consuming), you are better off displaying it on demand in the secondary window unless it is frequently needed.

The two techniques for displaying all the data in a many-to-many relationship are not mutually exclusive. You can provide a list of customers for each product in a hierarchical display on the main form, and you can also provide a "top ten customers" display in a secondary window that users view on demand. As always, you must base your decisions on how you anticipate the form will be used.

Summary

Having looked in Chapter 16 at how you can organize forms based on the tasks users perform, in this chapter we've examined how to structure the controls on the forms, based on the structure of the entities they display.

The choices you make in structuring your forms will be determined primarily by the entities that are to be represented on the form and—if more than one entity is represented—how the entities are related. Secondarily, the form's structure will be determined by the number of attributes to be displayed, since best practice dictates that no more than 25 to 30 controls or control groups should be visible on a form at one time.

In the next chapter, we'll move to the next level of user interface design: choosing individual controls to represent different kinds of data.

Choosing Windows Controls

In Chapter 17, we looked at various ways to structure forms based on how the entities represented in them are related. In this chapter, we'll look at how to match specific controls to certain kinds of logical data.

Two basic principles apply to choosing controls. The most important is to choose the control that best matches the way users think about the data—in other words, to match the users' mental model. Secondarily, you should limit user input to the narrowest possible range of values.

People who work with databases tend to think of data as textual values. If you open a recordset in datasheet view in Microsoft Access, as shown in Figure 18–1, all the fields are shown as text. But in fact only the Customer-Name field has a Text data type. CustomerNumber is an AutoNumber field, DateOfFirstOrder is Date/Time, CreditLimit is Currency, and Preferred-Customer is Yes/No (Boolean).

When systems designers are manipulating data, we of course think about different data domains and don't try to join a date to a Boolean

CustomerName	CustomerNumber	DateOfFirstOrder	CreditLimit	PreferredCustomer
Alfreds Futterkiste	10061	8/25/1997	$5,000.00	No
Ana Trujillo Emparedados y helados	10062	9/18/1996	$2,000.00	No
Antonio Moreno Taquería	10063	11/27/1996	$10,000.00	Yes
Around the Horn	10064	11/15/1996	$15,000.00	Yes
Berglunds snabbköp	10065	8/12/1996	$30,000.00	Yes
Blauer See Delikatessen	10066	4/9/1997	$5,000.00	No
Blondel père et fils	10067	7/25/1996	$20,000.00	Yes
Bólido Comidas preparadas	10068	10/10/1996	$10,000.00	Yes
Bon app'	10069	10/16/1996	$25,000.00	Yes
Bottom-Dollar Markets	10070	12/20/1996	$10,000.00	Yes

Record: 11 of 89

Figure 18–1 This Datasheet Shows Several Data Types as Textual Values value. Despite this, there is a tendency to display values of different types the same way, usually in text boxes. This approach works—you can display any data type in a text box—but it isn't doing your users any favors. You should consider a text box to be the control of last resort and use it only after you've determined that the other, more specific control types are inapplicable.

Looking at a field declared on the Date/Time domain, you might see a string of characters formatted in a specific way, but users see a date. Their mental process is not at all the same when changing a date as when changing a text string. If a user has mistyped a name, she might think, "The J in 'Jary' needs to be an M." If a user needs to change a date, however, she's more likely to think along the lines of, "Oh, that really should be a week from Monday." You can make users' lives easier by choosing a control that supports the way they think about the data.

You'll also make users' lives easier by limiting the values they can enter. Data limitation isn't the same issue as data validation, which we'll discuss in the next chapter. Data validation is an after-the-fact check performed by the system to ensure that the value entered is reasonable. Data limitation prevents users from entering an unreasonable value in the first place.

The place to start is, of course, limiting the type of data that users can enter. For choosing controls, data can be organized into four groups: logical data, sets of values, numbers and dates, and text. We'll look at each of these in this chapter.

NOTE: It isn't possible for me to discuss the seemingly endless variety of widgets, gizmos, and gadgets available from third-party suppliers. I've limited my discussion to those provided by Microsoft Visual Studio .NET and Microsoft Access. However, I do encourage you to familiarize yourself with what's available. (The Microsoft Web site is a good place to start.) You'll find a lot of junk around, but a lot of seriously cool stuff, too—and you might find that a few hundred dollars spent on a third-party tool can save you weeks of development and testing.

Representing Logical Values

Although you can display logical values in a text box, it's not a good practice. For example, a Customer table might contain a field called CreditApproved that you declared as a Boolean value. You *could* use a text box to display the field and then use data validation to check that users have entered "Yes," "No," "True," or "False." But allowing unlimited data entry like this is just begging for users to enter "Provisionally" or "Deadbeat." Unless you're prepared to accept and interpret these entries, you can do the users and yourself a favor by choosing a control that's limited to two values.

Both Access and Visual Studio provide two controls that do a better job: check boxes and toggle buttons, which are shown in Figure 18–2.

Most people are familiar with check boxes, and they're a good choice for representing most logical values. Toggle buttons are used less frequently. They're more effective for Boolean values that equate to "on" and "off" rather than to "true" or "false." The problem with toggle buttons is that in their "off" state they're indistinguishable from command buttons. Since users expect that pressing a button will cause some action to be performed, many might be hesitant to press a button labeled "Credit Approved," thinking that doing so will initiate the approval process rather than simply indicate that it has been completed. For this reason, I prefer to use toggle buttons in sets, like radio buttons. This is, in fact, how they're implemented in Visual Studio. They are RadioButton controls with their Appearance property set to "Button".

On the subject of radio buttons (also known as option buttons), please don't use these controls to represent single logical values. Nothing in the Microsoft Windows environment actually prevents you from doing so, but it's unnecessary (check boxes do just as well) and inappropriate. Radio buttons are intended to represent a set of mutually exclusive choices. A single option button all by its lonesome looks peculiar.

Worse, if you're using option buttons to represent several logical values in the same area of the form, users are likely to erroneously believe that they are somehow related and that they can choose only a single option button at a time. They will also expect that selecting one option will automatically cause the others to be deselected. It's always disconcerting to users when a computer system doesn't behave as they expect.

Figure 18–2 Each Check Box and Toggle Button Control Is Used to Display a Logical Value

Representing Sets of Values

A number of controls allow you to display sets of values on a form. The choice is largely determined by whether you need to capture a single value (albeit drawn from a range of values) or several.

Capturing a Single Value from a Set of Values

The acceptability of a given value is often determined by its existence in a list. For example, the CustomerNumber value in an Orders record might be valid if and only if the customer number exists in the Customers table. Given that you want to limit the user input to the range of acceptable values wherever feasible, you'll want to present users with the list of Customers and allow them to choose one.

The controls most often used in this situation are the combo box and the list box, shown in Figure 18–3. The two have a few differences in functionality, the most important being that the combo box allows users to enter values that are not already in the list. As discussed elsewhere, this functionality can sometimes be used to create records for a linked entity. Even if entering new records isn't appropriate for your specific environment, the ability to find a value by typing it directly is preferred by most touch typists, who tend to find reaching for a mouse, or even looking at the screen, an inconvenience.

Visual Studio allows combo boxes to be configured to display their lists all the time or only on demand. Access allows only drop-down combo boxes. (Additionally, list boxes in Visual Studio can display check boxes next to each value; Access doesn't support this functionality.)

Figure 18–3 Visual Studio Provides Three Styles of Combo Boxes

The Windows Interface Guidelines for Software Design states that you should size simple combo boxes and list boxes to display between three and eight items. If you can't find the room on the form to do this comfortably, you should use a combo box with a drop-down list.

Even if you have the space to display the list permanently, you should use a drop-down combo box if the list is irrelevant once users make a choice. At times, it can be useful to allow users to see at a glance what values are possible, particularly if either the list itself or the value assigned to the record changes frequently.

In a library system, for instance, in which titles are assigned to a subject category from a list that is frequently updated and refined, users might want to see the most current list to determine whether a new category better defines a given book.

But if you're providing a list of customers on an Orders form, for example, users don't care what other customers are known to the system once they've chosen the customer they want. In these situations, you should use a drop-down combo box that hides the list once the user has made a choice.

An extremely useful capability in both Visual Studio and Access is being able to display a value other than the one being stored in the table. If you're using a counter or identity value as the primary key in the Customers table, for example, you'll need to store this value as the foreign key in the Orders table, but there's no reason to make users look at it. In the Orders form, you can easily display customer names (from the Customers table) for users to choose from instead.

In Visual Studio, you do this by specifying a different value for the DataField and ListField properties. In Access, you use multiple columns—one for the customer name and one for the customer number—bind the control to the Orders customer number column, and hide the customer number column by setting its width to zero.

The ability of Access combo boxes to display multiple columns is extremely useful, and it has always seemed a pity to me that it's not possible in Visual Studio. In showing a list of customers, for instance, it's nice to include some additional information, such as the city in which they live, to further identify the customer. In Visual Studio, you can do this only by using a calculated field that concatenates the values as the ListField property setting. Somehow this never seems to work quite as well as Access combo boxes, particularly if some values are empty.

As useful as list boxes and combo boxes are, they aren't practical if the list contains too many values. With more than a couple hundred items, you'll need to find some way of limiting the list. You could have users select

Figure 18–4 Option Buttons or Toggle Buttons Contained in a Group Box Can Display Short Fixed Lists

a letter of the alphabet, a sales region, or the state of residence, perhaps, and then filter the list items based on this selection.

If the list is very short—no more than five or six items—and if its values are fixed, you might want to use an option group rather than a combo box or list box. You can implement option groups using either option buttons or toggle buttons, as shown in Figure 18–4. Option buttons are the more usual choice.

However, although it's possible, at least in Visual Studio, to generate an option group at runtime, it's not a good idea to do so. It's disconcerting to users for a form layout to change, as it will do if you're adding and deleting options on the fly. So unless the option list is permanent (or at least fixed until the next release), you're better off using a list box or combo box. The size of these controls stays the same when list items are added or removed, so it's not uncomfortable for users if the list items change.

Capturing a Set of Values

If you need to capture a set of values, you're working with the many side of a one-to-many relationship. As we saw in Chapter 17, the first decision you must make in these situations is whether you need to display and capture the records all at once or one at a time.

If you want to display and capture the many-side records one at a time in Access, you can use a sub-form in single-record view. Set the LinkChildFields and LinkMasterFields properties, and Access does the majority of the work for you. In Visual Studio, creating such a sub-form requires a little more work (OK, a *lot* more work), but in return you get slightly more control. Either way, this is a good technique if you have several field values to capture, and particularly if you want to use a variety of control types.

If you need to collect multiple values per record and want to display multiple records simultaneously, you might be able to use a datasheet in Access or a DataGrid control in Visual Studio. Access datasheets are quite powerful (sometimes *too* powerful), and they allow several control types in addition to text boxes. Visual Studio DataGrid controls are, frankly, a bit painful to implement, but workable (and more stable than grid controls in earlier versions of Visual Basic).

Microsoft Access provides an alternative for when you want finer control over the form display. The Access sub-form control supports the display of sub-forms in continuous form view so that multiple records can be visible simultaneously. This is a good choice if you need to display multiple records and also need to use a control type—such as an option group—that isn't supported by a datasheet or grid control. To implement the same functionality in Visual Studio, you would need to create a User Control.

Another control that can be useful for displaying multiple records in some circumstances is the TreeView control. The TreeView control is most often used to display hierarchical data in outline form, but it can also be used to display selected details for each record. The TreeView is not an effective mechanism for editing this detail, but it can be very useful for navigating records. Using a paradigm similar to Microsoft Windows Explorer, you can show details regarding the selected record in another section of the form.

Finally, in situations where users need to select a set of items from a list, a linked pair of list boxes can be a useful structure. This structure, shown in the Sample Fields and Fields In My New Table lists in Figure 18–5, is frequently used in wizards. (The screen shown is from the Access 2000 Table Wizard.) It's easy for users to understand list boxes linked in this way, but be warned, they're difficult to implement.

A pair of list boxes like this is convenient during initial data entry, but it's not an appropriate structure for subsequent editing and display, if for no other reason than that it takes up too much space. This is why the technique is most often used in wizards, where each bit of data entry can be handled on a separate screen. Once the initial data entry is complete, the user probably won't need to refer to the full lists of chosen and un-chosen values, and you can more effectively use one of the controls listed previously or even a single multi-select list box.

However, because of the way selection works in multi-select list boxes, they can be dangerous. It's very easy for users to accidentally de-select all the currently selected items by single-clicking (rather than control-clicking) a new item. When the selections are bound to data, sorting out the record additions and deletions and reselections can be an absolute nightmare. A normal, single-select list box that only shows the items that have been

Figure 18–5 The Microsoft Access 2000 Table Wizard Uses Linked List Boxes to Allow Users to Choose Fields for the New Table

selected is a better solution, perhaps in combination with a text box or combo box for adding items.

Representing Numbers and Dates

Numeric values and dates are most often presented in text boxes. As always, it's better to constrain the numeric values users can enter wherever possible. If the range of values is too broad, however, you might not be able to.

The Input Mask property in Access and the MaskedData control in Visual Studio provide a certain amount of control over numbers entered by means of a textbox—you can at least prohibit the entry of alphabetical characters. Access is also pretty smart about interpreting the data entered, but of course, this is after-the-fact data validation and not the best option if data limitation options are available.

Visual Studio provides two additional controls for entering calendar data, the MonthView control and the DateTimePicker control, shown in Figure 18–6. Access provides a calendar control similar to the MonthView control in Visual Studio.

You can think of these controls as calendar equivalents of list boxes and combo boxes—the DateTimePicker displays the calendar only on demand, while the MonthView displays it at all times. Both controls handle only dates, however, not dates and times. This can lead to some

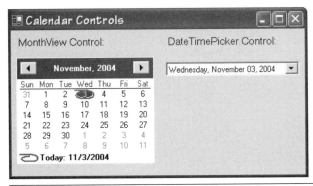

Figure 18–6 The MonthView and DateTimePicker Controls

odd complications when they're bound to Date/Time fields, so you need to be careful during implementation.

Visual Studio and Access also provide the Microsoft UpDown control (sometimes called a spinner control) that can be used for entering both numeric and Date/Time data. Most users will be familiar with UpDown controls from having set the date and time in Windows, as shown in Figure 18–7.

UpDown controls are particularly useful if values are not incremented evenly—a date that can only be on a weekday, for example, or a numeric value that must be rounded to the nearest hundred.

A final set of Visual Studio controls that can be used for entering numeric data includes slider controls and scroll bars, shown in Figure 18–8.

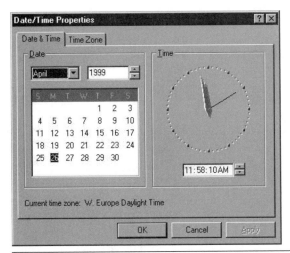

Figure 18–7 Windows Uses UpDown Controls for Controlling Time Values

Figure 18–8 Slider Controls and Scroll Bars Have Limited Value in Database Applications

These controls have a fairly limited value in database applications. They're essentially only graphic mechanisms for setting numeric values, and as such could theoretically be used to enter any numeric data. (You probably don't think of scroll bars as numeric tools—that's not their manifest model—but they actually return numeric values to the application in the background.)

I find them most useful when users can compare a set of values whose relative position is more important than their precise values—that is, "This field value is more important than that field value." For example, I have occasionally used sliders for match checking, allowing users to set the relative importance or required tolerance of the fields to be compared in finding a match for a particular record.

Representing Text Values

Finally, we turn to those controls of last resort, text boxes. Text boxes aren't evil; they're just overused. Most data in a typical database is textual, and text boxes are the appropriate controls for representing those values. The exception is when the field is a foreign key, in which case a combo box or list box is usually a better choice, as described earlier.

The basic principles of choosing controls apply equally to text boxes: Use them when they match the users' mental model, and employ whatever data limitation techniques are possible.

Data limitation is provided in Access by the Input Mask property of the text box control. It isn't directly supported in the current version of Visual

Studio. Input masks allow you to specify a pattern that controls the form of data entered. An American social security number, for instance, follows the pattern ###-##-#### (three digits, a dash, two digits, a dash, and four digits).

Input masks are useful in certain situations, but these situations are less frequent than some people seem to think, and it's easy to limit the data entry too much. Phone numbers are a good example: It's tempting to use an input mask for these values, but before doing so you must make sure that the system needs to accept phone numbers only from within the same country. Phone numbers in different countries often do not have the same format. Even within a single country, you need to think about possible variations—extensions and access numbers, for example, or simply different conventions. (It used to make me crazy that in Australia some people format a seven-digit number as 999-9999 and some use 99-99-999 instead.)

Remember, your goal in providing an input mask is to make life easier for users. Preventing them from entering perfectly valid—but unexpected—values is a hindrance.

In addition to standard text boxes, both Access and Visual Studio support using a Microsoft Rich Textbox control for entering text that combines different typefaces and styles. Implementing a Rich Textbox control is more complex than using other controls because you must also provide an interface for setting the text properties.

In addition to the added complexity in the interface, a Rich Textbox control also adds some complexity to the data manipulation, since the text formatting is embedded in the control. For this reason, I recommend restricting the use of Rich Textbox controls to situations in which the added functionality is of tangible benefit to users. Furthermore, you should use them only for values that will be treated as "chunks" of text that are displayed in various places but are not searched or joined with other values.

For example, rich text can be useful for managing boilerplate paragraphs of text that are combined to produce standard letters. The actual paragraphs to be included would be stored as rich text but chosen by users on the basis of descriptive or categorical information stored as standard, unformatted text.

Summary

In this chapter, we've examined the various types of controls you can use for displaying and capturing information. Your choice of controls should be based on matching users' mental model of the data and limiting the data entry to a valid range of values wherever possible.

In the next chapter, we'll look at what you can do when data limitation isn't possible, as we examine when and how to implement data validation.

Maintaining Database Integrity

Imagine that you're the owner of a small manufacturing company, and you've been working very hard to lure a certain customer away from a larger, better-established competitor. You finally convince the customer to give you a try, but you have to deliver the merchandise within 48 hours. You check with manufacturing and they can do it (just barely), so you break out the champagne.

Ten minutes later, there's trouble. It seems the accountant won't sign off on the order until the customer's credit has been approved, which will take a week, and without a signed order manufacturing can't proceed. What do you do? You'll probably start by explaining to the accountant that the situation requires bending the rules a little. If that doesn't work, you'll explain that requiring a credit check before completing an order is *your* rule, and because it's *your* company, you can break it as you see fit. If nothing else works, you'll sack the idiot and issue the paperwork yourself.

I have it on good authority that accountants are people and that they have families and mortgages like the rest of us, so the scenario I've just outlined isn't very likely. People don't just flatly refuse to carry out their boss' orders (or at least not very often). But computer systems do, regularly. They stamp their little electronic feet, stick out their little electronic lower lips, and refuse to comply with perfectly reasonable requests, all in the name of "maintaining data integrity."

After telling you earlier in the book about what data integrity is, how to model it, and where to implement it, I'm now going to tell you something *really* scary: Maintaining data integrity isn't very important.

I'll pause now and wait for the howls of protest to die down.

I'm not saying you should *eliminate* data validation. I'm saying that maintaining the integrity of the database is far less important than helping users do their jobs, and you should design your system accordingly. Data does need to be valid *eventually*, but it doesn't necessarily need to be completely valid at the moment it's entered.

Stop for a moment and think about why your database system is being developed: to help people perform some task. Data validation that helps people perform tasks is good; it supports the system's goals. Data validation that prevents people from performing tasks in the order that makes sense to them, or from doing something perfectly reasonable, but unexpected, is bad. It's as simple as that.

Your system should *never* prevent the user from entering data just because it isn't complete or you didn't anticipate it. Of course, like most things, doing this is sometimes easier said than done. In this chapter, we'll look at various types of integrity constraints and at how you can balance protecting the data from accidental errors with maintaining the reliability and usability of the system.

Classes of Integrity Constraints

In Chapter 4 we divided integrity constraints into six different types based on their logical levels in the relational model. In this chapter, we'll use a different organization. We'll separate integrity constraints into two classes: intrinsic constraints and business constraints.

Intrinsic constraints govern the physical structure of the data and are derived from the relational model. The rule that prohibits users from deleting a record from the Customers table if any related records exist in the Orders table is an intrinsic constraint, since referential integrity is a function of the relational model. If a user deletes the customer record without deleting the dependent order records, the database is destabilized. If a customer record is added later that has the same primary key as the deleted customer record, the orphaned order records will be associated—incorrectly—with the new customer record. This can easily happen if, for example, you derive the primary key value from the customer's name.

Even if the primary key is never reused, orphan records can cause the database to return spurious results. Queries that calculate the total number of products sold over a given period of time will return different results depending on whether or not the Orders table is joined to the Customers table, for example. For a detailed listing of the number of each product sold to each customer, the Customers and Orders tables are usually joined using a natural join. Only the Orders records that have a matching record in the Customers table will be included in the calculation of total sales. The orphaned Orders records don't have an associated record in the Customers table, so they'll be left out of the calculation. For a summary sales listing that links the Orders table only to the Products table, on the other hand, these orphaned records will be included in the total sales calculation. Thus the system will provide two different answers to the question, "How much did we sell in June?" depending on how the question is phrased, which is clearly unacceptable.

Business constraints (also known as **business rules**), on the other hand, are derived from the problem space. A rule that prohibits a customer record deletion from cascading to the Orders table unless all the relevant orders have been filled or canceled is a business constraint. Business constraints say "we don't do that here," whereas intrinsic constraints say "it can't be done."

In practice, the distinction between intrinsic constraints and business rules isn't always clear and isn't at all important. What is important is that one class of data integrity constraint derives from the problem space. You implement these constraints as a convenience to users, and you can safely ignore the constraints when doing so is convenient for the users. Deleting a customer who has open orders isn't convenient—it could very well be a disaster. But adding a sixth employee when a business rule says each manager can have only five employees *could* be convenient. In fact, not being able to enter that employee could be very inconvenient indeed.

The point is that overruling business constraints won't jeopardize the stability or reliability of the database. If a user deletes a customer record and also deletes associated outstanding orders, the system has lost important data but none of the remaining data is threatened. The relevant Customers and Orders records can be restored or reentered, and everything will be fine.

The two classes of data integrity constraints—intrinsic constraints and business constraints—must be handled differently by the system. Intrinsic constraints can't be ignored without jeopardizing the reliability of the data. Business constraints can, and often should, be overridden at the discretion of users. We'll examine each class of integrity constraint in detail in the following sections.

Intrinsic Constraints

The class of validation rules I'm referring to as intrinsic constraints controls the physical structure of the database. This class includes the rules governing the type, format, and length of data; the acceptability of null values; range constraints; and entity integrity and referential integrity.

Data Type

Provided you've chosen appropriate control types, users normally don't run afoul of data type constraints. I've never known anyone to intentionally try to enter a date in the Amount Due field or enter text in a check box. Someone might, however, try to enter "eleven" into a text box that was expecting a numeric value, which is why the choice of data entry controls is so important, as we saw in the last chapter.

Format

Formatting doesn't usually pose a problem, particularly if you can re-format the entry as users leave the field (Microsoft Access and Visual Studio both make this easy to do) or provide an input mask to guide user input. Be careful not to impose data formats too rigidly, however. If the data entered doesn't quite fit the format you've defined, you might be better off to match the data to the format as best you can and allow the users to fix it as they see fit. You don't want to do this if the invalid format indicates invalid data, but this situation is rare. A user who enters a telephone number as 9-9999-99999-99 could simply be dealing with a funky new phone system.

Length

Length constraints—particularly those on character fields—consistently cause problems. No matter how generous you've been, a perfectly valid entry that's too long to fit always seems to come along. You can sometimes avoid the length constraint problem by using Character fields, allocating the maximum field length (255 characters) and setting the field to a variable-length type. In Microsoft Access, all text fields are variable length. In SQL Server, you must explicitly set the field type to VARCHAR. Both engines will allocate space only for the characters stored, so no space is wasted.

Variable-length character fields aren't appropriate in all situations, of course. First, a certain length might be required. For example, Social Security Numbers are always nine characters long. If a user has a 10-character Social Security Number, length isn't the problem; the data is invalid. Allowing it to be entered would be unwise. Second, because of the way SQL Server handles updates of records containing variable-length character fields, using them can result in slower performance. In most situations, the performance hit is negligible, but in performance-critical applications that require updating the data frequently using fixed length fields is preferable. (There's no performance difference in *adding* data, only in *updating* it.)

Finally, although allowing very long field lengths can improve usability, this isn't always the case. Sometimes, in fact, it can wreak havoc with usability. Screen and report formats can get ugly (especially reports, because it isn't possible to scroll the data), and finding records that contain particular information can be a nightmare.

When it isn't appropriate to allow long data values, try to provide conventions or policies for handling data that doesn't fit. If a customer name really is longer than the allotted space, you might work with users to establish reasonable conventions for shortening it, such as eliminating articles such as "The", always abbreviating "Company" to "Co", and truncating all the characters after the word "Company." This will help ensure—but not guarantee—that "The Really, Really Long Name Company, Incorporated" will always be entered as "Really, Really Long Name Co" and not as "Really, Really Long, Inc" one time and "Really Long Name Company" the next.

Nulls

Missing values is the next area in which users often have trouble with intrinsic constraints. We've discussed null values at great length elsewhere, and I've tried to make it clear that I believe nulls should be allowed wherever values can reasonably be unknown in the real world, at least where doing so won't make the data completely irrelevant to the system. If you choose to ignore this sage advice, however, you must consider how the system can assist the poor user who is trying to create a new record without all the data being available.

The issue here is *when* the data is needed. You know from analyzing the system's work processes that certain bits of information are required before a given task is completed. But that doesn't mean *all* the data required by *all* the tasks is required when the record is first created. You need new employees' bank details before you can pay them. So bank detail fields can't be null come payday. But just because the employee doesn't have the information handy when a user first creates the record, the database system shouldn't prevent a user from entering the rest of the employee's details or from performing other tasks. The user might need to produce a security card so that the person can get into the building. The bank details aren't needed for that task. The bank details will be needed *eventually*, just not necessarily on the first day of work. Don't let your system throw a tantrum; everything will be fixed up in time—the employee will see to that!

If you're unwilling to accept null values, even temporarily, the easiest way to handle this constraint is to provide some reasonable default value. One possibility is for the system to declare a single value as a default in the database schema. Alternatively, the system can present a selection of values to the user—perhaps "UNKNOWN", "NOT APPLICABLE", and "YET TO COME". Sometimes the system can calculate a reasonable default value on the fly.

Ranges

Specified ranges are the other attribute-level constraints—in addition to Null values—with which users often have trouble. Some range constraints are explicit in the data type—255 is the largest value that can be stored in a short integer, for example. When a data type determines a range constraint, you can't do much beyond explaining the constraint to users. If larger values are required, you must identify a data type with a higher range in the database schema. I do *not* recommend trying to have your application do this on the fly.

If, however, you have defined the range constraint as a validation rule or CHECK constraint in the schema, or you have implemented the constraint in the application instead of in the schema, chances are that it's a business rule rather than an intrinsic constraint and you have a lot more room to maneuver. (We'll examine business rules in the next section.)

Entity and Referential Integrity Constraints

You'll remember that entity constraints ensure that each record in a table can be uniquely identified, while referential integrity constraints prohibit records from referencing records that don't exist in the same or another table. You must consider how to handle entity constraints and referential constraints without unnecessarily imposing on the user. They are most commonly handled by allowing users to select from a list of valid items. However, as we saw in the last chapter, this isn't always possible, usually because the list would be too long to be practicable.

When constraining users' entries in a list isn't possible or appropriate, check the data as soon as possible after it's been entered and notify the user of any problems. A record entry that appears to duplicate an existing record in the database is an entity constraint problem. The system's best response is to offer to display the existing record—or just the pertinent fields—to the user and allow the user to decide whether the new record really is a duplicate, as shown in Figure 19–1.

Be careful not to overwrite the data the user has entered for the new record when you display the existing record. Display the existing record in a separate window, and allow the user to decide whether to overwrite the new record. Notice, too, that the dialog box in Figure 19–1 allows the

Figure 19–1 This Dialog Box Allows the User to Decide Whether the New Record Is a Duplicate

user to continue entering data without viewing the suspected duplicate. The user might already know about the other record, and you don't want to disrupt him any more than absolutely necessary. (Repeat after me: "The computer does *not* know best, the computer does *not* know best, the computer....")

The user who is trying to leave a primary key field blank presents a slightly different problem. That a primary key field value can't be empty is the best argument I know for using a system-assigned primary key. Using an AutoNumber field (an Identity field in SQL Server) ensures that users can do anything they require to the natural primary key fields without compromising entity or referential integrity. If using AutoNumber (or Identity) fields isn't appropriate in your system, you must ensure that users enter some value into each primary key field. Simple default values can't be used, obviously, because the default would be accepted only once for each table. You *could* have the system calculate a value on the fly, but if you're going to use an arbitrary value you might as well use an AutoNumber field. Your only other choice is to query users for an acceptable value.

When a referential integrity problem occurs, a user is usually trying to reference a record that doesn't exist. This can be accidental—the user might have misspelled a name, for example—or it can be more or less intentional. The user might not realize that the referenced record doesn't exist or might not have gotten around to entering the data yet. The dialog box shown in Figure 19–2 shows one way of handling this situation. This dialog box gives users four options: They can have the system add a new record and add the details now, they can have the system add a new record and

Figure 19–2 This Dialog Box Allows the User to Choose How to Handle a Referenced Record that Doesn't (Yet) Exist

update the record later, they can change the reference, or they can fix the reference later.

Note that overriding the constraint is not an option for the user. This constraint can't be overridden because doing so can make the database unstable, as we've seen.

If you are unable to have the dialog box present a complete list of valid items to users because the list would be too long, your dialog box can instead display a list of items that are close matches to the entered data. Any number of algorithms for performing these searches exists, from a simple SQL LIKE statement to a SOUNDEX search.

In some situations, it is not necessary to display a referential integrity validation dialog box at all. In fact, it's generally better to avoid doing so and thereby avoid disrupting users' work. If you can predict with reasonable certainty that users will want to add the new records and update the details later, *and* you have provided adequate facilities for undoing the system's actions if you've guessed wrong, the system can simply add the new record quietly, in the background, without making a fuss. After the user completes the record, you might want to display a message in the status bar that the record has been added or display the message in a dialog box if you want the information to be more obvious. But whatever you do, don't interrupt users while they're entering the records if you can avoid it; it's unnecessarily rude and is scary for users.

The flip side of users trying to reference a record that doesn't exist is users trying to delete or change a referenced record. A user might be trying to delete a record for a customer that has outstanding orders, for example, or change the ProductID value for a product that is referenced in the OrderItems table.

The Microsoft Jet database engine supports cascading updates and cascading deletes that allow updates and deletes of referenced records to be handled without user intervention. You can implement the same functionality in SQL Server using triggers. If cascading updates and deletes make sense in your application, using them is by far the best solution. However, if only the users can decide the best course of action, be sure to explain to them the implications of their choice, as shown in Figure 19–3.

The dialog box in Figure 19–3 lets users cancel the deletion, cascade the deletion, or reassign the dependent records to a different customer. Notice the dialog box warns users that open orders can't be deleted (which is a business rule) and provides the option of canceling the orders (essentially overriding the rule) or reviewing them.

You might also display the open orders, or all the customer's orders, in the validation dialog box. Your goal is to provide users with as much information as you can to allow them to make an informed decision.

Figure 19–3 This Dialog Box Explains the Implications of Each Option and Allows Users to Choose

Business Constraints

In the previous section, we looked at the intrinsic constraints that protect the structure and integrity of the database. You can do little to assist the user with data that violates an intrinsic constraint. Data must, at least eventually, be made to conform to the requirements of the relational model. Data that violates a business constraint, however, is a very different matter.

As I've said, you derive business constraints from the problem space rather than from the relational model itself. Remember that a data model is just that—a simplified model of some part of the real world. As a system designer, you'll do your best to capture all the relevant aspects of the problem space in your model, but despite your best efforts you won't always succeed. Even if your model is perfect in every respect when it's first implemented, business conditions change. To be successful, your system must be able to handle the unexpected gracefully.

There are two reasons users might try to enter data the system isn't prepared to handle: either they entered the data by accident, or reality doesn't match the system model. (Actually, there are three reasons if you count intentional sabotage, but the pessimism of the average system analyst notwithstanding, sabotage is *extremely* rare, and, in any event, business rules are not the best way to handle it.)

Accidental Entries

If users enter the unexpected data accidentally, your only concern is to make it as easy as possible for them to correct the problem. At the very least, this means you should explain exactly what the problem is and what needs to be done about it. Where you can, you should also provide reasonable alternatives that can be implemented directly by the system. The dialog box shown in Figure 19–4, for example, might be triggered when a user enters the month and day of a date field backwards. The dialog box makes a reasonable guess about what the user meant to enter and allows the user to select the revised date with a single click.

When users enter the data accidentally, it might be a genuine accident, or it might be that they don't really understand what was expected. The dialog box shown in Figure 19–4 goes some way toward explaining the purpose of the DeliveryDate field, but it also includes a Help button to allow the user to find more detailed information. We'll talk about user assistance in detail in Chapter 21.

Figure 19–4 This Dialog Box Explains an Entry Error without Issuing Ultimatums

Reality vs. the System Model

The second reason users might enter unexpected information is because reality doesn't match the system model. For example, users might be trying to correct a situation in which an order has already been delivered but for some reason wasn't entered into the system. The delivery date for this order will be earlier than the order date, which could break a business rule. If you don't provide users with some guidance, they'll enter any meaningless delivery date they can get the system to accept, and the integrity of your database will be compromised. So it behooves you to be as creative as possible in thinking of as many exceptions as you can and help the user resolve them consistently. Figure 19–5 shows a possible response to a user entering a DeliveryDate earlier than the OrderDate. This example assumes that the OrderDate is set to the current system date by default and that the user ordinarily can't edit the field.

Not all business rules can (or should) simply be overridden. Some business rules *can't* be broken, because the situation is impossible or because of statutory regulations, for example. But sometimes the question is not so much "whether" a rule can be broken as "by whom?" In Figure 19–6, for example, a user has tried to enter information about a sixth employee reporting directly to a manager, in violation of the rule that no manager can have more than five employees.

The current user doesn't have the authority to override the rule. But the system makes available a secondary dialog box that allows a password and authorization code to be entered by someone who does have the authority—presumably a supervisor or manager. Because individuals in authority aren't always available on demand, the first dialog box also allows the user to

Figure 19–5 This Dialog Box Allows the User to Backdate an Order

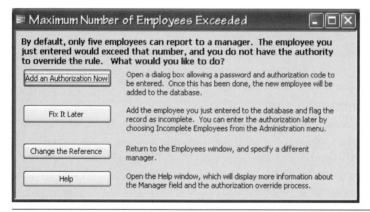

Figure 19–6 This Dialog Box Indicates that Only Someone with Appropriate Authority Can Override the Business Rule

save the current record and provides instructions for entering the authorization code at a later date.

Providing the ability to override business rules can add significantly to the usability of the system, but it does so at the cost of adding complexity to the data model. In this example, you must add a field to the Employees table to contain the authorization code and include in the integrity constraint a reference to the authorization code. You must also provide a mechanism for putting records in abeyance if the authorization is delayed.

One approach is to add a single Boolean field to the Employees table to indicate that the record is not (yet) valid. This flag can be used to find the invalid records later, when the user is ready to resolve the outstanding problems, or to filter the records when producing reports. Sometimes it's useful to know why the record is invalid, and in this case you can use a code field—"MA" for "awaiting Manager approval" or "CC" for "Credit Check Outstanding," for example. This second approach provides more flexibility in handling the records.

The changes required to hold records in abeyance might seem straightforward, and for the most part they are, but they can propagate through the system in unexpected ways. Should the records held in abeyance be included in reports, for example? An abeyance code field can be useful when deciding how to handle these reports, since it allows you to determine which records should be excluded from a particular report or query.

If records in abeyance *are* included in reports and queries, you must also consider whether they should be marked as unreliable in some way, perhaps by grouping them together under a separate heading.

If you've determined that records held in abeyance, or a particular type of record held in abeyance, are not to be included in a report, you must then decide whether any associated records should be excluded. For example, if the problem is a record for an as-yet-unauthorized sixth employee, should only that employee record be excluded or all the records for employees reporting to the same manager?

All these issues must be considered before you decide to include the ability to override a business rule. The ability to do so increases the usability of the system, but the added complexity might not be justified. In simple systems it might be better to reject the record that doesn't comply with a business rule and handle the exception outside the computer system. If you decide to handle exceptional cases outside the system, be sure to say this in a data validation dialog box. Don't leave the user guessing how to proceed.

Summary

In this chapter, I've taken the admittedly unorthodox position that database systems shouldn't necessarily enforce database integrity constraints. We've looked at two different classes of constraints: intrinsic constraints that govern the physical structure of the data and derive directly from the relational model, and business constraints that derive from the problem space.

We've seen that allowing users to override intrinsic constraints is dangerous but that allowing records that violate business constraints to be held in abeyance and resolved at a later date often makes sense. We've also looked at several examples of how you might handle holding records in abeyance.

In the next chapter, we'll look at various aspects of reporting on the data the system maintains.

Reporting

Only when the facts stored in a database system are combined in meaningful ways do they become information; before then, they are only trivia. In this chapter, we'll look at various issues involved in providing those meaningful combinations of facts—that information—to your users.

NOTE: When I use the term "reporting" in this chapter, I don't mean only the production of printed reports. I'm using the word in a more general sense, to mean the provision of information based on data stored in the database. This information *might* be provided in the form of a printed report, but it might also be provided in a form or as a recordset shown in datasheet view.

In the days when computers cost much more than employees and computing time was an extremely scarce resource, database systems produced a few reports at regular intervals. If you wanted the system to do anything special, you could pretty much whistle for it. The backlog in the average MIS department was several years, so if you needed a report "just like this one, only sorted by Customer and subtotaled by State," you'd give it to your secretary, who would type it up for you.

These days, computers are cheap and plentiful and secretaries are extremely scarce resources. A user must now be able to tell the computer system, "I'd like a report just like this, but..." and that means your job as a database designer has gotten a little harder. But hey, it beats taking shorthand dictation. (You can trust me on this one.)

There are two general approaches to providing reporting functionality in a database system: attempt to predict all the possible reports in advance; or allow users to create them as needed. Most systems require a combination of both approaches.

The reports you can predict when designing the system can be created during implementation. I call these types of reports **standard reports**. You can also provide some mechanisms for users to create their own reports after the system has been implemented. I call these types of reports **ad hoc**

reports. We'll look at both types of reports in this chapter, but first we'll examine mechanisms for the sorting, searching, and filtering of data that reports require.

Sorting, Searching, and Filtering Data

When you're writing SQL statements, sorting, searching, and filtering data is relatively straightforward: You simply specify the appropriate criteria in either the WHERE clause or the ORDER BY clause. When you want to provide this capability to your users, however, you need to provide a buffer between them and the logic of the SQL SELECT statement.

The difficulty here is that SQL logic is a poor match to natural language. When a Sales Manager asks for a listing of all the company's distributors in Wyoming and Florida, she expects a list containing both the distributors in Wyoming *and* the distributors in Florida. But the SQL SELECT clause is WHERE State = "Wyoming" OR State = "Florida". Linguistically, the correct usage is "and," but in the formal syntax the correct term is "or." This is a huge problem for users—SQL is just close enough to natural language to be hopelessly confusing.

Teaching users how to write SQL SELECT criteria clauses is possible to do. In fact, I know of at least one well-respected database designer who does this regularly and, by all accounts, with great success. I think it's preferable to save yourself, the documentation writers, and (most importantly) the users the hassle of directly using SQL syntax by providing a more intuitive interface.

Fortunately, you're not on your own here. Microsoft Access provides examples of interfaces for constructing SQL criteria clauses. While it isn't always appropriate to copy one of these user interface mechanisms directly to your own systems, these mechanisms at least provide a place to start, which is how I'll treat them here. While the Microsoft Visual Studio interface doesn't support any of these mechanisms, you can implement most of them in Visual Basic code with a little work.

Sorting Data

Access provides an excellent sorting interface through the Sort Ascending and Sort Descending commands. Users click in the control by which they want the data sorted, and then select the appropriate command from the Records menu or on the toolbar. It's hard to think of a simpler interface.

Filter By Selection

When it comes to filtering data, the simplest interface Access provides is the Filter By Selection command and its partner, Filter Excluding Selection. The interface for these two commands works very much like Sort Ascending and Sort Descending. If a user either selects the contents of a field on a form or places the insertion point in the field, and then chooses the Filter By Selection command, Access filters the form's underlying recordset to include only those records with a value that matches the selected field value exactly. In other words, the SQL WHERE condition is <fieldname> = <control value>.

If a user selects only the first part of a field's contents, Access limits the recordset to those records with a field value that begins with the selected characters. If a user selects the first three characters of the product name "Chartreuse verte", for example, the equivalent SQL WHERE clause would be WHERE [Product Name] LIKE "Cha*". In the Northwind sample database, this query returns records containing the product names Chartreuse verte, Chai, and Chang.

If a user selects any other characters within the field, Access returns all the records that contain the selection anywhere within the field. If a user selects "ar" in the previous example, for instance, the equivalent SQL WHERE clause would be WHERE [Product Name] LIKE "*ar*". In the Northwind sample database, this would return the 10 records shown in Figure 20–1.

Product ID	Product Name
18	Carnarvon Tigers
39	Chartreuse verte
58	Escargots de Bourgogne
24	Guaraná Fantástica
32	Mascarpone Fabioli
72	Mozzarella di Giovanni
73	Röd Kaviar
20	Sir Rodney's Marmalade
62	Tarte au sucre
7	Uncle Bob's Organic Dried Pears

Record: 6 of 10 (Filtered)

Figure 20–1 These Records Are Returned If a User Chooses the Filter By Selection Command that Has "ar" Selected in the Product Name Field of a Form or Datasheet

NOTE: Don't assume that Access is actually issuing SQL SELECT statements when a user chooses the Filter By Selection command. I think that's what's happening, but I can't guarantee it. There's just no telling what those wizards on the development team are up to.

Filter By Form

Filter By Selection is a simple, elegant interface that's easy for users to learn, but it limits them to filtering on a single field. Users can issue additional Filter By Selection commands to progressively narrow the data set, but this can get tedious. For users who want a more powerful filtering interface, Access provides the Filter By Form command. Figure 20–2 shows the Customers form from the Northwind sample database after a user has chosen the Filter By Form command from the Records menu.

In a Filter By Form window, users can set filter values for multiple fields on multiple tabs in the window. The values on the Look For tab will be combined with a logical AND, while those on separate Or tabs will be combined with a logical OR. This approach doesn't completely eliminate the differences between the linguistic and formal uses of AND and OR, but it comes pretty close.

By default, the Filter By Form window displays each text box from the source form as a combo box that contains all the current values for the field.

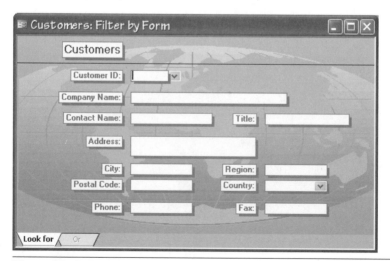

Figure 20–2 The Filter By Form Command Allows Users to Filter Information in Multiple Fields

You can turn this behavior off by setting the text box control's Filter Lookup property to Never. If the Filter By Form window displays a combo box, qualifying records must match the value a user selects exactly. If a text box is displayed—that is, if you set Filter Lookup to Never—users can either enter a value that must be matched exactly, or enter an expression such as LIKE "CHA*" or IS NOT NULL. Your decision on whether to use combo boxes in the Filter By Form window depends on the size of the underlying recordset (you don't want users to wait while Access populates a 100,000 item combo box) and the flexibility your users require.

Advanced Filter/Sort

Filter By Form, or an interface based on it, is sufficient for the majority of situations. However, if your users are familiar with Access' query design, or if you're using the Filter Lookup property to allow users to select values from a combo box in Filter By Form and also want them to be able to enter criteria expressions, the Access Advanced Filter/Sort window, shown in Figure 20–3, can be useful.

The Advanced Filter/Sort window provides a subset of the functionality provided by the Design View for a query: It controls only the WHERE and ORDER BY clauses of the SELECT statement. It does not provide the ability to change the basic structure of the returned recordset by changing the field list or joining additional recordsets.

Figure 20–3 Microsoft Access 2000 Displays This Window If a User Chooses Advanced Filter/Sort with the Customers Form Open in the Northwind Sample Database

The Advanced Filter/Sort window is one filtering interface that I would *not* attempt to duplicate in Visual Basic. It could be done, I suppose, but it would certainly be a nontrivial exercise. If you need this functionality, you should probably choose Access as your development tool or find a third-party product to plug in to the system.

Microsoft English Query

If you choose SQL Server as your database engine, consider implementing Microsoft English Query. More than just a sorting and filtering interface, English Query provides a full-blown natural language interface to the database.

To implement English Query in your application, you will need to map the language of the problem space to the database schema by creating what English Query calls an "application file." Creating an English Query application file isn't difficult, but it isn't trivial, either. Like a good help file index, it requires spending a lot of time predicting the words users will use to reference the entities and attributes in the schema.

Once you create the application file, integrating English Query into your database application is easy. Your database application simply submits a user's natural language question to the English Query engine and receives a SQL statement in return. Well, in theory it's that easy. In reality, your application might receive an error message indicating that a user (creative little creatures that users are) has phrased the question in terms the engine doesn't understand.

In the right environment, English Query is a wonderful tool. If you have a complex database schema and a lot of novice users making inquiries, the natural language interface provided by English Query can be a superb solution.

Producing Standard Reports

Almost every database system has a certain number of reports that you can define in advance. You will have discovered most of these standard reports during the work process analysis, but it's worthwhile spending some time going over the database schema with users to consider whether any other reports would be useful to them.

Listing Reports and Detail Reports

For each entity in the system, consider using both listing reports and detail reports. A listing report is just a list of every instance of the entity—that is, every record in the table. Sometimes you can simply arrange these listings in alphabetical order. More often, you should group listings in some way. Customers might be grouped by state, region, or salesperson, for example.

If you expect a report's source table to contain more than a few hundred records, provide users with the option of printing only a selected range of records. A salesperson is most likely going to want a list of only his own customers, for example, not of every customer in the system.

Whereas a listing displays a few details for every instance of an entity, a detail report shows all (or at least most) of the details about a specific entity. Again, you'll usually want to provide some way for users to select the records to print. A multi-select list box is often a good mechanism for selecting records because it doesn't require contiguous selections.

Remember to bear in mind the practical limitations of list boxes, however. If the table contains thousands of records, you must use a set of list boxes to allow users to progressively narrow the range of records. Alternatively, you could use some other type of control. You might consider using a text box similar in functionality to the one used by Microsoft Word in the Print dialog box to specify print ranges, for example. Parsing a range of records separated by a dash, or single records separated by commas, is not difficult to implement.

Summary Reports

A little more complicated to implement than listing and detail reports, but often more useful, are what I think of as "slice and dice" reports: summary data combined and compared in various ways. The percentage of sales by region or salesperson and the number of customers who purchase each product category are examples of this type of report.

Summary reports are good candidates for graphical representation, and Microsoft Graph and various third-party tools make the implementation of graphical reports straightforward. However, I recommend that you provide graphics *in addition to* textual data rather than *instead of* it. A text-based sales summary might not be the easiest thing in the world to look at, but it can be exported to a statistical analysis tool or a spreadsheet such as Microsoft Excel for further manipulation.

Form-Based Reports

In addition to the reports derived from the database schema, consider also the forms in the system as a source of useful reports. I provide the ability to print copies of the majority of forms in a database system as a matter of course. They're easy for you to implement and extraordinarily useful to users for checking their work or getting a quick printout to show to someone else.

Sometimes an entity detail report contains the same information as a form, and you can use the detail report rather than creating a new form report. Most often, however, entity detail reports contain additional information or are formatted differently than a form report. Reports based on forms are so cheap and easy to provide that I usually give my users both detail and form reports. The form-based report is the default printed when a user clicks the print button on the toolbar, and the detail report is available from a menu (and perhaps also from the toolbar).

Reporting Interfaces

Making reports available within the user interface is not very tricky. Like any command, you have three methods for making the command available to users: via a menu, a toolbar button, or a command button on a form.

Of course, a command that prints a report must always make clear to users *which* report is to be printed. This is easy to do on a menu: simply use the report name as a Reports menu item. You can use the report name as a toolbar button's ToolTip or a command button's caption as well, but you should preface the name with the verb "Print". "Customer Listing" is sufficient as a menu item on a Reports menu, for example, but the corresponding ToolTip or command button caption would be "Print Customer Listing". In addition to being compliant with Windows guidelines, this text makes it clear to users that the system will print a report, as opposed to opening a window containing the report.

In addition to *where* you make the system's reports available to users (via a menu, a toolbar, or a command button), you must also consider *how*. A database system often contains dozens, even hundreds, of reports and listing them all in one huge umpteen-column menu isn't sensible. Fortunately, limiting the list of available reports to those that make sense within a user's current context is usually easy to do. A user is unlikely to want to print a list of employee phone numbers in the middle of entering sales orders, for example.

If you think making all the system reports available at once is appropriate, you could provide a dialog box that presents a categorized list of the reports and allows users to choose the report they want to print. This approach can also be useful if users need to print multiple reports at once. By allowing them to select any number of reports at once in the report dialog box, you enable them to click the print button once and then go about their business.

For reports that are often printed as a set—such as month-end summaries—I use a variation of this technique. I present a dialog box with all the reports that are usually printed as a set selected by default. Users can add any relevant reports that are printed only occasionally, or de-select a standard report, before sending the whole set to the printer.

Listing each report in a set imposes a little more overhead on users than batching the reports from a single menu item does, but I find that the additional flexibility for users is generally worth the single extra mouse click involved. A single report in a batch often needs to be reprinted because of a printer fault or because somebody spilled coffee on it. A dialog box that groups these report sets but allows each report to be printed individually eliminates the need to list each report on a menu, or worse, print an entire report set because there's a problem with only a single report.

Handling Printer Errors

Your system must always be able to handle printers messing up or printouts being messed up, and because of this, certain common printing situations can be very tricky to handle. A user might want to print all the invoices that haven't already been printed, for example. This is a common request, but one of the most difficult for a system to handle gracefully because it can't know whether any given report has actually been printed. The system knows only that it sent the report to the print spooler, and that's not the same thing at all.

Some designers handle possible printer errors by displaying a message box after the reports have been sent to the printer, asking for confirmation that the reports printed successfully. This approach will work, but it requires that users stop using the system until they have the printouts in their hand. If the print job happens to be behind somebody's 1000-page manual in the printer queue, a user could be in for quite a wait. Furthermore, since most reports *do* print correctly the first time, the delay is unnecessary 99 percent of the time.

I prefer to handle printing problems as the exception that they are. To return to our earlier example, if the system needs to print only unprinted invoices, you'll need to add a field to the appropriate table anyway. If the system is relying on user confirmation that the invoices have printed successfully, all that's required is a Yes/No or Boolean field. But it's easy enough to store a date or print job number instead. You can then add a command that allows users to record printing problems on either a print-job or an invoice-by-invoice basis.

If a report is printed no more than once a day, you can use the current date as a flag. It's safer, however, to generate a unique number for each print job and store that instead. If anything goes wrong, a user simply selects the appropriate print job and the system can set the fields containing that print job number back to Null. The records containing a Null will automatically be included in the next print job. Alternatively, the system can display all the records that were included in the problem print job and allow the user to select only specific records to be reprinted.

How does a user recognize a particular print job? You could include the print job number in a report footer, but I prefer to set up a system table that stores the name of the report, the print job number, the date on which the report was printed, and (if it is available) the name of the user who initiated the job. You can then present a descriptive list of print jobs to users rather than making them remember a meaningless number. It's fairly easy to choose "the invoices I printed on Wednesday morning."

Sometimes more is at stake than whether a given record is included in the next print run; they're part of a work process. Accounting systems sometimes include report generation as part of end-of-month processing, for example. Once the month is rolled over, certain values will be reinitialized, and there might be no way (or at least no *easy* way) of regenerating the reports. I think this is an extremely poor design strategy, but it's a common one.

Because of the unreliability of printing, I try very hard to keep report generation and record updates (other than "record printed" updates) as completely separate tasks, and I recommend you do the same. If the work process absolutely requires that updating a record be linked to printing a report, the safest approach is to hold up further system processing until the person printing the report confirms that the report has printed successfully.

Confirming a successful print job might be possible to do as a background process, so you don't hold up the system until the job is confirmed. You could, for example, place an icon in the status bar that, when clicked, displays the confirmation dialog box and completes the table update. Be sure to display a message to users explaining what they need to do.

Automatic and On-Demand Printing

Another consideration in producing standard reports is whether they should be printed on demand, automatically, or both. As a general rule, I make all reports on-demand. The only exception I make is for a report that is clearly part of a work process, such as an invoice produced after a user enters a sales order. Such an automatic report should be available on demand as well, in order to deal with those pesky printer problems.

Note that reports tied to a work process, such as invoices, can be printed one at a time or as a batch. For example, you can print each invoice as the corresponding sales order is entered or you can batch all the unprinted invoices and print them at the end of the data entry session. I've used both approaches successfully. I tend to print each invoice individually if users have a local printer and to batch print invoices on a network printer. You should probably make the choice configurable by users—printer setups are subject to change.

Some designers choose to have the system automatically produce reports that are printed at regular intervals—weekly or at the end of each month, for example—but I prefer to make these on-demand as well. Having the system produce reports automatically is a complex task. The system must calculate when the report needs to be printed (allowing for weekends and holidays) and track whether the report has yet been printed on the correct date. If multiple people use the system, it must also determine which user or category of user should trigger the print job, and what to do if no users of that category log on to the system on the required date.

Compared with all the problems associated with automatic report generation, having the users select Print Weekly Reports from a menu at their convenience is trivial. In any event, you'll need to provide the menu item (or a reporting problem dialog box), since users will need to be able to regenerate the reports in case of printing problems.

Users aren't very likely to forget to print the weekly, monthly, or quarterly reports, but it's a good idea to allow users to specify the period for which the report is to be run, in case they do forget. By using the current period of time as a default value and allowing users to change the value, you enable them to easily correct any oversights. This technique also allows reports that are printed at regular intervals to be printed before the end of the current time period. To be able to check performance against budget while there's still time to do something about potential cost overruns can be useful.

Producing Ad Hoc Reports

The work processes a database system is intended to support are sometimes extremely well defined, and you can specify in advance all the reports the system must produce. More often, however, you will need to provide some level of flexibility for users to configure or design reports themselves.

Just how much flexibility is required must be determined by the needs of your users and will vary from system to system. The degree of flexibility can range from providing users with a full-blown report designer to simply allowing users to specify additional filter criteria for predefined reports.

Report Designers

Providing users with a report design tool is an easy option to implement if you can use a commercially available tool such as Microsoft Access or a third-party report designer, such as Crystal Reports.

Report designers give users essentially unlimited freedom in designing whatever reports they need. Unfortunately, this flexibility has a price. It's not so much that the base cost of the reporting tool is high, although if you provide a full copy of Microsoft Access to hundreds of users who otherwise don't need it, the base cost is certainly not insignificant.

The cost is more the result of having to train users to design reports using sophisticated tools. Not only must users know how to lay out the report using the report designer, they must also have at least a superficial understanding of the database schema to access the specific data they need. None of this is beyond the capabilities of the average user given adequate time and training. But these people already *have* a job, and building custom reports isn't it.

Customized Report Design

To make the report design process efficient for users, implementing a custom report design utility is often more appropriate than using a commercial tool. Theoretically, it's possible to provide a report design tool that has the same flexibility as the Microsoft Access report designer and is customized to support the database schema of the system. Such an exercise would be expensive, however, and it's difficult to imagine a situation in which the cost would be justified. A more usual solution is to provide a set of predefined report layouts and allow users to specify the data to be displayed.

The Access Report Wizard is probably still too close to the implementation model for customized reporting, but it is an example of a useful approach to providing predefined layouts. The Report Wizard provides extensive formatting capabilities but avoids much of the complexity of report design by allowing users to select from a list of predefined report layouts and styles. Once the Report Wizard generates the report, users can further manipulate it using the Access interface.

Allowing users to specify the layout and style of a report separately provides a fine degree of control to users. Alternatively, you can combine layout and style in various ways to simplify the process. Most users require "custom" reports that are really only variations of standard reports. In other words, they need one of those famous "just like this, but..." reports and what follows the "but" is either sorting or filtering criteria.

The taxonomy I use in my own work is therefore quite different from the one used by the Access Report Wizard. I divide an ad hoc report into two components, which I call the "format" and the "criteria." The format rolls together the layout and style components of the report and also specifies the fields (and by extension the table or query on which the form is based) to print. It is, in fact, a report object that is modified at runtime based on the criteria specified by the user.

The criteria specify the sorting and filtering to apply to the format. I almost always provide the user with a means of storing and reusing criteria. We'll see how this works a little later. Allowing users to define grouping levels is sometimes appropriate as well, but as a general rule I have found this unnecessary.

Because users are specifying only two components, I use a dialog box for generating custom reports. A general structure for this dialog box is shown in Figure 20–4. (If you adopt this approach to ad hoc reporting, you should modify the sample to conform to the user interface of your system.)

The dialog box is divided into three sections. In the left pane, a TreeView control presents users with a list of formats to choose from. You could use a list box or even a set of radio buttons rather than a tree view control. In the example, the formats are grouped into categories. This technique is useful if you have a lot of formats. Grouping the formats into "Administrative Reports,"

Figure 20–4 I Use This Basic Structure for Providing Ad Hoc Reporting to Users

"Month-End Reports," and "Sales Reports," for example, makes it easier for the users to find the report they want.

The lowest level of the hierarchy shown in Figure 20–4 is "reports." A report, in this context, is the combination of a saved criteria and format. Having specified "Southwest" for the Region in the criteria of a sales report format, for example, the user can save a report as "Southwest Region Sales." If you have complex criteria specifications, this capability can save users a great deal of time.

The middle pane of the dialog box allows users to specify the sorting and filtering criteria. You can sometimes use a single set of controls in the criteria pane for all formats, although it might be necessary to disable certain controls that don't apply to the format a user has chosen. Sometimes each format will require a completely different set of controls for establishing the criteria. In my work, I tend to walk a middle path. As shown in Figure 20–4, I divide the report formats into categories, and it is the category that determines the criteria controls.

The right pane of the dialog box in Figure 20–4 contains a set of command buttons. The Print button displays a subsidiary dialog box allowing users to set print options, such as the number of copies or the printer. If these options aren't available, it's probably better to provide two command buttons, Print and Print Preview, and save the user the additional step of displaying a dialog box.

The Save Or Restore Criteria command button displays a dialog box that would be similar to that shown in Figure 20–5. This simple dialog box provides the same criteria controls displayed on the main custom reporting form in the middle pane. The criteria that users have already saved are shown in a list box in the left pane. Selecting a criterion in the list box displays it in the middle pane. The Save As... button first asks the user for a name and then saves the criterion specified, while the Restore button loads a criterion into the main form.

The ability to save criteria in this way is quite straightforward to implement. You simply need a table for each category, with fields for each control on the pane. In a multi-user situation, you need to decide whether to have the saved criteria be available to everyone or allow each user to maintain his own set. If the criteria are shared, the tables should be kept in the main database along with other shared data. If each user maintains his own set of criteria, the tables should be stored locally, in the front-end database (or a local database if your application is written in something other than Microsoft Access).

The two techniques are not mutually-exclusive. You can easily provide both shared and user-specific criteria either by including the user's name in the

Figure 20–5 This Dialog Box, Called from the Main Custom Reporting Form, Allows a User to Save and Restore Report Criteria

criteria table or by displaying a UNION of the shared and local tables. I usually include the user's name in a shared table because it makes it easier to support "roaming" users, who may use more than one computer to access the system.

Saving and restoring criteria allows users to save criteria on a category basis. The criteria thus saved can be applied to any report in that category (assuming that the reports share criteria specifications).

Sometimes, however, it's more appropriate to link the criteria with a specific report format, which is what the final command button in Figure 20–4 does. Again, this is straightforward to implement. You will need tables for each type of criteria (you can reuse the tables used for saving criteria if you've implemented that functionality) and a table that links the report formats and the criteria. The structure is shown in Figure 20–6.

The ReportCategories table contains a field called CategoryTable-Name. This allows the system to identify the specific criteria table that contains the criteria for that category of format. If all your reports have the same criteria structure, this field isn't necessary. On the other hand, if all

ReportCategories	ReportFormats	NamedReports	CategoryCriteria
CategoryID	CategoryID	FormatID	CriteriaID
CategoryName	FormatID	ReportID	Field1
CategoryTableName	FormatName	ReportName	...
	PhysicalName	CriteriaID	FieldN

Figure 20–6 This Table Structure Allows User to Save Criteria and Reports and Has the Added Benefit of Allowing Reports to be Added to the System at Runtime

your formats have different criteria structures, this field should be in the ReportFormats table.

The table structure shown in Figure 20–6 also allows the reports available within the system to be configured at runtime, which is what the FormatName and PhysicalName fields in the ReportFormats table are all about. If your report formats are defined independently, either as objects in the database (as with Access reports) or as separate files (as with many third-party reporting tools), you can use indirection to enable adding reports to the system at any time. To do so, you base the list of formats shown in the form dialog box on the ReportFormats table rather than hard-coding the list.

To add a new report format, you need only create the format object (a report in Access, or a separate operating system file) and then add a record to the ReportFormats system table. The new format will automatically be available within the system without anyone having to touch core system functionality. The FormatName field contains the text to be displayed to the user, while the PhysicalName contains the actual name of the object and perhaps its file path if the objects are stored externally.

The approach to custom reporting described here, while simpler for users than a full-blown report design tool, is overkill for some applications. All your users might need is the ability to occasionally specify additional filter criteria for the predefined standard reports. You can often accommodate these simple criteria by adding a few controls for specifying the criteria to a custom print dialog box, rather than implementing a full custom reporting user interface such as the one I've described.

Standard Letters

A special type of custom report is the standard letter. Sometimes the text of standard letters is fixed, but more often users need to select from boilerplate paragraphs and have the system combine them to create the letter. Whether the text is fixed or not, I am of the opinion that a database report is not the best means of producing correspondence.

Although database report formatting capabilities are becoming increasingly powerful, they do not equal the formatting capabilities of a word processor specifically designed for this task. Furthermore, most users want the ability to add text to letters before they are printed, but allowing them to manipulate the database reports is not a good idea because any changes to the standard structure would be permanent.

By all means, use the database to maintain names and addresses, and even to store the boilerplate paragraphs. But outputting this data to a word

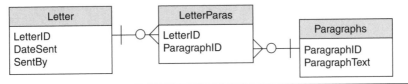

Figure 20–7 This Structure Can Store the Paragraphs Included in a Specific Letter

processor such as Microsoft Word allows more sophisticated formatting and lets users manipulate the text before printing it.

Fortunately, sending standard letters to a word processor is becoming increasingly easy to implement. Gone are the days of struggling to send Dynamic Data Exchange (DDE) command strings to some uncooperative, poorly documented application. In Microsoft Word, for example, you can directly specify an Access table or query as the data source for a mail merge with a document. You can then use Visual Basic for Applications (VBA) to merge the document with the data from your database application and then either display the result to users for subsequent manipulation or send it directly to the printer.

In some circumstances, you might need to keep track of the standard letters that are created by the system. If you aren't allowing users to customize the letters before they print them, there's no need to store the letters themselves in the database. You need to store only the fact that a letter was sent, and perhaps the date and the name of the user who sent it. On the other hand, if users create the letters by combining boilerplate paragraphs, you can model this process using a complex entity, as shown in Figure 20–7.

If the system allows users to customize letters before they are printed, it's better not to store the text of the letter in the database, since neither Access nor Microsoft SQL Server is particularly efficient at handling large amounts of text. Better to store only the location and name of the physical document file, but this means the system must be prepared to handle the file being moved, renamed, or deleted, usually by asking users for assistance.

Summary

In this chapter, we've looked at various aspects of providing information to users based on the data stored in the database. This usually means the production of printed reports, but it can also mean information provided by way of a form or a recordset shown in a datasheet.

We began by examining the techniques provided by Microsoft Access for sorting and filtering data. Even if your application isn't being implemented in Access, these techniques provide useful examples of the kind of functionality that you might want to provide.

We examined various kinds of standard reports that might be provided by the system, including listing and detail reports, summary reports, and reports based on the forms in your system. We then looked at how reporting can be integrated into the user interface of the system and some of the issues involved in handling reporting errors. The production of ad hoc reports was discussed in some detail, and I presented the technique that I use for providing this functionality. Finally, we looked at the production of standard letters by combining the data management functionality of a database with the advanced formatting capabilities of a dedicated word processor.

In the next chapter, we'll turn to the subject of user assistance and look at the explicit forms of user assistance that can be incorporated into the user interface of your database system.

User Assistance

In a sense, everything we've talked about in Part IV of this book comes under the heading "user assistance." Your goal in designing the user interface and choosing windows structures and controls should always be to assist users in accomplishing their tasks. Most of the discussion of data integrity in Chapter 19, for example, was couched in terms of your system helping users avoid accidents without getting in their way. In this chapter, we'll look at more explicit forms of user assistance that you can incorporate into the user interface.

User Levels

We have discussed three categories of people who will be using your systems. Beginning users need to know *what* the system does. Intermediate users need to know *how* to perform specific tasks, and expert users want to know how to perform tasks *quickly*. Different types of assistance are appropriate for each level of user. The introductory screens and guided tours that are so helpful to beginners will get in the way of intermediate users and drive advanced users to distraction.

You must consider not only the support mechanisms that you will provide for each type of user, but also the best way for the various mechanisms to coexist. The introductory dialog box that you display for beginners on application startup, for example, should contain a "Don't show me again" check box that enables more advanced users to get the dialog box out of the way. The ToolTips and status bar messages that support intermediate users usually don't cause problems for more advanced users, but you might consider providing a mechanism for turning off ToolTips and status bar messages just to be sure. We'll discuss the customization of the user interface for different types of users in greater detail later in this chapter.

In addition to the coexistence of support mechanisms, consider how your system can help a user move from one level of competence to another.

You could rely on the system documentation and external training, but they're really not very effective mechanisms for increasing competence, for reasons we'll examine later. A better technique is to assist users from within the user interface itself.

Most systems of even moderate complexity will provide multiple paths to each command. For example, saving changes to a record might be accomplished by choosing Save from the File menu, clicking a toolbar button, or typing Ctrl-S. Each of these paths is called a **command vector**, and each command vector is appropriate for a different level of user.

Beginning and intermediate users tend to rely on menus to remind themselves of what functionality is available; intermediate users will make greater use of toolbar buttons; and experts will use the shortcut accelerator keys. To assist users in moving from one user level to another, you can consistently display all of these vectors for each command throughout the system.

Figure 21–1 shows the default File menu in Microsoft Access. Note that the Save item shows all the command vectors for the command. The mnemonic keyboard access Alt-F-S is indicated by the underlined capital letter S in the word Save. (The F in the File menu name is also underlined.) The icon used for the command on toolbars is also shown, as is the Ctrl-S accelerator. By displaying all the command vectors on the menu, the user interface itself helps users learn faster ways of performing tasks.

NOTE: Visual Studio .NET doesn't allow toolbar icons on its intrinsic menus, although implementing an OwnerDraw menu that displays them isn't too difficult. Additionally, there are several third-party controls available that do support icons on their menus.

The menu creation paradigm in Microsoft Access allows you to include icons, but the selection of built-in icons is so ridiculously small that you'll almost certainly have to use the Button Editor to draw your own. Both Visual Studio and Access make it easy to create accelerators that are automatically displayed on the menu.

Displaying multiple command vectors doesn't present any coexistence problems because it is a passive mechanism. All user assistance mechanisms can be divided into **passive mechanisms** that form part of the user interface, **reactive mechanisms** that are invoked in response to some user action, and **proactive mechanisms** that attempt to anticipate a user's needs. We'll discuss each of these mechanisms in turn in this chapter and end with a brief discussion of training materials and user customization.

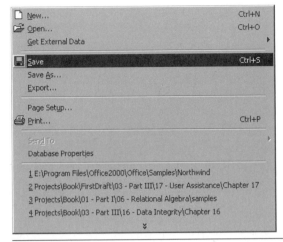

Figure 21–1 The Default File Menu in Microsoft Access 2000 Displays All the Command Vectors for the Save Command

Passive Assistance Mechanisms

Passive assistance mechanisms include all the clues, pointers, and explanations that you embed in the user interface to guide users in their tasks. Unlike reactive assistance mechanisms, passive assistance mechanisms don't require users to do anything—hence the name.

Control labels, menu names, and even the titles of your forms and dialog boxes are passive assistance mechanisms, and therefore you should give due consideration to how you name these elements. Choose names that describe as clearly as possible the action to be performed or the data to be entered.

In addition to names, many other passive mechanisms are available. We'll examine just three: mnemonic access keys, ToolTips, and status bars.

Mnemonic Access Keys

Mnemonic access keys provide both direct functionality and passive assistance to users. Because they allow users to navigate through the system quickly, access keys provide direct functionality. Because they are always underlined in control labels, access keys also provide passive user assistance. Any user with even moderate experience with Microsoft Windows will be familiar with the "Alt-underlined character" paradigm.

You should provide mnemonic access keys for all menu items and all controls. Choose which letter to use as the access key in the following order of priority:

1. The first letter of the menu item or control label.
2. A distinctive consonant in the menu item or control label.
3. A vowel in the menu item or control label.

Defining access keys is trivial to do in both Access and Visual Basic: You precede the access key character in the label with an ampersand (&). In both environments, the system will underline the character in the label and handle the navigation for you. (To display an ampersand character instead of an underlined character in a label, by the way, you use two ampersands. "Nuts & Bolts" will be displayed as "Nuts_Bolts", but "Nuts && Bolts" will be displayed as "Nuts & Bolts".)

ToolTips

The ToolTip for the Save button on the Access Form View toolbar is shown in Figure 21–2. The principle behind ToolTips is straightforward: They function as labels for toolbar buttons and other controls that don't have labels.

Not terribly exciting, is it? But unexciting and straightforward as ToolTips might be, their impact on the usability of the system is immense. If you've ever had to choose icon images to represent system functionality, you know how difficult it is for an icon to convey information. Choosing an icon for "Save" isn't too hard (at least it isn't now that we've all seen the disk icon used in Microsoft Office), but what about an "Open Customer Form" button? You might use a little figure, but what if you also need images for opening the Employees and Vendors forms? Your visual metaphors can get a little tenuous.

Fortunately, ToolTips take off a lot of the pressure to find a self-explanatory icon. Given half a chance, most people are pretty good at making up little stories to associate an image with an idea—that's the principle behind one method for remembering people's names—and ToolTips give them that half a chance.

Figure 21–2 ToolTips Indicate the Purpose of Controls that Don't Have Labels

So you're using the little fish icon in Access to represent Customers. (What *did* Access designers have in mind?) That a fish represents the Customers form is never going to occur to users the first time they see your toolbar, but the ToolTip will explain the icon's meaning. Provided you reinforce the association by using the image everywhere customers are referenced—the menu, the forms, and the documentation—users will adjust with no problems.

To implement ToolTips in either Access or Visual Basic, you simply set the appropriate property. The ToolTip text should be short—just a word or two. Remember that the ToolTip functions as a label: Its purpose is to remind users of what the control represents, not to teach them how to use it.

If the control duplicates a menu item, use the same word or phrase in the ToolTip as in the menu item. If the control doesn't duplicate a menu item, use the noun or verb that best describes the control's functionality and distinguishes it from other controls. If a toolbar contains three buttons that open the Customers form, Suppliers form, and Employees form, for example, you could use the ToolTips "Customers", "Suppliers", and "Employees". If, on the other hand, one button represents opening the Customers form and a second button represents printing a customer list, you would need to use the ToolTips "Open Customer Form" (or perhaps "Maintain Customers") and "Print Customers" to distinguish between the two buttons.

A note on images: In associating images with ideas, as in all other areas of user interface design, consistency is critical. Each image that represents an entity in the system should be used wherever your system references the entity, as should each image associated with a verb.

Best practice is to select a range of images for each category—entities and verbs—and combine images from the two categories where necessary. If I were to associate an X image with the delete action, and a person's profile image with the Customers table, for instance, I would superimpose one image on the other to indicate "Delete Customer," as shown in Figure 21–3.

Figure 21–3 Combining Images Can Be Very Expressive

Status Bars

A status bar is a common mechanism for providing passive assistance to users. Displayed at the bottom of the window, a status bar can display modal information such as the state of the Num Lock key, the Caps Lock key, and the extend selection mode. The status bar also displays messages for users. Figure 21–4 shows an Access status bar. Note that the Categories form is maximized, so the status bar at the bottom of the window appears to be part of the form. However, the status bar is actually part of the Access window itself.

Access makes it easy for you to display descriptive information in the status bar for each control on a form by setting the control's StatusBarText property. If you don't explicitly define the StatusBarText property for a control bound to a field, that field's Description value (which you specify in the table's Design view) will be displayed in the status bar. You can't, to the best of my knowledge, set the status bar text from code in Access, however, so there is no way to use status bar text for an extended description of a menu item or for general messages to users.

In Visual Basic, you control the text displayed in a status bar by explicitly setting the Text property of the appropriate panel of a StatusBar control. You can therefore use the status bar to display explanatory messages throughout the system, not just to describe the active control as in Access.

Figure 21–4 The Status Bar Is at the Bottom of the Main Window

A trade-off for this additional flexibility is that you must always set the text in code, and there is no way to tie text to a control and have Visual Basic display it automatically. Admittedly, this extra work can get tedious, but it's a fairly small price to pay for the expanded functionality.

The greatest advantage of a status bar is that it doesn't intrude on users. Unlike a message box, the status bar doesn't capture keyboard input or require explicit user dismissal. In fact, in Access (and Visual Basic as well, if you provide the functionality) a user can choose not to display the status bar.

In Visual Basic, you can use the status bar to display extended descriptive information to users or to keep them informed about processes that are operating in the background. You can also use the status bar to display error messages, although you must allow for the possibility that users won't have the status bar visible. It's dangerous to use status bar text for anything users *must* see. Even if the status bar is visible in the main window, users might not notice a message displayed there.

Displaying messages in the status bar does have its uses, however. If, as I recommended in Chapter 19, you suspend rather than reject records that violate integrity constraints, the status bar is a good place to explain the situation and how to resolve it. I sometimes display the "problem" field contents in red, and when the user selects the field, describe the problem in the status bar and suggest how to fix it. Because space in the status bar is limited, however, I also make available a dialog box with more extensive instructions, usually having it appear when a user presses a function key.

Of course, Visual Studio .NET supports the ErrorProvider control, which provides the same functionality (highlight the problem control and display an error message) in a slightly different way. It has the advantage, of course, of requiring significantly less coding.

Reactive Assistance Mechanisms

Reactive assistance mechanisms, unlike the passive mechanisms we've been discussing, are displayed only as a response to some action by a user. Intermediate or advanced users are more likely to use reactive mechanisms than beginners, who might not know how to invoke them or even that they exist. For this reason, they're not particularly good mechanisms for the kind of "what's this all about, then?" assistance that beginning users require.

Most reactive assistance is provided as some form of online help. Several paradigms for providing this type of online assistance exist, and we'll look at two in this section: traditional online help and the newer What's This tips.

Although not often considered in that light, error messages are also a kind of reactive assistance, and we'll look at them at the end of this section.

On-Line Help

Traditional on-line help is essentially a transfer of printed documentation to the computer, and as almost always happens when a real-world object or activity gets computerized, this transfer makes some things easier and some things harder.

On-line help is more accessible than printed documentation, and the ability to display cross-referenced material with the click of a mouse is certainly a benefit. On the other hand, on-line help is a lot more difficult to browse, and you can't take it with you to the lunchroom when you go to get a cup of coffee.

Careful design of the help system can go some way toward ameliorating the disadvantages of on-line help. (It's still only as portable as the computer is, however.) Designing and writing help systems is a huge topic, most of which lies outside the scope of this book. All I can do here is give you some general guidelines, point out a few peculiarities of writing help for database systems, and refer you to the Bibliography for more detailed information.

The first and most important consideration when designing on-line help for your system is that no matter how tightly linked the help might be to your system, you should never consider it an integral part of the user interface. That is, your system must be able to stand on its own and never force users to resort to on-line help (or any other documentation, for that matter) to complete a task.

Remember that beginning users might not understand what on-line help contains, so they might not think to press F1 when they get confused. You should consider on-line help as a support for the user assistance provided within the system itself, not as a replacement for it. It's all too common for designers to think that having an on-line help system relieves them of the burden of making the system self-explanatory. In my experience this is a mistake and leads to ugly, unusable software.

The second consideration when designing on-line help is what type of support you want it to provide. On-line help topics can be roughly divided into two types: task-oriented and function-oriented. Task-oriented topics tell users how to complete a specific task, such as how to print an invoice or schedule a meeting. Function-oriented topics provide detailed information regarding a specific function (such as the Print command on the File menu) or control (the CustomerID text box on a form). The two types correspond roughly to Users Guides and Reference Manuals in printed documentation.

Both task-oriented and function-oriented help have a role in supporting database systems. If your system supports many work processes, or if the work processes it supports are complex, task-oriented help can be of considerable assistance to users by providing a kind of roadmap to the procedures. It's still important to provide support and guidance within the system itself, though. It's not acceptable to merely present users with an alphabetical list of forms like the one in the Access Database window and rely on on-line help to tell them in which order the forms must be completed. (Well, it's not acceptable if you're working for me, anyway.)

Ideally, task-oriented topics should not include conceptual or introductory material. Remember, this isn't the right tool for teaching your users what the system does. The only purpose of task-oriented help topics is to provide a summary of the "how" of a procedure, not to explain the "what" or the "why."

Using multiple help topics for complex subjects will keep the topics readable on the computer screen. If the work process being explained is complex and has multiple paths, it's best not to try to explain all paths in a single topic. Just explain the simplest or most usual path in the main topic and provide links to topics explaining the variations.

Whereas task-oriented topics concentrate on the "how" of using your system, function-oriented topics concentrate on the "what" and the "why." For database systems, most function-oriented topics will refer to data items and controls rather than functions per se. Few database systems will require topics such as those provided by Access help, for example, where it's necessary to explain the precise syntax of the Mid$ function.

Systems *do* require topics that explain the meaning of every entity and attribute in the system and the constraints that pertain to each of them. They might also require topics to explain the use of various control types used by the system—how to navigate through a tree view control, for example, or how to pick a date using a calendar control.

In planning these data-oriented topics, it's important to think about why users would ask for help. If a user is looking at an Orders form text box with the caption "Desired Delivery Date," it's really extraordinarily unlikely he would press the F1 key because he doesn't understand that this is the date the customer would like the goods delivered. If this is all that your topic tells users, it's worse than useless—it's an irritating waste of time.

So why might the user have pressed F1? Maybe he doesn't understand why the date is already filled in—so explain the default and how to override it. Or maybe the customer has told him to have the goods delivered "any time after the first of the month"—so explain that he should enter the earliest date or whatever rule applies in your environment. The better you are at thinking about the questions users might really be asking, the more effective your help system will be.

What's This? Tips

What's This? tips are much like task-oriented on-line help except for how they are invoked. What's This? tips are invoked by clicking the question mark icon in the window's title bar and then clicking a control within the window. Figure 21–5 shows the What's This? topic for the Windows In Taskbar check box in the Options dialog box in Access 2000.

I like the idea of What's This? tips a lot because they are so tightly integrated with the user interface of the system. I've seen novice users stumble upon What's This? tips on several occasions. I've never seen novice users find on-line help by pressing F1 by accident, and I imagine it might be a little scary if they did, what with strange windows opening up all over the place.

For simple systems, a good set of What's This? topics might be all the help you need to provide, particularly if the system doesn't support a lot of complex work processes. What's This? topics must be fairly short, however, since they're displayed on top of the associated window and can't be scrolled. If you need to explain complex constraints, you simply won't have

Figure 21–5 What's This? Tips Are Displayed in Dialog Boxes by Clicking the Question Mark Button in the Title Bar and Clicking a Control

the space and you'll need to back up the What's This? topic with one or more longer on-line help topics. (Be sure to add "Press F1 for more details" or words to that effect to the end of the What's This? topic.)

The specific question a What's This? topic attempts to answer is—as you've probably guessed from the name—"What is this thing?" Think of a What's This? tip as a paragraph-long control caption. Because of space constraints, you usually can't be highly creative in responding to the questions you think users might be asking. But with a little thought, you can do better than just providing a reworded control label.

Describing the Desired Delivery Date as "the date on which the customer desires delivery of the goods" is just as evil in What's This? tips as it is in on-line help. At the very least, try saying "the earliest date on which the goods are to be delivered. This value defaults to three days after the order date, but you can change this value by clicking the field and typing a new date. Press F1 for more details."

Audible Feedback

Audible feedback—using a computer tone to describe some system state—is an extremely powerful mechanism for assisting users, but designers can use its power for good or evil. The "Beep, you blew it" dialog box that's displayed when the system detects a "user error" is a prime example of using audible feedback for evil purposes. Users do not enjoy having attention drawn to their mistakes, and a beep not only draws a user's attention to the problem, it also notifies anyone within earshot. Besides, the default beep is a *really* annoying sound.

Turn audible feedback on its head, however, and it can be a wonderful tool. Instead of having the system blow a computer raspberry at a user when it gets confused, try having the computer emit a soft sound (I think of it as a purr) when something goes right. Say that during data entry the system is checking each field as the user exits the corresponding control. If the data complies with all relevant constraints, the system can issue a soft "I'm OK" sound. (The sound shouldn't be very loud.) If any problems occur, the system makes no sound but instead displays a message in the status bar. Silence is sufficient notification of the problem, and the user will check the screen.

The best analogy for this positive feedback technique (for which I am indebted to Alan Cooper) is the keyboard. As you press each key, the keyboard makes a soft click. You're probably not consciously aware of the sound, but if it were to stop, you'd notice it immediately and investigate the problem.

The example of the keyboard ought to calm any fears you might have regarding the cacophony of a room full of data entry operators. As I've said, the "I'm OK" sound needn't be obtrusive to be effective. I've successfully used positive audible feedback in a system designed for a call center with over 100 users in a single room.

Error Messages

Most people don't consider error messages as a means of providing assistance to users, which is a pity. But then, most error messages *don't* assist users, they chastise instead, which is an even greater pity. Instead of treating error messages as an opportunity to point out users' faults, treat them instead as a plea for users' assistance. The system has got itself into trouble, and it needs user help in getting out.

A well-behaved person, when requesting another's assistance, doesn't make cryptic statements or issue demands. A well-behaved person doesn't try to imply that it's someone else's fault that she is confused or in trouble. A well-behaved person explains a problem as clearly as possible, requests assistance politely, tries not to impose any more than necessary, and takes pains to explain the implications of her requests.

A well-behaved computer system ought to do no less. In fact, because computer systems are deserving of less respect than people, they ought to do more. (Groveling is not inappropriate here.) When issuing "error" messages, the system has an obligation to:

■ Explain the situation clearly, in terms users will understand.
■ Request assistance politely, without implying that users are at fault.
■ Not impose on users by asking them to do anything the system could reasonably do for itself.
■ Describe the implications of any action users might take.

The system will sometimes get itself hopelessly confused, or some environmental factor such as a shortage of memory or a disk failure will at times make it impossible for the system to continue operation without assistance from the user. When these events occur, you have little choice but to display a message to the user. This is a wonderful opportunity not only to get the assistance the system needs, but also to provide the user with the information *she* needs to help the system stay out of trouble in the future.

By explaining the situation clearly and not using confusing jargon, the message you display to users will allow them to resolve the problem right away. Having understood the problem the first time, a user will be in a

position to avoid having the same problem in the future—assuming the situation is avoidable. Invalid data entry formats are avoidable; hard disk failures generally aren't.

By explaining the implications of users' choices, the system is far more likely to receive the most sensible response. Remember that a lot of things that seem perfectly obvious to you won't be obvious to the user. Don't talk down, of course, but don't be afraid of stating the obvious.

Wording the message politely and not imposing on users are just good manners. Remember when your mother told you that you'd catch more flies with honey than you would with vinegar? If users perceive your system as generally polite and helpful, they'll be inclined to forgive that one weird GPF that you never were able to track down. (Nobody's perfect.)

Proactive Assistance

Passive and reactive user assistance are relatively well-understood categories of user support, although they become increasingly sophisticated as our knowledge of computer-human interaction grows and new implementation tools become available. The final category, proactive assistance, is very much the new kid on the block and very few systems currently implement it.

The principle behind proactive user assistance is simple: The computer system monitors users' actions and acts proactively to assist, either by making suggestions for more efficient use of the system or by undertaking tasks on the users' behalf. The Microsoft Office Assistant gives proactive assistance by offering users tips based on their actions.

One type of proactive assistance currently receiving a great deal of attention is the intelligent agent. An intelligent agent is a piece of software to which users can delegate a task. Intelligent agents are most often implemented as a specialized Web user interface that answers such requests as "Find me the best price for this item" or "Suggest a book that I might like to read." But nothing restricts them to the Web environment. You might, for example, implement an agent that assists students in organizing a class schedule based on their preferences—"Don't schedule any math before noon, and I prefer language courses in the evening."

Microsoft provides two tools for creating interfaces based on animated characters, the Microsoft Office Assistant and the Microsoft Agent. Most people are familiar with the little bouncing paperclip representing the Microsoft Office Assistant (the character can be changed by a user), but not everyone realizes the Office Assistant has a programmable interface. The

Office Assistant is available only within Microsoft Office applications, however, and can't be distributed with the Access runtime engine.

If you're working in Access (or in any other development environment that can use Microsoft ActiveX controls, including Visual Basic), you might want to download the Microsoft Agent SDK from the Microsoft Web site. It's quite a bit more powerful than the Office Assistant.

Microsoft Agent is a very cool toy. You can design and animate your own characters in addition to the ones provided in the SDK. Microsoft Agent also supports speech recognition, which has fascinating potential for database applications. I'd love to see a Microsoft Agent interface to the Microsoft English Query tool (which provides natural language processing of SQL queries) included in Microsoft SQL Server. Imagine representing the database itself as a Microsoft Agent character.

Be forewarned, though. Neither the Office Assistant nor Microsoft Agent provides any direct support for you to monitor and react to user actions. They provide simple interfaces to sophisticated character interactions with users, but when it comes to actually implementing the intelligence in your intelligent agent, you're strictly on your own.

User Training

The requirements for user training are no different for database systems than for any other type of software. Initial user training can be provided by documentation, classroom instruction, or the computer. And of course these options aren't mutually exclusive.

If you decide to implement computer-based training mechanisms, remember to be clear about both the scope and the audience of the project. Beginning users are primarily interested in what the system does and only secondarily interested in how to do it.

The scope of training aimed at beginning users varies with the complexity of the system and with the budget. Many systems require only an introductory screen or two explaining the system. More complex systems will benefit from more extensive training mechanisms, perhaps a guided tour or even formal computer-based training with exercises and quizzes and what-not.

Intermediate users are primarily interested in how to perform specific tasks, and in many cases task-oriented help can meet their requirements. In fact, the distinction between "help" and "training" is somewhat arbitrary. Complex systems, however, might require the same kind of formal computer-based training implemented for intermediate users as for beginning users.

Whatever the scope of the training you implement, keep the training reasonably separate from the system itself. Users should certainly be able to initiate the training from within the system's user interface, perhaps from an item on the help menu. But the existence of training materials should never interfere with normal use of the system.

Summary

In this chapter, we've examined three types of explicit user assistance: passive assistance that is built into a system's user interface, reactive assistance that occurs as a result of some user actions, and proactive assistance that is initiated by the system itself.

We began by looking at three types of passive assistance: mnemonic access keys, ToolTips, and status bars. We then examined reactive assistance, which is usually implemented in the form of on-line help or What's This? Tips, but can also include audible feedback and *should* include error messages. Finally, we looked briefly at the new area of proactive assistance and user training.

Bibliography

Part I: Relational Database Theory

Date, C. J. *An Introduction to Database Systems*. 7th Edition. Reading: Addison-Wesley Publishing Company, 1999.

Date, C. J. and Hugh Darwen. *Foundation for Object/Relational Databases: The Third Manifesto*. Reading: Addison-Wesley Publishing Company, 1998.

Fleming, Candace C. and Barbara von Halle. *Handbook of Relational Database Design*. Reading: Addison-Wesley Publishing Company, 1989.

Teorey, Toby J. *Database Modeling & Design*. 3rd Edition. San Francisco: Morgan Kaufmann Publishers, 1999.

Part II: Designing Relational Database Systems

Gilb, Tom and Susannah Finzi. *Principles of Software Engineering Management*. Reading: Addison-Wesley Publishing Company, 1988.

Haught, Dan and Jim Ferguson. *Microsoft Jet Database Engine Programmer's Guide*. 2nd Edition. Redmond: Microsoft Press, 1997.

McConnell, Steve. *Rapid Development*. Redmond: Microsoft Press, 1996.

Pressman, Roger S. *Software Engineering: A Practitioner's Approach*. 3rd Edition. New York: McGraw-Hill, 1992.

Sommerville, Ian. *Software Engineering*. 6th Edition. Reading: Addison-Wesley Publishing Company, 1996.

Soukup, Ron. *Inside Microsoft SQL Server 6.5*. Redmond: Microsoft Press, 1997.

Part III: Designing the User Interface

Cooper, Alan. *About Face: The Essentials of User Interface Design*. Foster City: IDG Books Worldwide, 1995.

Heckel, Paul. *The Elements of Friendly Software Design*. New York: Warner Books, 1991.

Mandel, Paul. *The Elements of User Interface Design*, New York: John Wiley & Sons, 1997.

Microsoft Corporation. *The Windows Interface Guidelines for Software Design*. Redmond: Microsoft Press, 1998.

Shneiderman, Ben. *Designing the User Interface: Strategies for Effective Human-Computer Interaction*. Reading: Addison-Wesley Publishing Company, 1980.

Glossary

abstract entity   An entity that models relationships between other entities.

ad hoc report   A report that is configured by the user after implementation of the application.

aggregate function   A SQL function that returns summary values.

alternate key   A candidate key of a relation that is not used as the primary key of a table.

application   The forms and reports with which the user interacts.

attribute   A column in a relation.

base relation   A relation that is instantiated as a table in the database.

binary relationship   A relationship having two participants.

Boolean expression   An expression that results in either True or False.

business constraint   A constraint derived from the problem space.

business rule   An integrity constraint that originates in the problem space rather than from relational theory.

candidate key   One or more attributes that uniquely identify a relation.

cardinality of a relation   The number of rows in a relation.

cardinality of a relationship   The maximum number of instances of one entity that can participate in a relationship.

Cartesian product   A relational operation that combines every record in one recordset with every record in a second recordset.

cascading delete   The automatic deletion of records in a foreign table when the corresponding record in the primary table is deleted.

cascading update   The automatic updating of records in a foreign table when the corresponding record in the primary table is changed.

closure   The principle that all operations on a relation result in a relation and can be used for further manipulation.

command vector   A path to the execution of a command in a user interface, for example, a menu item or a toolbar button.

composite entity   A single entity in the problem space that is modeled by one or more relations.

composite key A candidate key composed of two or more attributes.

concrete entity An entity that models an object or event in the real world.

conventional value An arbitrary value used to represent a nonexistent or unknown value.

database The combination of the database schema and the stored data.

database access object model A software library used to communicate between a database engine and a development environment.

database application The forms and reports with which the user interacts.

database constraint An integrity constraint that references multiple relations.

database engine The software that handles the physical storage and manipulation of data.

database schema The physical layout of tables in a database.

database system The combination of the database application, database engine, and database.

data integrity The rules used by a database to ensure that the data is, if not correct, at least plausible.

data model The conceptual description of a problem space in relational terms.

declarative integrity A method of defining integrity constraints by explicitly declaring them as part of a table definition.

degree of a relation The number of columns in a relation.

degree of a relationship The number of participants in a relationship.

derived relation A virtual relation that is defined in terms of other relations.

domain The range of values from which an attribute can be drawn.

domain constraint An integrity constraint that determines the range of possible values for a domain.

entity Anything about which the system needs to store information.

entity constraint An integrity constraint that ensures the validity of the entities being modeled by the system.

equi-join A join between two tables on the basis of equality.

field The physical representation of an attribute in a database.

foreign relation The relation that receives the primary key of the other participant in a relationship.

full outer join An outer join that returns all fields from both participants.

functional dependency A relationship between two attributes such that the value of one attribute determines the value in the other.

inner join   A join that returns records only when the result of an operation is True.

integrity constraint   A data integrity rule.

intrinsic constraint   A constraint that governs the physical structure of the database.

join dependency   A cyclical relationship between three relations.

junction table   A table that represents a relationship in the database.

left outer join   An outer join that returns all fields from the first recordset listed in a SELECT statement.

logical data type   A generic indication of a domain such as "String" or "Number", without reference to specific physical data types.

logical operator   An operator that returns a Boolean result.

lossless decomposition   The ability to divide relations in such a manner that they can be recombined without loss of information.

multivalued dependency pairs   Mutually independent sets of attributes participating in functional dependencies.

natural join   A special case of an equi-join in which the join is performed on the basis of equality, all common fields participate in the join, and only one set of common fields is included in the result set.

normal forms   Rules for defining the structure of relations in order to eliminate update anomalies.

normalization   The process of structuring a database schema to ensure data integrity, remove redundancy, and assist in data retrieval.

orphan entity   A weak entity that is not related to an entity in the primary relation of a relationship.

outer join   A join that returns all the records of an inner join plus all the records in either or both of the other participants.

partial participation   The entity can exist independent of its participation in the specified relationship.

participant   An entity that is associated to another in a relationship.

passive user assistance   A user assistance mechanism that is an intrinsic part of the user interface.

primary key   The candidate key of a relation that is used to uniquely identify the records in a table.

primary relation   The relation whose primary key is stored in the other participant in a relationship.

proactive user assistance   A user assistance mechanism that attempts to anticipate the users' needs.

problem space   The portion of the real world that is to be modeled by a database application.

procedural integrity   A method of enforcing data integrity by creating procedures that are executed automatically when a record is updated, inserted, or deleted.

query   A derived relation in Microsoft Access.

reactive user assistance   A user assistance mechanism that is triggered by some action by the user, such as an invalid entry or the request for online help.

record   The physical representation of a tuple.

recordset   The generic term used in Microsoft Access to mean the physical representation of a relation.

referential integrity   The integrity constraints that ensure that relationships between entities remain valid.

regular entity   An entity that can exist without participating in a relationship.

relation   A logical construct that organizes data into rows and columns.

relation body   The tuples comprising a relation.

relation heading   The definition of the attribute and domain at the top of a relation.

relational database   A physical implementation of the relational model defined by Dr. E. F. Codd.

relational difference   A relational operation that returns the records of one recordset that are not matched in another recordset.

relational divide   A join that returns all the records in one recordset that have values that match all the corresponding values in the second recordset.

relational intersection   A relational operation that returns the records two recordsets have in common.

relational union   The concatenation of two recordsets.

relationship   An association between two or more entities.

right outer join   An outer join that returns all fields from the second recordset listed in a SELECT statement.

scalar value   A single, non-repeating value.

schema   The physical layout of tables in a database system.

simple key   A candidate key composed of a single attribute.

standard report   A report that can be defined and implemented as part of the database application.

table   The physical instantiation of a relation in the database schema.

task   A discrete step in a work process.

ternary relationship   A relationship having three participants.

theta-join   Technically, any join based on a comparison operator, but normally restricted to joins based on operators other than equality.

three-valued logic   A model for logical evaluation that allows the values True, False, and Null as results of expressions.

total participation   The entity cannot exist unless it participates in the specified relationship.

transaction integrity   An integrity constraint that controls the validity of multiple operations on the database.

trigger   Procedural code that is executed when a specified database event occurs.

tuple   A row in a relation.

type-compatible domains   Domains that can be logically compared.

unary relationship   An association between a relation and itself.

update anomaly   Problems with data manipulation resulting from a poorly designed data model.

view   A derived relation in SQL Server.

weak entity   An entity that can exist only if it participates in a given relationship.

work process   Something that is to be done using the database application.

Index

Symbols

= (equal) operator, 87

A

abstract entities, 14
abstract relations, 51
accelerator keys, 321–322
Access (application), 7
access keys, 321–322
Access Report Wizard, 312
accidental entries, correcting, 297
ActiveX Data Objects (ADO), 8
ad hoc reports, 301–302, 311–317
additions, tracking, 218
ADO (ActiveX Data Objects), 8
ADO.NET, 8
Advanced Filter/Sort window, 304–305
advanced users, designing for, 239, 319
aggregate functions, SQL, 99–100
AllowZeroLength flag, 78
alternate keys, 33
AND operator, 87
ANSI_NULLS option, 88
applications, 5
architectures for user interfaces, 247–259
AS keyword (SQL), 101
assistance. *See* user assistance
attributes, 11, 14–18
   candidate and primary keys, 32–34
   constraints on, 213, 291–292
   defining data objects, 179–184
   of dimensional tables, 131–132
     changing, 136–138
   for entities, determining, 190–191

   in fact tables, 117
     dimension keys, 117–118
     fact attribute characteristics, 118–126
   functional dependency, 34–35
   of relationships, determining, 187
   restrictions on value ranges, 193–194
audible feedback, 329
audience, for system design, 221–222
auditing, 218–219
AutoLookup operation (Jet database
   engine), 91
automatic report printing, 310–311
AutoNumber fields, 34

B

base relations, 85
beeping, as user feedback, 329
beginner users, designing for,
   238, 319–320, 332
benefit analyses, 162–164
binary relationships. *See* one-to-one
   relationships
bit flags, 37
body, relation, 12
Boolean logic, 86–88
Boyce/Codd normal form, 41–42
building data models, 148, 179–195
   data object identification, 179–184
   domain analysis, 191–193
   entity review, 188–191
   normalization, 195
   relationship definition, 184–187
   value range restrictions, 193–194
business intelligence, 112–114

Also available from Rebecca Riordan and Addison-Wesley

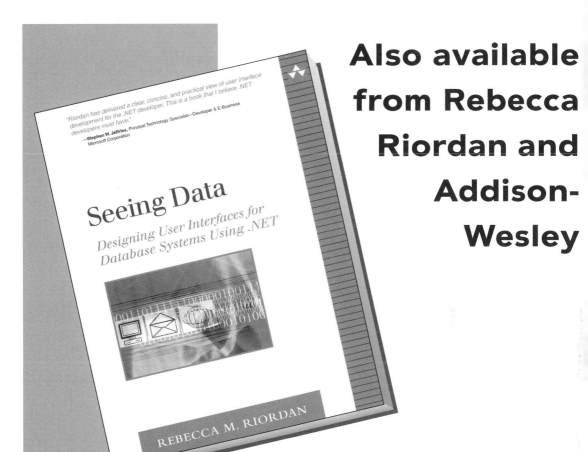

In **Seeing Data,** Microsoft MVP Rebecca Riordan shows how to use .NET's advanced UI tools to build applications that reflect today's interface design best practices. She offers visual examples, code, and techniques for every .NET project. Riordan presents dozens of Visual Basic .NET examples—all designed for easy, quick reuse, and downloadable from the book's companion Web site.

"Riordan has delivered a clear, concise, and practical view of user interface development for the .NET developer. This is a book that I believe .NET developers must have."
> —**Stephen W. Jeffries,** Principal Technology Specialist—Developer & E-Business, Microsoft Corporation

"Rebecca provides an invaluable resource to help developers focus on a commonly overlooked but vital part of an application—the user experience."
> —**David Sceppa,** Program Manager, Microsoft Corporation

"Rebecca Riordan takes UI programming and practices to new heights. She has gone beyond simply explaining the theory behind UI programming practices, providing code samples that are practical, well-documented, and can be immediately incorporated into a development project."
> —**Wendy Chun,** AVP/Product Development, SunGard Insurance Systems

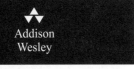

BOOKS ONLINE

ENABLED

THIS BOOK IS SAFARI ENABLED

INCLUDES FREE 45-DAY ACCESS TO THE ONLINE EDITION

The Safari® Enabled icon on the cover of your favorite technology book means the book is available through Safari Bookshelf. When you buy this book, you get free access to the online edition for 45 days.

Safari Bookshelf is an electronic reference library that lets you easily search thousands of technical books, find code samples, download chapters, and access technical information whenever and wherever you need it.

TO GAIN 45-DAY SAFARI ENABLED ACCESS TO THIS BOOK:

- Go to **http://www.awprofessional.com/safarienabled**

- Complete the brief registration form

- Enter the coupon code found in the front of this book on the "Copyright" page

If you have difficulty registering on Safari Bookshelf or accessing the online edition, please e-mail customer-service@safaribooksonline.com.